God and Creation
in Christian Theology

Kathryn Tanner

God and Creation in Christian Theology

Tyranny or Empowerment?

FORTRESS PRESS

Minneapolis

GOD AND CREATION IN CHRISTIAN THEOLOGY
Tyranny or Empowerment?

Fortress Press ex libris publication 2005

ISBN 0-8006-3737-2
The Library of Congress has catalogued the original publication as follows:

Library of Congress Cataloging-in-Publication Data
Tanner, Kathryn E.
        God and creation in Christian theology: tyranny or empowerment
        Includes index.
        1. Languages—Religious aspects—Christianity.
        2. God. 3. Creation. I. Title.
        BR115.L25T36 1988   231'.014 87-33839
        ISBN 0-631-15994-0

Manufactured in the U.S.A.

09   08   07   06   05   1   2   3   4   5   6   7   8   9   10

Contents

Acknowledgements — vii

Introduction — 1

1   Method in the Study of Theology — 10

2   The Transcendence and Creative Agency of God: the Basic Structure of Christian Discourse I — 36

Greek Problematic and Christian Resolution — 37
Analysing Theological Cases — 48

3   God and the Efficacy of Creatures: the Basic Structure of Christian Discourse II — 81

The Coherence of Christian Talk about the Creature's Power and Efficacy — 84
Rules for Talk about God's Agency and Created Efficacy — 90
Rules as Resources of Complexity — 104

4   The Modern Breakdown of Theological Discourse — 120

A Modern Framework for Discourse — 124
Historical Examples of the Transformation of Theological Discourse in Modern Times — 132
The General Effects of a Modern Framework on Theology — 152
A Strategy for Faithfulness — 160

Conclusion — 163

Notes — 170

Index — 191

Acknowledgements

I would like to thank the following people for the effort they expended in providing both criticism and encouragement during the conception and writing of this project: Hans Frei, George Lindbeck, David Kelsey, Louis Dupré, Gene Outka, John E. Smith, William Christian, David Burrell, Maurice Wiles, David Dawson, Gene Rogers and Cyril O'Regan.

The book is dedicated in memory of Elaine Prassas Tanner (1924–76).

Introduction

In the end we are always rewarded for our good will, our patience, fairmindedness, and gentleness with what is strange; gradually, it sheds its veil and turns out to be a new and indescribable beauty. That is its thanks for our hospitality. Even those who love themselves will have learned it in this way; for there is no other way. Love, too, has to be learned.

Friedrich Nietzsche, *The Gay Science*[1]

What is 'familiarly known' is not properly known, just for the reason that it is 'familiar'. When engaged in the process of knowing, it is the commonest form of self-deception . . . to assume something to be familiar, and to let it pass on that very account. Knowledge of that sort, with all its talking around it never gets from the spot, but has no idea that this is the case. . . . To display an idea in its original elements means returning upon its moments.

G. W. F. Hegel, *Phenomenology of Mind*[2]

This work concerns Christian talk about God as an agent in relation to created beings, particularly those assumed to have their own power and efficacy. It was prompted by the sense that modern discussion of the topic has taken an odd turn, a turn that requires, therefore, some account beyond appeals to the self-evident logic of modern conclusions on these matters.

The charge that Christian theologians speak incoherently about the nature of God and the created world has become a commonplace, almost a cultural given of contemporary times. Christian theologians have often claimed that God's power in creating and governing the world is unconditional and unlimited. At the same time they speak of creatures operating on their own and of men and women who are free and therefore responsible for the character of their lives. To modern ears, such assertions of God's power imply a coercive tyranny that must block a creature's exercise of its own proper powers and in particular a human being's capacity for free self-determination. When philosophers of religion bring the clear light of rational analysis or the speculative dialectics of a grander metaphysics to bear on the question of the sort of divine agency compatible with creatures that are active and free, the options seem to exclude traditional Christian understandings of God and God's relation to the created world. The idea that a radically transcendent God exercises a universal and unconditional agency tends to go by the board in modern philosophical strategies for resolving the alleged conflict. In an attempt to make talk about God and world coherent, the philosophers (and those theologians who accept the philosophers' critique) either limit the power and extent of divine agency, or deny that divine and created operations are ultimately distinct. In the first case, a space is cleared for creatures to operate apart from divine interference. In the second, the capacity of the creature to act and the scope of its activity cannot be reduced by the intensity and magnitude of God's power since God's work becomes in some sense the creature's own.

From the time of the Reformation, the Christian church itself has been divided along lines that suppose a similar either/or option between a traditional account of divine agency and the affirmation of free, active creatures. In modern times the existence of opposed Christian communions and of persistent theological factionalism within and between them has often been justified by mutually exclusive claims to theological propriety on issues of this sort. Theological opponents accuse each other, in the terms used in this work, of deforming a basic structure of discourse about God and world that is essential to appropriately Christian life and belief.

Protestant voices, for example, charge Roman Catholic theology with sinfully elevating the powers of the creature at the expense of God's sovereignty. The fault is often attributed to its seduction by Aristotelianism or some other philosophical system: an overarching ontology including both God and world leads the Roman Catholic theologian to bring the divine down to the level of created being.[3] Roman Catholic critics, on the other hand, accuse Protestant theologians of emphasizing the sovereignty of divine agency to the extent of denigrating the creature and its capacities given by God through nature or grace. Protestant theologians, according to a Roman Catholic diagnosis, confine Christian insight within the bounds of philosophical nominalism: on those terms there can be nothing real in the creature to correspond to what God is said to have done for it.[4] The theological inadequacy of the nominalistic principles that infiltrate Reformation Protestantism is confirmed for such Roman Catholic critics by the surprising reversal in later Protestant churches and culture of a properly Christian emphasis on divine sovereignty. For Protestants who deplore this sort of trend in Protestant liberalism, the fault lies with the corruption of Reformation theology by theoretical assumptions shared with Catholicism; the same theoretical assumptions are behind the tendency of Roman Catholic and liberal Protestant theology alike to aggrandize human autonomy and achievement at the cost of the creature's absolute dependence upon God. Mutual accusations like these of a basic surrender of either divine sovereignty or the dignity of the creature are reproduced in stubbornly persistent disputes about God's providence, grace and predestination, within the Roman Catholic Church and both between and within the major Protestant communions.

The Christian theological tradition thus seems disordered and fragmented in modern times by unresolved controversy of a very fundamental sort. Absent is any unifying theological self-definition on these issues that effectively excludes what would have been regarded as heresy in pre-modern forms of Christian self-description. Theological factions may intend to be 'orthodox' – that is, to speak in ways that are permissible within the field of Christian discourse according to established dogmatic guidelines or previous paradigmatic examples of acceptable sorts of discourse on these matters. They rarely seem able, however, to carry through such intentions effectively. This lack of success becomes apparent in a mutual failure of recognition, i.e., in the refusal of the various factions to accept each other's orthodoxy. In general, there is a curious inability to arrive at a consensus in modern times about what it is permissible to say on theological issues that had previously been resolvable. To be sure, difference and dissension do not in this way erupt for the first time within a hitherto monolithic orthodoxy in theological statement. A rich diversity in theological forms of Christian self-expression has always existed; orthodoxy in the sense of limits to acceptable Christian statement has never demanded uniformity. What is odd about the modern situation is the degree to which difference takes on the character of mutual exclusivity. Disputes of the fundamental sort under discussion here are never finally resolved one way or the other by a consensus opinion concerning the boundaries of acceptable statement.

The incoherence of Christian theology seems the conclusion to draw, then, not just from the external standpoint of philosophical critique without specifically Christian commitments, but also from an internal, 'in-house' reckoning of theological argument in recent centuries. The present project hinges on the idea that both these internal and external evidences of incoherence are to be accounted for in terms of a specifically modern common source. Problems in asserting a transcendent God's sovereign agency together with the creature's own power and efficacy arise historically, I shall argue, with a certain body of interrelated presumptions that form a framework for modern discussion of the topic. This framework of presumptions will be specified in chapter 4. Problems of intelligibility arrive on the scene as an earlier tradition of discourse in Christian theology is subtly but quite significantly transformed: a modern interpretive frame skews the sense of traditional Christian claims about God and the world for both philosopher and theologian. As a result, what Christians have said begins to appear incoherent to philosophers; Christian discourse actually comes to be incoherent in the hands of those theologians who intend to remain faithful to the traditional claims in reformulating them for a contemporary audience.

If, as I argue, these developments are historically circumscribed, problems in intelligibly co-affirming traditional Christian notions of God and creature are not endemic to Christian theism per se. Radical revisions of those traditional notions are not required, then, to remedy any essential incoherence of Christian discourse, made clear for the first time through the honest rigours of logical analysis. I shall suggest that those who reject the coherence of the Christian account have already misconstrued it according to assumptions that underlie their own revisionist understandings of God and God's relation to the world.

The fragmentation of discourse within the Christian church since the Reformation suggests, however, that this misconstrual cannot be dismissed as an external attack by the hostile or the misinformed, an attack from which, therefore, theologians might have gained safety by fideistic retreat within the confines of the church. Granting the general accuracy of *both* Protestant and Catholic accusations of distortion in Christian discourse, it is difficult to accept *either* side's diagnosis that the source of error lies with some philosophical seduction of Christian purity. The general disruption of Christian discourse that occurs in mutual charges of impropriety between Christian factions crosses all philosophical lines distinguishing those factions. This general disorder suggests, not the accidental corruption of any particular theological faction through the untoward outside influence of flawed philosophical principles, but a curious forgetfulness about the rules for proper Christian talk on the part of the church itself as a whole. A plausible explanation for general disruption is a wide ranging breakdown of the church's own discursive habits. If those with no compelling sentiment of allegiance to past traditions of Christian theology – Christians and secular philosophers alike – find credible only radically revisionist understandings of God and God's relation to the world, this may well be due, then, to the lack of clear witness to the coherence of traditional Christian theology within the church itself.

Christian theology's own forgetfulness should, therefore, be centrally important for discussion of these issues even from an external standpoint. The present work will concentrate, accordingly, on the character of Christian coherence. The claim that theology has been forgetful of the coherence of its own forms of discourse will be supported by arguing that (1) there are ruled relations among traditional forms of theological statements sufficient to provide internal coherence for Christian discourse, and (2) these ruled relations have generally undergone a radical transformation during the last five centuries. The deleterious effect of this transformation for the coherence of traditional theological claims will become clear.

My initial sense that modern theology proceeds under strange circumstances will be confirmed in going behind modern commonplaces to the historically conditioned presuppositions that make traditional Christian talk incoherent. From a modern standpoint, it is traditional Christian accounts of God and creation that seem recondite and unfamiliar, disquieting in their attempts to bring together obvious incompatibles. This very charge of unintelligibility will become for us an odd fact to be accounted for, when that modern standpoint loses its fixity as a 'natural' given for thought.

In the chapters that follow, the problem of Christian coherence will not, then, be *solved* by engaging in arguments from *within* a framework of modern common sense. Instead, the absolute claim that traditional ways of formulating Christian statements about God and world are simply incoherent is to be *dissolved* by disturbing the complacent self-evidence of modern assumptions used to interpret traditional Christian language. The possibility of coherent Christian discourse of a traditional sort is recovered by viewing the supposedly inevitable conclusions and natural givens of modern culture as temporally conditioned, historically funded results: any presumption that they reflect either 'the way things are' or 'the simple logic of the matter' is undercut.

Just as the possible coherence of traditional Christian theology appears when modern assumptions are put in question, so what is taken for granted in a modern context comes to light when genuinely questioned by traditional forms of Christian theology initially alien to it. By formulating rules for coherent Christian discourse in subsequent chapters certain assumptions of modern discourse are exposed. Presuppositions of a modern framework, which escape notice because they ordinarily serve as a backdrop for judgements, are rendered possible objects for critical scrutiny in being confronted with forgotten possibilities from the past. A certain modern framework of discussion is disenchanted of its obviousness when an initially strange discourse is allowed to make a claim on it.

The attempt here to show the coherence of Christian discourse according to certain ruled uses of language is, therefore, at the same time a project for increasing practical wisdom, for furthering the critical self-understanding of modern 'prejudice' (in the non-pejorative sense used by Gadamer).[5] To uncover an interpretive context for the coherence of traditional Christian theology is also

to overcome the closure to which a modern viewpoint is susceptible. Indeed this is the only general way to overcome closure once
finite human understanding renounces the Cartesian dream of an
external, neutral vantage point for self-scrutiny. One overcomes
calcified or rigid prejudgements, not by suppressing either
prejudgement or the historical determination of context, but by
continually extending and enriching one's point of view. This
happens through open conversation and subsequent understanding of the alternatives for thought presented by other, not least
past, traditions of discourse.

It should be clear, then, that my proposals do not require any
anachronistic return to a world-view purportedly better able to
support the coherence of traditional Christian claims. Christian
coherence does not demand that the theologian be anything less
than modern since the potential for such coherence involves the
present perspective's opening up to include past theological possibilities as its own. But there is a more important point to be made
in this connection.

Later chapters will show that the coherence of Christian theology hinges on principles that regulate the construction of theological statements *whatever* the particular vocabulary or conceptuality or metaphysical substrate of beliefs about human beings and
the world. Theologians do not need to reproduce forms of
traditional theological statement along with the baggage of some
previous cultural outlook in order to repeat the success of pre-
modern forms of theological discourse in conforming to those
rules. *In principle* the rules for coherent talk about God and the
world that I will lay out can operate successfully in *any* cultural
context, however initially unfavourable a rhetorical climate it may
be.

For example, a typically modern preference for explanations
that remain within the natural order, and high esteem for the
self-determining character of human action, can be incorporated
in theological statements that conform to our rules for discourse as
well as can any cultural outlook that lacks them. A preference for
'this-wordly' explanation and an appreciation for human powers
of self-determination seem to imply the irrelevance of divine
agency in ways that conflict with traditional theological claims
about God's sovereignty. This conflict is only apparent, however,

when those theological claims are unpacked according to the Christian rules for discourse to be specified later. We shall see that a modern context did present special problems for theological language. The problems, I shall argue, were more the result of basic habits of interpretation than material claims about the nature of human beings and the world. Habits of interpretation hindered the correct assessment and appropriate new use in modern times of the rules for discourse present in the theological tradition.

Conforming to such rules in new contexts has always been more a matter of training in the tradition of Christian theology than a matter for conscious deliberation. Some sort of 'grammar', stating the rules *as* rules, should help, however, to block the subversion of a ruled use of language to which Christian theologians have shown themselves prone. Such a grammar, as this book hopes to show, may be a contribution of modern theology, situated as it is in an interpretive context where attention to linguistic form or media has all but supplanted consideration of what language is used to talk about.

Other aspects of the contemporary cultural scene favour the critical modification of cultural givens necessary if discourse borrowed from other contexts is to conform to rules for theological coherence. The pretension to absolute inviolability, made by cultural forms of various times, is dissolved both by the 'historical consciousness' of modernity and by recent emphasis, in the human sciences and in philosophy after Wittgenstein, on the importance of attending to specific historical and linguistic contexts when assessing the significance of statements generally.

The point I am making by rehearsing arguments for extended discussion later on is that, rhetorical tone aside, the present project is not an attempt to 'repristinate' theology – in the double sense of either a return to origins or a recovery of former purity. Just as modern theology is implicated along with general secular culture in the subversion of theological discourse, so the very feasibility of the theological project undertaken here supposes that pre-modern theology is neither privileged nor innocent.

Let me outline the stages of the presentation to follow. The complicated scenario of this introduction is made more manageable by the recommendations for the study of theological language discussed in the first chapter. The second and third chapters argue that traditional Christian claims about God and creation can be coherently maintained together in theologies that restrict in certain ruled ways the implications their language would suggest in non-theological contexts. The fourth chapter lays out the modern assumptions according to which traditional forms of discourse are misread and their structure altered by new theological construction, so that Christian discourse becomes genuinely incoherent. My concluding remarks should make clear those options for theology at the present time that follow from the analyses of the second, third and fourth chapters.

1

Method in the Study of Theology

Metaphysics is the finding of bad reasons for what one believes on
instinct, but to find these reasons is no less an instinct.

F. H. Bradley, *Appearance and Reality*[1]

Teach me, Lord, how I can conceive that to be possible which I
perceive to be necessary.

Nicholas of Cusa, *The Vision of God*[2]

On the way towards showing how Christian language has been
broadly tranformed in modern times, we will be studying a
number of historical cases of theological discourse about a transcendent God who creates, governs and saves the world. My
intention is to isolate ruled structures in such talk and their overall
function, while respecting the differences and historical particula-
rities of theological language. Methodological guidelines for a
study of this sort are sketched now. By the last chapter it should
be evident what general contributions such recommendations
make towards understanding what theology can do, how it works
and the conditions for its success. Because it concerns procedures
for the study of theology, the discussion in this chapter is, by
necessity, abstract; readers impatient with a discussion of that sort
may prefer to start with chapter 2 where the modes of investigation proposed here begin to be employed.

How is theology being approached, if, as I have just said, my
object is to specify the ruled structures of theological talk and their
function? The approach has two aspects: first, theological language
is the focus of investigation; second, an attempt is made to specify
the work such language performs. Let us discuss the ramifications
of these two points in turn, so as to get a better sense for them.

In studying theology I am concentrating, not on what theologians are talking about, but on the way they say it. My direct concern is not for the object of theological discourse – e.g., God, the world, eternal life – but for theologians' talk about it. The approach is characterized, then, by what is called in American analytic philosophy a linguistic turn (Bergmann, Rorty) or semantic ascent (Quine) from what language concerns to language itself.[3] The referents of theological statements are put in brackets for the purpose of uncovering ruled relations among those statements.

In this regard the present approach dovetails with a number of currently influential intellectual trends noted, sometimes infamous, for their 'non-referentiality'. The language orientation of modern American analytic philosophy is merely a case in point. Examples cover a wide range of philosophical styles and preoccupations – from Dewey's pragmatism to Nietzsche's enthusiasm for the will to power at work in active interpretation, from Hegel's phenomenology of forms of human experience to structuralist analyses of linguistic systems and Derridian proclamations of nothing outside the text. For all their differences, these intellectual trends are interested far less in reality (supposing that notion remains a meaningful one for them) than in the shapes it takes according to modes of human intercourse which vary over time and place. Statements are not viewed as ideally transparent pointers to their objects of real concern, but tend to become opaque human artefacts bound up with forms of life (for Wittgenstein), institutional and cultural frameworks (for sociologists and anthropologists), and linguistic systems (for language philosophers).

The study of theological language undertaken here does not align itself with any particular current of these trends, although the discussion to follow will often be expressed in terms associated with American philosophy of an analytic or pragmatist stripe. The attention given to theological language is justified primarily by certain theological assumptions.

The talk of theologians becomes an object for discussion in keeping with the reservations they express about their own abilities to comprehend the nature of divinity thereby. Theologians seem to know that it is appropriate to say certain things about God without quite knowing what they mean by doing so. They may abjure all positive knowledge of the nature of God and insist their statements tell us nothing but what God is not; their statements inform us of our own ignorance. Theologians may make affirmations about the nature and existence of God but maintain that their analogical status prevents any specification of their positive content. In that case, theologians may claim to know *that* their statements refer to God and are true of God's nature, but they do not claim to know in what way they refer or *how* they are true. In Thomistic language, they affirm that the *res significata*, i.e., the reality signified by their terms, properly applies to God, but they deny or remain agnostic about the application of the *modus significandi* of those same terms, i.e., about the application to God of the way those terms signify for us in virtue of what we mean by them. On this apophatic or agnostic reading, theological statements are not conveying information about God so much as they are suggesting how to talk in circumstances where we do not pretend to understand fully what we are saying.

It makes sense then to recast the 'material mode' of a theologian's statements *about* God and world into a 'formal mode' whereby they express recommendations for *talk* about these matters.[4] Statements about God and world become rules for discourse, proposals about what should and should not be said. Theological recommendations for talk about God's agency in relation to creation will be our specific area of concern in what follows.[5] I will have more to say in a moment about the general nature of theological statements understood as rules for discourse.

Although the referential character of theological discourse is crucial to the whole enterprise (what would be the point of doing theology if one were not really talking about God?), the informational vacuity of such talk should shift the focus of someone investigating it away from epistemological questions of truth and meaning. Theologians simply assume that what they say about God is meaningful and true: they have no way of actually specifying what they are talking about (the *res significata* of their statements) apart from the meanings of the terms they use and it is just those meanings whose applicability to God they admit to failing to understand. The attention of the investigator is directed consequently to the practical effects of theological statements: as proposals for talk, those statements are helping to build a distinctive Christian practice of discourse and, by extension, forms of life congruent with it. By making recommendations about how to talk, theological statements work to establish Christian vocabularies and the usage rules appropriate for those expressions. In doing so, frameworks for discourse are constituted within which it makes sense to talk *about* God and try to conform oneself to Christian *truths*.

A linguistic turn in the study of theology therefore suggests a pragmatist focus on the behaviours theological language influences and the purposes behind the particular context of inquiry that theological statements serve to promote.[6] Theology, according to this pragmatist approach, helps us to get along in the world as Christians; it works to expedite the task of forming ourselves as people who believe and act and approach life in a Christian way.

This brings us to the second aspect of our approach to theology: the emphasis on the functions of theological language. Theology does not merely help to set up a distinctive Christian practice, as our pragmatist focus on theological language maintains; Christian practices that are already established specify jobs theology is to execute. Theology is an integral part of Christian life in community – a function of it, one might say. It takes its place within that context by undertaking the tasks the community sets for it, i.e., by doing certain things, performing certain functions that community practice requires.

On this functionalist approach theology and the practice of Christian life are not separate, subsequently conjoined spheres. Theologians' statements about God and world do not form an independently constituted body of speculation which gains relevance for Christian life by a kind of secondary application. The theologian is not engaged on his or her own in a free theoretical pursuit, propelled by a drive for knowledge that proceeds where it may, blindly, for the truth, before being brought together after the fact with a particular context of practical interests. Theological speculation is called forth by Christian practice and returns to it.

Theology may be called to do many different things within the context of a Christian form of life – to make first-order claims about God and world, recommend courses of action, criticize or support the practice of the community, regulate the church's belief and action, police itself etc.[7] Congruent with the linguistic turn of our study of theology in which statements about God and world become statements about how it is appropriate to talk, theology can be understood as called forth by Christian practice to be a kind of reflection upon it. The subject matter of theology becomes community practices. The primary task for theology in such a case is to explicate in an organized fashion the essentials of what is said and done by Christians in their daily lives.

Theologians start with unreflected Christian habits of speech, action and affection; they work outwards from that given. Theology, like philosophical reflection, must start somewhere; it has presuppositions which tend to form the limits of its own discussion. Those starting points, in the theologian's case, correspond to assumptions basic to Christian forms of behaviour, claims implicated in the shape of Christian life as we know it. Philosophers take as their starting points the presumptions of a less narrowly defined practice; those beliefs, for example, about self-identical things, personal identity, free will, the reliability of our faculties etc., that appear to be the presumptions of any sustained human enterprise.

Theologians work over in a reflective way the know-how that Christians exhibit. Those engaged in a Christian form of life have been trained to do so by listening to, watching and being corrected by those who already know what it means to live in a Christian manner. Those who are learning to be Christians hear what is said about God and world from the pulpit, in the liturgical practices of their communities; they have before them the example of Christian uses of scripture, the example of Christian behaviours and attitudes and proclamations of belief. Through these means an unreflective habit of conduct is acquired. One discovers how to go on in a Christian fashion, for the most part without hesitation or deliberate effort, in the course of one's own life. One now knows what dispositions and forms of comportment are appropriate to Christians, what it is proper to say about oneself, about the world and the object of one's religious devotion. It is a knowledge that shows itself in one's deeds; a knowledge constituted by one's ability to act.

A specifically linguistic competency is part of this knowledge of performance. Training in a Christian form of life makes one a competent Christian speaker. One gains the ability to discriminate between well-formed and ill-formed Christian statements, and to generate statements of the former sort in the appropriate circumstances.

The theologian reflects on this competency. In talking about how Christians talk, he or she tries to make explicit what Christians are doing in choosing to speak in certain ways and not in others; the theologian tries to formulate in a principled manner the Christian grasp on language that goes with use. In part this involves articulating the sort of things that Christians are prone to say about God and world in the various 'language games' of Christian life – e.g., in the creeds, doxologies, catechesis, prayers, proclamation and witness of Christian communities. In part it involves an intellectual ordering of the multiple, uncoordinated forms of talk about God and world that figure in these different linguistic arenas.

In addition to the primary performance of Christian worship and belief, the theologian supplies, then, a kind of map of how it is done. In this capacity the theologian supplies something like a logic or grammar covering Christian linguistic competency. The theologian reflects on customary forms of Christian statements to codify prevailing standards of linguistic behaviour. He or she elucidates Christian intuitions regarding well-formed Christian statements and their interconnections by formulating rules of speech that make sense of the variety of statements Christians make.

Throughout this process the existence of an already relatively well-defined Christian community of discourse exercises a crucial determinative influence. The end point as well as the starting point of theological speculation is the given practice of Christian behaviours and beliefs. A theological grammar of Christian linguistic competency is acceptable only to the extent that its principled reflection matches the intuitions of competent Christian speakers about well-formed statements and offers an ordering of the variety of such statements without oversimplification or distortion.

In this process the data of an already existing sphere of Christian discourse are controlling in the aggregate; they are not, however, individually sacrosanct. Within a regulative ideal of by-and-large conformity, theological discourse may suggest revisions of Christian linguistic practice. Such suggestions prove correct to the extent Christian practice is altered to conform to them. Thus the doxology 'Glory be to the Father and to the Son and to the Holy Ghost', which coordinates the persons of the Trinity through the use of 'and' connectives, became standard after the fight against Arian theology which subordinated the Son and the Holy Ghost to the Father.[8] Modifications of the creed used in liturgy after the *filioque* controversies provide another case in point: the Nicene

Creed was altered in the West to read 'from the Father *and* the Son' to reflect a growing theological consensus there about the procession of the Holy Spirit.[9] Whether theological discussion between East and West will continue to confirm the need for that change, and whether it might in any case prove permanent, are questions that may be left open here. The point is that a feedback structure exists which provides some room for mutual determination and accommodation between theology and the fundamental discourse of the Christian community.[10]

Theology as this self-reflective moment of Christian practice is not simply the product of a natural desire on the part of Christians for self-understanding. It is a theoretical activity shaped by the practical needs of community contexts; it is itself the working out of practical interests. Theology can be viewed in this regard according to the perspective a pragmatist like Charles Peirce takes towards inquiry in general: theological reflection, like any form of inquiry, arises to meet problems that threaten a practice as an ongoing concern.[11] Thought intervenes in a generally conservative fashion to re-establish habits of conduct by overcoming the obstacles that interrupt their functioning. After reflection the very same practice may be reinstated; sometimes a revision of what has been done may be required to set a practice back on track. Within the overall context of an attempt to maintain the basic shape of a Christian form of life, the theologian offers reasoned defences and critical evaluations of Christian conduct.

Such attempts to bolster a faltering practice may take a variety of forms. Theological reflection, like other kinds of thought, may work to justify patterns of behaviour and affirmation when they begin to seem bereft of reason, or to shake off those potentially disruptive confusions to which a sphere of discourse is prone for lack of careful discriminations, or to maintain what we already want to believe in the hope that it does not extend, as we fear it might, beyond the realm of real possibility. Thought arises after the fact in all these cases to give the cast of knowledge to prior opinion that might otherwise appear suspect.

The problems of Christian practice that prompt theological reflection are legion. If we narrow them down to those that afflict religious discourse, it is possible to give a rough classification of them. First, Christians may exhibit a tendency to mis-speak: they may make statements whose well-formed character or Christian authenticity is a matter for dispute. Second, they may deploy well-formed Christian statements inappropriately. Third, they may be unsure how to speak, how to continue the practice of Christian discourse, in strange or novel circumstances. Fourth, they may make Christian statements whose well-formed character is undisputed and yet fail to understand how those statements are compatible with one another. In all four cases, Christian discourse begins to sputter; theological reflection becomes necessary as a result.

The linguistic practice of Christians is set back on its feet in such cases by principled reflection on Christian linguistic competency. Such reflection can help extend linguistic practices so that it becomes clear how to speak in a Christian manner under new conditions. It can help to establish conclusively *whether* a particular statement is Christianly authentic or misapplied, and *why*. Misapplication could be shown by setting out explicitly the principles that underlie a statement's proper employment. Demonstrating misuse might involve pointing out that the attitudes and behaviours promoted by that use are inappropriate to a Christian life. Thus, to take an example of special importance to followers of Martin Luther, a theologian might conclude that statements about God's wrath are improperly employed to address those who trust that Christ has saved them despite their sins; talk of that sort would serve to reanimate a terrified conscience and worried scrupulosity which are no longer appropriate. Where the Christian authenticity of statements is under dispute, the resulting disruption of Christian linguistic habits is also dispelled by reflection upon those habits. Judgements of inauthenticity require the theologian to show that, although a statement seems to follow from authentic Christian statements, it conflicts with too many others of crucial importance to Christian forms of life, and/or with liturgical practices and forms of comportment that are equally essential. Thus, although Pelagian claims about sin and the influence of our own efforts on salvation seem to follow from biblical injunctions to be morally perfect, Augustine argued that they undermine the importance of Christ's death and resurrection and conflict with the Lord's prayer, practices of infant baptism, and Christian humility.

The fourth sort of problem afflicting religious discourse is centrally important to the study of theological language undertaken here. It is prudent to discuss it more thoroughly before outlining how theological reflection on the linguistic practices of Christians might be a way of resolving it.

The problem is basically one of an apparent incoherence among statements that competent Christian speakers recognize as well-formed or authentic. Such problems are particularly acute when the statements in conflict lie at the core rather than the periphery of Christian belief. They are, in other words, not merely well-formed statements but ones crucial to Christian worship and belief – statements like 'Jesus Christ died for us' rather than statements like 'Jesus walked on water'. Giving any of them up would have drastic repercussions for the rest of Christian belief and worship. The task for theological reflection is to explain how they are consistent with one another.

Philosophical reflection is often prompted by the same sort of concerns.[12] Philosophers seek to confirm claims essential to human life as we know it in the face of their apparent conflict with other beliefs we hold. For example, we speak of ourselves as agents with free will: using the vocabulary of an internal perspective we affirm our freedom. Yet we also employ an external vocabulary that implies our insertion in a causally determined network of actions and reactions: we view ourselves and others from the outside in a way that appears to conflict with our belief in a human capacity for free self-determination. Because both ways of speaking are implicated in a vast array of human practices, the philosopher usually does not want to give up either. The task becomes to show with what right we hold on to both despite their apparent incompatibility. The theologian does much the same thing: the tasks are simply set by a more specialized sphere of discourse – a specifically Christian one.

The problems that prompt attempts to explain the compatibility of Christian statements are thus theoretical ones; they represent a kind of disease of reflection. As such, however, they affect the functioning of Christian linguistic practices. Should a believer reflect on the variety of things he or she says, inconsistencies may emerge. For a reflective individual, recognizing that Christian statements do not hang together very well may cause a kind of stammering: the believer may hesitate, waver as he or she tries to go on as a Christian speaker. The practical force of Christian statements in promoting Christian forms of affection and behaviour may also be blocked by a failure to resolve this sort of problem.

To show how this might work, let us take as an example Philippians 2:12 – 13: 'Work out your own salvation with fear and trembling, for God is at work in you, both to will and work for his good pleasure.' The statement recommends certain attitudes and actions. It tells Christians that they have to do something: they must not be quietistically complacent, they must not sit on their hands, they must work, they must take responsibility for themselves. On the other hand, they must do so 'with fear and trembling': they should not trust in their own accomplishments since everything, including it seems their own power and activity, is given to them by God. What the statement recommends is complex but practically possible.

If one reflects upon what the statement suggests about God and human beings, a theoretical problem of consistency seems to arise. The first half of the statement assumes that human beings are agents with their own capacities and responsibilities for action; the second half, that God's activity extends everywhere, even to cases where Christians are themselves supposed to be at work. How can both halves be true at once? It would seem that to the extent a Christian believer is genuinely responsible for working out his or her salvation, God must not be, and vice versa. A Christian tendency to say both might in that case incline a reflective Christian to believe that Christian linguistic habits do not make sense and are therefore ill-advised.

If theological reflection fails to show how the two sorts of claims are compatible, Christian behaviours and attitudes may be skewed accordingly. The appearance of a contradiction splits the two sides of the recommendation apart. The Christian may take the first part seriously and neglect the second. In that case the statement merely recommends that the believer work his or her own salvation. Despair over one's failings or pride in one's accomplishments will be the result. He or she may adhere to the second part while discounting the first. In that case God works the Christian's salvation and there is nothing left for him or her to do. The believer's own enterprises become *adiaphora* where his or her own salvation is concerned; one is free to do as one likes without repercussions, free to fall even into a quietistic stupor, since salvation or damnation is purely a matter of God's will. In either case, an intellectual problem that might disquiet a reflective Christian has potentially harmful practical consequences for Christian behaviours and attitudes: the spontaneous, unreflective practice of Christian comportment threatens to derail.

Unless reflective questions are simply to be squelched – an impractical suggestion given a natural human tendency to reflect and the needs of Christian practice that reflection serves – more reflection is the only solution to problems of this sort.[13] Problems of incompatibility among Christian statements will be solved only if the theologian can show *how it is possible* for Christians to affirm certain statements while holding on to others that seem to conflict with them. What the theologian has to do is to show *with what right* Christians say what as competent speakers they feel inclined to say. Christians want to make those statements that seem implicated in a Christian form of life. A statement of that sort becomes problematic by appearing to conflict with at least one other statement Christians also wish to affirm. The theologian steps in to supply conditions of possibility that justify the need Christians feel to meet certain linguistic obligations.

In so far as they supply conditions of possibility for problematic affirmations, the arguments theologians provide have the general shape of transcendental arguments. An analysis of such arguments in a philosophical venue may therefore make more perspicuous what is involved in the theologian's attempt to explain the compatibility of apparently conflicting Christian statements. Immanuel Kant will be of help in this respect.

Kant employed transcendental arguments in two different ways. One of these corresponds to our theological case. Transcendental arguments on the whole supply conditions of possibility for something; but the rhetorical force of their employment varies depending upon whether that something is problematic or taken for granted prior to the argument. If that for which conditions are supplied is problematic, the point of the argument is to support it by providing those conditions. If conditions are supplied for something unproblematic, the purpose is to argue in support of those very conditions themselves. That is done in showing they are preconditions for what is solid for us, for what we take for granted and cannot imagine giving up. In this second case, the *ad hominem* strategy of a transcendental argument is this: if you do not want to renounce what seems impossible for you to give up, then you must accept this, its precondition. In the first case, the strategy is, 'if you accept this proposed precondition you will be justified in your desire to hold on to what otherwise appears problematic.' Theological arguments that support problematic affirmations of Christian linguistic practice by supplying conditions for their compatibility conform to this first sort of use.

Kant in his *Critique of Pure Reason* attempts a transcendental argument of the first sort in order to support the necessary and universal applicability of scientific and mathematical principles. Kant wants mathematical principles and the basic laws of Newtonian science to have necessity and universality; such claims do not seem justified, however, given the usual sources of human knowledge. Principles derived empirically cannot claim universality or necessity. Principles formed by explicating the senses of terms can indeed make such claims but only by renouncing that pretension to extend our knowledge of the world that mathematics and science make. To resolve this apparent incompatibility between claims made for science and mathematics and their potential derivations, Kant argues that the concepts and forms of intuition basic to science and mathematics are involved in the very constitution of objects of experience for the human mind. Mathematical and scientific principles *must* be applicable to *every* object of experience if sense data are worked up to form such objects by way of the very categories and forms of intuition employed by those principles. Within an overall argument of this first sort, Kant includes transcendental arguments of the second sort I mentioned. He argues for most of the first *Critique* that certain categories, forms of intuition and principles should be accepted in so far as they are necessary conditions for the possibility of experience of objects in general which no one wants to dispute.

To increase the argumentative force of this second use of transcendental arguments, which forms the linchpin for his other projects, Kant makes two highly dubious assumptions. Our corresponding account of theological arguments will not follow him here. He assumes (1) that the preconditions of experience he adumbrates are necessary preconditions, the only preconditions of our experience of objects, and (2) that there are no alternative modes of meaningful human experience that cannot be accounted for with reference to the conditions of possibility he specifies. In modern times a recognition of cross-cultural and historical diversity in forms of meaningful human experience undercuts Kant's second assumption. Against the first, Stephan Körner has shown conclusively that transcendental deductions cannot prove that the conditions of possibility sufficient for a given are also necessary or unique.[14]

These two considerations weaken markedly the force of what I have been calling the second use of transcendental arguments. Support for conditions of possibility via a transcendental argument is only as strong, in the first place, as it is difficult to abandon the supposed givens of human life for which preconditions are supplied. If there are alternatives to a supposed given of human practice (e.g., if the scientific experience of a world of objects, which Kant held so dear, has no exclusive claim on the way human beings make sense for themselves), the power of a transcental argument of the second type is weakened accordingly. Conditions of possibility can be rejected along with what they condition. Were there to be something absolutely fundamental to human practices in all times and places to serve as the inviolable given of a transcendental argument of the second type, its force would nevertheless be trivialized by the second consideration we noted. Because there may be other sufficient conditions for its possibility, accepting a given does not require us to accept as well any particular precondition offered.

The recognition of cross-cultural and historical diversity in human practices which weakens transcendental arguments of the second type increases, however, the importance of those of the first type as strategic moves. All givens of human practice are rendered problematic, and therefore potentially in need of transcendental arguments that provide support by specifying conditions for their success. Even the experience of a world of spatio-temporal objects, which Kant assumed as an unproblematic given to fuel other projects of cultural justification, is no longer thought to be so inviolable that it would not also benefit from that sort of Kantian argument.[15] Thus, theological versions of the first use of transcendental arguments are understood to offer support for a Christian practice that is 'optional', i.e., one practice among others capable of providing a framework for a meaningful and fulfilling human life.

The other reservation about Kant's claims holds for transcendental arguments of the first type, too: preconditions offered as support for what is problematic cannot be assumed to be necessary or unique. Although this reservation weakens the force of arguments of the second type, it can only work to facilitate the task of providing arguments of the first sort – the reservation simply expands the possible range of conditions sufficient to support a problematic affirmation. If transcendental arguments in theology are understood accordingly, one has to admit that it is possible for a problematic claim of Christian practice to be buttressed in a number of different ways.

Combining the modifications that result from both reservations, transcendental arguments of the first type become tools for a particular purpose: the elucidation and support of problematic human practices – in the case at hand, the elucidation and support of the linguistic practices of Christian communities. Once the pretensions of finding unique conditions for an absolute given are deflated, transcendental arguments become devices for setting out the structures of various discursive spheres. They show how each such sphere of discourse may be held together. In this capacity as expository devices, transcendental arguments uncover assumptions that permit the acceptance of claims characteristic of a particular form of life. A particular sphere of discourse is shown to be made up of an internally consistent network of implications and suppositions within which such claims are held firm.[16]

A comparison with other forms of argument might help make clearer what we are left with. Qualified so that proposed conditions are not considered necessarily unique, transcendental arguments in theology bear some resemblance to the use of empirical hypotheses in science. In science a hypothesis is constructed to explain why something is the case, with the recognition, commonplace in the philosophy of science at least since Quine, that any such theory is empirically underdetermined.[17] In other words, empirical data are not enough to specify any particular theory as the one peculiarly correct account of the evidence. As in our qualified versions of transcendental arguments, there is a potentially infinite number of theories which could equally well account for the same empirical data. Of course, unlike transcendental arguments in support of community practice, the express aim of hypothesis formation in science is to produce explanatory theories with a predictive range well beyond the body of empirical facts from which one starts.[18]

There is, however, a more important point which distinguishes qualified transcendental arguments from not only empirical hypotheses but also demonstrative proofs. Transcendental arguments do not, as may be the case with empirical hypotheses, simply explain the *fact* or occurrence of something. They aim rather to show how something *can* be true, how something is possible given some other things which apparently conflict with it. For the same reason, it is not sufficient for transcendental arguments, as it is for demonstrative proofs, simply to provide premises from which something may be deduced. A proof may simply confirm something that one already believes without showing what one wants to understand – how that belief is specifically compatible with other beliefs which apparently exclude it.[19] For a proof to amount to a transcendental argument of our sort, (1) the premises from which something is deduced must include those things that appear at first to conflict with it and render its possibility problematic, or (2) the problematic affirmation and what it appears to conflict with must both be deduced from certain other premises, thereby demonstrating their compatibility.

Transcendental arguments of the sort we are interested in are not coextensive with deductive proofs because the problems addressed by transcendental arguments are always ones essentially of internal coherence. Something Christians want to affirm appears not to hang together very well with what else they affirm. Supplying conditions of possibility for that problematic affirmation therefore involves exhibiting the orderly arrangement of Christian discourse that includes it.

Does this difference from deductive proof insulate theological argument by ruling out public debate with non-believers? Does a preoccupation with internal coherence seal off theological discussion, in other words, from those who are not Christians? The theologian's enterprise has some relevance for non-Christians to the extent problems of compatibility within Christian discourse arise because Christians want to affirm what non-believers affirm as well. Non-Christians as well as Christians want to affirm, for example, the freedom of human beings and the genuine agency or causal efficacy of beings within the world. Such claims often prompt the feeling among Christians that traditional Christian claims about God's all-powerful sovereignty must be given up.

A demonstration of Christian coherence is, moreover, an argument for Christian belief to the degree that disbelief is engendered or justified by charges that Christian beliefs conflict with one another. The non-believer points out apparent incompatibilities among claims that are a part of Christian practice. These problems of compatibility, while reasons for non-belief, are also prime matters for the Christian bureau of internal affairs. By explaining how these claims can possibly be made together, theology as a kind of transcendental argument answers the objections of the non-believer and supplies thereby an apologetic for belief in simply going about its ordinary business.[20]

Because of another difference from deductive proof, theologians employing transcendental arguments in this manner need not argue on the unbeliever's own ground or beg the question by arguing from premises that the unbeliever would not accept. A simple proof designed to persuade someone of a conclusion must argue from premises that person accepts. Belief in the premises will be transferred to the conclusion by way of the logical connection that is shown to hold between the two. In such a case an argument from premises the non-believer does not accept will be open to the charge of vicious circularity or begging the question.[21] When transcendental arguments of our sort incorporate deductive proofs in the two manners we mentioned above, the sequence of what is believed does not follow the direction of logical consequence in the same way.[22] Where a problematic affirmation is supported by a transcendental argument that makes it the conclusion of a deductive proof, that conclusion is believed prior to its deduction from the premises, rather than the reverse; often indeed, the premises for the conclusion are hypotheses that gain credence from belief in the conclusion. The theologian who addresses such an argument to an unbeliever as an argument for Christian belief need not be directly persuading the unbeliever on the basis of the beliefs he or she already holds. The transcendental argument takes on a secondary function of recommending Christian belief on the grounds of its internal integrity.[23]

In making our comparison with qualified transcendental arguments, we have yet to discuss the general nature of the conditions of possibility theologians might offer to support problematic affirmations of Christian practice. Transcendental arguments in their classic Kantian formulation talk of fundamental structures of human cognition supplying conditions of possibility for necessary and universal knowledge of the world. Theological arguments accounting for the compatibility of apparently conflicting Christian claims offer nothing in the way of this sort of Kantian metaphysic of cognitive structures. Transcendental arguments are shifted in our case to a linguistic arena: conditions for coherent Christian talk are themselves linguistic.[24]

Conflict among Christian claims is not solved by further discussion of the subject matter in question; it is dissolved by rectifying mistakes in language practice according to proper rules for Christian usage. The theologian's failure to know quite what he or she means in talking about God prevents any straightforward 'ontological' explanation of theoretical difficulties posed by fundamental claims of Christian discourse. Following Austin Farrer, one cannot pretend, for instance, to reconcile God's agency with the creature's active powers through any material explanation of the actual mechanism found in some 'causal joint' between the two.[25] Because of the theologian's failure of comprehension, the compatibility of divine and created agencies cannot be established in any positive fashion that specifies the 'how' of their interaction.[26]

Linguistic solutions to problems of inconsistency among Christian claims are in keeping with the linguistic origin of those problems. Theologians elaborate claims implied in a Christian form of life by borrowing language in use elsewhere. In those other contexts that language already has established senses. Linguistic habits have formed a sediment of sense. Language has begun to run along certain well-worn tracks that direct expectations of use. One anticipates, more or less, from that past use what can and cannot be done with a statement – what else can be said, the possible associations, presuppositions, implications that form a statement's semantic horizon. The theologian breaks those habits, rechannels expectations, stirs up those sediments of sense in speaking of an extraordinary subject matter. The appearance of inconsistency that haunts theological statements is the result of this struggle with previous linguistic habits. The expectations of linguistic practices the theologian is working to revise always suggest that theological statements violate the canons of good sense. If those statements are to hang together consistently, the theologian must restrict apparent but nevertheless inappropriate implications of the language he or she presses into service. The theologian as grammarian of Christian usage shows how that is to be done.

Linguistic rules governing the formation of Christian statements are therefore the conditions of possibility which theologians supply in support of the coherence of Christian claims. Theologians show the coherence of Christian claims by following usage rules that block some of their apparent implications according to prior linguistic habit. The rules for their elaboration, which a theologian's discourse establishes, are what explain the coherence of Christian claims that otherwise appear to conflict with one another.

We can say these rules are rules for working over those in use elsewhere. They are transformation rules, rules for violating or fracturing the rules of non-theological linguistic practices. Any sphere of discourse with a measure of integrity exhibits ruled relations among its expressions. Parameters for appropriate word combinations and sentence connections, for instance, settle out from any sustained linguistic enterprise. Rules for word combinations establish the limits of proper sentence structure. Rules for sentence connections establish meaning: the import of a sentence and of the terms it employs becomes clear according to rules governing that sentences's elaboration – rules for further statements about its implications, presuppositions, associations. Theological rules of this latter sort are peculiar in that they are so often skewed versions of those found in other discursive spheres.

The rules we hope to specify are not the same as first-order statements about God and world (although they may come to be formulated by theologians in a material mode as if they were). They are rules *for forming* first-order statements; they direct the construction and interconnections of statements about God and world. Like mathematical functions or formulae of several variables, they work to produce theological 'equations' (first-order statements) of various sorts depending upon the concepts, vocabulary, ontological claims etc. of a particular theological context that are substituted within them.

The coherence of Christian claims about God and world does not require, therefore, any particular body of first-order claims about them; it requires, whatever the nature of those claims, that they be regulated according to certain rules. Thus, we will see later that God's transcendence understood as a rule for making first-order statements amounts to the following: whatever you say about God and world, do not simply identify or oppose their attributes. All the rules we will formulate are rules like this that direct the formation of statements without specifying their matter.

An analogous distinction used in logical theory may highlight in a rigorous way this difference between first-order statements and rules in theology. Consider the law of non-contradiction and the principle of excluded middle: they may work both as first-order claims within particular logical systems and as meta-level rules for the formation of such claims in any logical system. How are the two uses distinguished?

The difference is clearest in cases where the meta-level rule is followed while the first-order claim is denied. Thus, a logical system may not include a law of non-contradiction (e.g., $-\{P \ \& -P\}$) among the principles that constitute it as a particular logical system; the law of non-contradiction is not, in other words, a first-order principle of such a system. Every logic in so far as it is a formally consistent system conforms, however, to the law of non-contradiction as a meta-level rule governing the way principles within it are formulated. The law of non-contradiction on a meta-level simply keeps a logical system from affirming both a proposition and its negation. This meta-level principle is being followed even where a logic includes among its own principles a law contrary to that of non-contradiction, so long as that logic remains consistent in not also affirming the same law.

A distinction between first-order propositions and meta-level rules occurs with similar clarity in the case of many-valued logics. Many-valued logics do not include a principle of excluded middle: some value other than truth or falsity is admitted. To the extent that they are consistently formalized, they do, however, conform to a meta-leval version of the same principle, that 'if you do not class a proposition as true, you must class it as false and conversely.' Many-valued logics that are consistent simply apply this meta-level rule to the case of a first-order principle specifying values in addition to truth and falsity.

From these two cases of non-contradiction and excluded middle we can see that logical principles of a meta-level sort must not be equated with first-order versions of those principles in particular logical systems. Logical systems are abiding by those meta-level principles even when they deny first-order versions of them.[27] Logical systems may conflict on the level of first-order principles – one may deny the first-order principle of non-contradiction or excluded middle that the other affirms – yet the same meta-level rule may be governing the way those first-order principles are proposed in both systems. The first-order statements that theologians form according to rules and those rules themselves should be similarly distinct.

Our technical discussion of logical theory also points up the formality of the rules we seek in a theological arena. Like meta-level logical principles, rules governing theological statements are formal in that they have the capacity to structure talk of materially different sorts. The rules we seek do not themselves determine the specifics of discourse that follows them: what the rules leave open must be filled by the variable contexts of their use.

The case of logical theory suggests, moreover, the primarily negative function of rules in theology. The meta-level principles of logic again provide a model: the meta-level function of the laws of non-contradiction and excluded middle is to exclude inconsistently formalized logics; those laws do not of themselves pick out for special distinction any particular logical system.[28] Similarly, we will see that the theological rules narrow the range of what is admissible by eliminating a number of possible theological proposals without singling out any one for acceptance. They direct the formation of theological statements by way of normative constraints that simply rule out unacceptable statements as they are proposed.

Finally, the example of logical theory helps to clarify a distinction between the grammar of theology and the various theologies formed through its use. The same meta-level logical rules may structure very different logical systems – many-valued and two-valued logics, logics that include a principle of non-contradiction and those that do not. Similarly, the same theological rules conerning talk about God and creation may structure very different theological schemes, schemes distinguished by their first-order claims, by vocabulary, philosophical frames of reference etc.

If it is the grammar of a theologian's talk that ensures the coherence of apparently conflicting Christian assertions, no one theological scheme can claim an exclusive right to the applause of the faithful on that score. Here the linguistic emphasis of my approach dovetails with my functionalist emphasis on the job theology performs for Christian practice in the attempt to show the coherence of Christian claims, and with my account of that attempt as a qualified transcendental argument.

A particular theology – identified as such by discrete texts or by author or by theological school or denominational affiliation – may supply conditions of possibility for certain problematic Christian affirmations. From our discussion of transcendental arguments it is clear we cannot assume those conditions to be necessary or unique. There may be other theological schemes capable of supplying similarly sufficient conditions.

A functionalist approach generalizes this sort of conclusion. A task does not specify a single means. Different theologies may be functionally equivalent or analogous in that they perform the same job while using different tools. The functional equivalence of theologies in showing the coherence of Christian claims parallels in that case the functional equivalence of social forms that social scientists look for in studying the mechanisms of social cohesion. Shared beliefs, the organic interdependence of social sectors, the police, institutions of surveillance, may be the diverse but functionally equivalent mechanisms of social solidarity in different societies.[29]

The possibility of functional equivalence gives our study of theology an ecumenical slant. We have no a priori reason to privilege any particular theologian or theological school when trying to determine whether and how theologians establish the coherence of problematic Christian claims. There may be any number of quite different theologies fit to do the job. Theologies that solve potential coherence problems in talk about God and the world may span differences of historical and geographical context, differences of metaphysical commitment and denominational affiliation.

I have ventured to suggest, however, the general nature of the theological means used to solve problems of coherence in Christian talk about God and world – rules for discourse formation. I will go on in chapters 2 and 3 to specify one body of such rules and to argue that it is shared by all theologies successfully solving the particular problems of coherence I indicate. These proposals do not reinstate narrow rights of privilege. In keeping with my qualification of transcendental arguments I will not claim this body of rules is a necessary or unique condition for the solution of those problems – just that it is sufficient and makes sense of the theological cases studied. The claim that the same rules are found in all theologies that talk coherently of these matters is no more than an empirical generalization to be supported by the analysis of various theologies in subsequent chapters. I hope to show by that claim that Christian coherence is brought about not by wholly discontinuous mechanisms, but by a genuine tradition of theological discourse. In making this claim I recognize that the function of ensuring the coherence of Christian claims does not determine the particulars of theological discourse; I presume, however, that a purpose to be fulfilled places some constraints on discourse. A common objective will be mirrored in common linguistic features. If rules for discourse are what constitute those common features, it makes sense that theological positions of very different sorts might show coherence equally well. Rules for discourse will account for the functional equivalence of theologies that are very different in vocabulary or conceptuality employed, metaphysical assumptions, assertions made etc.

My functionalist and linguistic approach will show that if a tradition of coherent Christian talk exists, it has not been bought at the price of a static uniformity of linguistic expression or assertion by theology. Rules of discourse that ensure coherence cut across differences of context: the same rules may structure discourse, as I have said, whatever its particular assertions, vocabulary or conceptual frame. Our discussion of logical systems suggested that identical rules may operate even in schemes of thought that conflict on the level of first-order claims. On a functionalist account, theologies are compared for their success in completing a task rather than for their accuracy in describing a state of affairs. Although descriptive equivalence requires that theologies be reconciled on the level of content, on the level of claims made, functional equivalence does not. Functional equivalence does not demand semantic uniformity, an equivalence on the level of messages conveyed. Any number of very different theological accounts may be capable of explaining the compatibility of Christian claims about God and world. Even logically incompatible theological schemes (that is, schemes that cannot be included within one logically consistent system of discourse) may yet be functionally equivalent: each may be doing the same thing, performing the same explanatory function, in virtue perhaps of shared rules for discourse.

Although our stress is on rules that are held in common, the concrete particulars by which theologies differ will not be ignored on that account. Our search for rules does not isolate what is common to various theologies by progressively diminishing their content, by dropping as irrelevant those elements that make for their specific identities. The commonalities we hope to specify are not the residues left over from a negative process of stripping down the concrete particularity of theological positions. What theologies share are the rules by which their own constituent particulars are arranged. Those rules may traverse differences in theologies but they do not therefore make those differences any less essential. The rules will not function apart from a reference to the particulars that serve to differentiate theological positions. The rules we seek are therefore the very principles by which that diversity appears.

The pragmatic aspect of rules for discourse in my account supports much the same point – that such rules do not reduce the disparate theologies of the Christian tradition to a dreary succession of the identical. Rules of discourse shape a Christian form of life; in doing so they perform specific functions determined by the needs of that community life. One of those needs, I have said, is to show the coherence of apparently incompatible claims implicated in Christian practice. The rules that perform a function of that sort may also serve certain secondary, theology-specific purposes.

The rules that show the coherence of Christian talk about God and world may be used differently, they may be used with a quite significant diversity of emphasis, depending upon a theologian's assessment of the particular needs of the time and situation of the audience addressed. Rules within the body of those that ensure Christian coherence may differ in their individual practical effects. A theologian's particular priorities under the circumstances in which he or she writes will therefore influence the degree to which individual rules form his or her discourse.

Thus, it might be the case that in a context in which assertions of human power threaten to suggest that not everything is owed to God a theologian will form his or her discourse predominantly by those rules for coherence that highlight divine sovereignty. Another theologian or the same one in a different setting may primarily employ those rules for coherence that point up free human agency in the process of exhorting Christians to do all that they can in obedience to God's commands. In this way the same body of rules makes sense of very different theological agendas within an overall project of showing how claims of a Christian form of life hang together. Theological positions that are hard to reconcile when understood as flat descriptions of what is the case become functional complements serving situation-specific theological ends. The diversity of theological positions that may be functional complements in this fashion will come in for extended discussion in chapter 3.

Finally, our claim that Christian coherence is brought about by rules and the structure of discourse they form should not suggest a structuralist refusal of the complications of history. A tradition of coherent Christian talk cannot run counter to what the history of theology reveals. That history provides less evidence, it might be argued, for linear or cumulative developments, faithful discipleship and mutual understanding, than it does for the impoverishment of tradition by attempted clarifications, mutual misapprehension among contemporaries and the deformation of a precursor's discourse through a curiously self-deceptive forgetfulness.[30] An account of a tradition of Christian coherence cannot gloss over the ruptures of history.

Discontinuities in the use of Christian statements become a distinct possibility on our analysis of theological language. Theological statements are unusual linguistic formations. The theologian is violating the sense of terms garnered from previous non-theological linguistic practices, skewing the established usage rules for them. Often no specifically theological sense of the terms has yet to settle; the theologian is actively reconstructing usage rules for them in the very process of forming a body of statements. The sense of any theological statement is, therefore, peculiarly dependent upon the particular context of its use. Nothing except a theologian's further statements or use of a statement in a particular historical setting makes clear what it does or does not mean. The significance of a theological statement may vary fairly dramatically, therefore, depending on the network of statements in which it is embedded or the historical circumstances of its use. Theological statements gain in this way an unusual plasticity of import and function: with changes of context they tend to change their sense significantly and, thereby, the particular theological purposes they serve.

Unselfconscious reversals in the use of theological statements are not uncommon. Implications that were prohibited in a previous use come to be permitted; what was permitted is now prohibited. Rules for use change and thereby a subsequent function becomes the opposite of a prior one.

Take for example the statement 'whatever God does with created causes, God could do without them.' That statement might be used to imply our direct dependence upon God, even in cases where human beings are themselves at work; divine sovereignty is thereby highlighted. Carried over into a new linguistic context, the same statement might be used with the contrary aim of stressing our power to determine our own destiny apart from any specific gift of God. The statement might now suggest the previously unacceptable claim that men and women have the fundamental capacity to become holy through their own efforts apart from God's gift of new or renewed powers for action. God does not have to rework or reissue the created causes of rectitude (our habits of action) in order for us to gain it.[31]

In chapter 4 we will have the occasion to document reversals of this sort in the carrying over of Christian statements. A Christian tradition of similar sounding statements will be shown to provide only a spurious continuity. Usage rules are skewed; the function of explaining Christian coherence is no longer fulfilled.

Historical factors are also crucial determinants of the success of theologies' attempts at explaining the coherence of Christian claims. The functional equivalence of theological schemes in virtue of shared rules for discourse does not rule out historical grounds for preferring one over others. Even when all theological candidates abide by the same rules for coherent discourse, not all those candidates will provide an explanation of coherence in a form adequate for a particular time and place. Rules for coherent discourse operate in the live settings of producers and receivers of theological language; rhetorical factors will therefore affect the relative explanatory success in a particular situation of theologies that conform to those rules.

Take, for example, a theology that explains the compatibility of human freedom and divine power by employing language that suggests, according to its usual usage rules, the genuine freedom of human agents, but only indirectly, by skewing those rules, the sovereignty of God. Theological explanation of that sort may be especially appropriate in a historical context in which the freedom of human agents is denied, and their moral efforts discouraged, by an emphasis on the sovereignty of divine agency as a sort of coercive determinism. While exhibiting coherence, it will shore up threatened human dignity. The same form of theological explanation would be far less appropriate in a historical context in which the autonomy of human agents was stressed to the detriment of God's sovereignty and the humble, trusting thankfulness owed by men and women *coram Deo*.

Situational factors affecting the relative success of theologies that follow the same rules for coherence will become important in chapter 4 and in the conclusion. If we can isolate rules for coherent Christian discourse, we will need to assess the likelihood of a successful use of those rules at the present time. We should turn now to the prior question. Can Christian claims about God and world be shown to make sense together? If so, in virtue of what body of linguistic rules?

2

The Transcendence and Creative Agency of God

The Basic Structure of Christian Discourse I

Non enim esse suum est finitum per aliquam naturam determinatam ad genus vel speciem, ut possit dici quod *est* et *non est* illud, ut sunt determinatae etiam substantiae spirituales.
Thomas Aquinas, *In Librum Beati Dionysii De Divinis Nominibus Expositio*[1]

. . . a supreme example of power . . . is not bounded by circumstances contrary to its nature.
Gregory of Nyssa, *An Address on Religious Instruction*[2]

Methodological preliminaries of a general sort out of the way, we are ready to begin in this chapter an argument about Christian coherence. We will inquire how Christian claims about God and creation may hang together intelligibly. My treatment of the topic falls into two parts: this chapter considers the consistency of Christian talk about a transcendent God who creates the world; the next chapter, the consistency of that talk when the world God creates is said to include creatures with their own power and efficacy.

Claims of this kind about God and world make sense together, I shall argue, if certain rules for their elaboration are followed. These rules for discourse are shared, moreover, by Christian theologies that explain the coherence of those claims. To use the language of the last chapter, such theologies are functional equivalents in that they explain away the same potential problems of consistency via the same rules for discourse.

The arguments of the next two chapters have two main purposes, therefore: (1) to demonstrate how the coherence of Christian claims can be achieved through rules for Christian talk; and (2) to suggest that a historical tradition of Christian theology conforming to those rules exists. The first aim is met basically by conceptual arguments of my own devising: assuming that Christians want to say certain sorts of things about God and world, I argue that certain directives for discourse formation ensure that talk's coherence. The second aim requires the rules that result from these arguments to be shown at work in various historical cases of theological discourse.

In making the conceptual arguments I do not exclude the possibility that Christian coherence could also be achieved by some body of rules other than the one specified. The extreme diversity of theologies that we will discuss in terms of those rules suggests, however, that they may be enough to account for the success of any theology explaining the coherence of Christian talk. Examples will span differences of time, geography, church affiliation and philosophical affinity. The reader should try testing this last claim against his or her own familiarity with theological positions that will not be mentioned here.[3]

In the present chapter (but not the next) these two logically distinct parts of the agenda correspond to different sections. In a first section, I come up with rules for talk about a transcendent God who creates the world by looking at possible problems of consistency that might suggest themselves in the Hellenistic milieu of Christian theology's birth. In a second section, I discuss various ways those rules have actually been exhibited over the course of the history of Christian theology.

GREEK PROBLEMATIC AND CHRISTIAN RESOLUTION

The claims of Christian practice whose consistency we are concerned to evaluate in this chapter concern (1) God's transcendence, and (2) God's creative agency.

'God transcends the world' is an odd affirmation of primary Christian practice – apart from the reflections of theologians it is likely to be a rare utterance in the daily lives of Christians.[4] That

God is somehow beyond this world seems, however, to be at least a presumption of a number of common practices. God must not be of this world if God is to act as its saviour and judge. Biblical and liturgical doxologies proclaim God's 'otherness' in power and mystery. Prohibitions against idolatry forbid the ascription of divine attributes to things of this world. The mystery of God's ways is a presupposition of the Christian trust that, appearances to the contrary, the world is ruled by a good, just and loving God.

God's direct involvement with the world as the creator of all that is finds more explicit biblical and liturgical expression. God is the 'all-governing creator of heaven and earth, of all things visible and invisible', e.g., in the Nicene Creed. Christians confess 'the one God, the Father, from whom are all things and for whom we exist, and one Lord, Jesus Christ, through whom are all things and through whom we exist' (I Corinthians 8:6). They proclaim that 'the God who made the world and everything in it, being Lord of heaven and earth . . . gives to all men life, breath and everything' (Acts 22:24 – 5):

> By the word of the Lord the heavens were made and all their host by the breath of his mouth. He gathered the waters of the sea as in a bottle; he put the deeps in storehouses. Let all the earth fear the Lord, let all the inhabitants of the world stand in awe of him! For he spoke and it came to be; he commanded and it stood forth. (Psalms 33:6ff).

Let us assume, then, the Christian authenticity or well-formed character of claims of this sort: God transcends the world; God is directly involved with the world as its creator. We can leave unspecified the exact nature of these claims. They are vague in practice. Theologians, we shall see, work out rules for their elaboration in explaining their consistency with one another; in that manner their import is established for theological purposes.

What problems in Christian talk about a transcendent God's involvement with the world might prompt the theologian to try to account for its coherence? Potential problems of consistency become clear in non-Christian Hellenistic talk about much the same thing. In the cosmologies of the Hellenistic era, which were formed through the confluence of Platonic and Aristotelian categories, the transcendence and direct involvement of God with the non-divine appear to be mutually exclusive, to vary inversely in degree. The more transcendent God is the less God is directly involved with the world; and vice versa. Hellenistic views of divinity in relation to the world seem to oscillate, as a result, between a characterization of divinity as a kind of being in the world that supposes their close connection and an oppositional definition of divine transcendence that separates them.

If Christian theologians are to affirm at once God's transcendence and direct involvement with the world without fear of self-contradiction, they must follow rules for the elaboration of such claims different from those in force in non-Christian Hellenistic contexts. Attention to a Greek problematic illuminates, therefore, the structural revisions of Greek ways of talking about divinity that are necessary for coherent talk about a transcendent God who creates. Apparent problems for Christian coherence that Hellenistic cosmologies suggest are resolved, we shall see, if Hellenistic forms of speaking about God's transcendence and involvement with the world are transformed in certain ruled ways.

Since my description of Hellenistic cosmologies is a means for elucidating the rule-governed character of Christian discourse, the primary concern here is not for the integrity of non-Christian ways of speaking. The reader should expect such descriptions to have only the general sort of schematic accuracy sufficient to make points about Christian discourse. With this caveat in mind, let us begin a kind of typology of Greek ways of talking about the transcendence of divinity and its relation to the non-divine.

In Greek and Roman religion and in Greek philosophy to a great extent, divinity refers to a kind of being distinct from others within the matrix of the same cosmos. Divinity characterizes that which is most powerful, self-sufficient and unchanging among beings, providing loci of intelligibility and meaning within an otherwise disordered world. As a distinct sort of being differentiated from others, like any other kind, within the same spectrum of being making up the cosmos, divinity is a predicate determined by commonality and susceptible of difference: it is the sort of thing which can be said to be shared generically with specifying differences of degree. Divinity is attributed univocally, in other words, to the realm of Ideas, the World-Soul of the *Timaeus*, celestial spheres and even human souls in so far as they are all characterized by rationality, permanence and stability in varying degrees of purity. According to the young Socrates of the *Parmenides* and to Aristotle's theory of substances composed of form and matter, forms with these properties of divinity behave like logical universals that may be shared by, or ingredient in, a number of instances.

Defined in this way, as a kind of finite being differentiated by common predicates from other sorts of beings, divinity may be intimately involved with the world. It may be the world's principle of unity and directing reason: the realm of the Ideas is the order by which the chaos of the world is formed in Plato's *Timaeus*; the World-Soul of Plato and the Stoics guides the cosmic harmony. In Platonism, the non-divine world, characterized by change and instability, may be effected directly by the divine: life from Life, man from Man etc., in virtue of a univocal participation in the Ideal Forms. Divine and non-divine may have a composite efficacy of a physical sort in a world to be worshipped: in Stoicism divine and non-divine interact in so far as they share the character of material substantiality, divinity being distinguished simply by its relatively fine or fiery composition. The limited transcendence that divinity has according to a univocal attribution of divine qualities results, however, in the limited efficacy of divine agency in Greek cosmologies of this type. As a sort of being within a complex system, the divinity of rational principles only order, and demiurgic craftsmanship merely works on, what pre-exists.

In contrast to this univocal characterization of divinity as a shared kind, divinity in Greek thought is often set off oppositionally, as a realm of eternal, changeless intelligibility, over and against the world as a whole characterized by the contrary predicates of becoming, uncertainty and instability.[5] This side of Greek thinking about divinity is reflected in Plato's theory of Forms as transcendent. The Being of knowable Ideas is simply contrasted with the physical world of Becoming apprehended in sense perception and opinion. Physical objects merely imitate an ideal which they are not, instead of participating in the commonality of pure form in virtue of what they are.[6]

This contrastive manner of specifying divinity tends to become spatialized in Aristotle and in the movement historians call Middle Platonism: divinity is localized as First or Primary Being within a cosmological hierarchy and characterized in an exclusive way that sets it apart from everything else. Divinity and the rest of the world taken as a whole are viewed as logical contraries within a single spectrum; this forces an a priori separation of the two.[7]

In Aristotle, for instance, there is a prima facie difficulty in connecting up divinity, understood as eternal, self-enclosed thought of itself, with its direct antithesis, a world of time and change, division and fluctuation. Although Aristotle objects to a Platonic separation of being and becoming, form and the physical world, he shares with Plato a general search for intelligibility via a dualistic distinction between an ordering principle and the unordered subjected to it. The ultimate tendency of this search for intelligibility comes to the surface in the Aristotelian account of God and universe. Although the world is itself intelligible and eternal by inherent forms, the divine unmoved sameness of thought thinking itself remains opposed to a world inclusive of materiality and change. If this oppositional characterization of God is to be retained, any direct influence of divinity upon the world as a whole must be limited to a final causality which presupposes what it attracts, and preserves to the greatest degree possible the solely self-referential isolation of an indifferent God.

In the terms used by the Middle Platonist philosopher Albinus, the 'generate' and begotten world is directly opposed to an 'ingenerate' and unbegotten God, in whom Plato's intelligible forms exist as a realm of eternal and changeless thoughts. For Albinus as for Aristotle, the transcendence of God in virtue of a direct contrast with the world makes God's involvement with it problematic. The generate world does depend on the ingenerate according to Albinus, but once again only for its rational organization. Even this limited relation of independence is qualified, however: God's effect on the world becomes indirect. Intermediate deities of inferior rank are necessary to mediate what is originally formulated as an unmediateable contrast. The Stoic Logos, treated now as the equivalent of Plato's World-Soul, takes on this mediating function: its activity must come between an ingenerate First God and a generate world. The manner and extent of divine influence is circumscribed in this way by a divine transcendence requiring some degree of isolation from the world: God must be insulated by a multiplication of intervening entities from the defilement that a direct relation with the non-divine would bring.

A third sort of characterization of divinity in Hellenistic cosmologies emphasizes a radical transcendence of God that is non-contrastive: God transcends the world as a whole in a manner that cannot properly be talked about in terms of a simple opposition within the same universe of discourse. Direct contrasts are appropriate for distinguishing beings within the world; if God transcends the world, God must transcend that sort of characterization, too.

It is to this end that the Neo-Platonic philosopher Plotinus develops the resources of Platonic thought – specifically, Plato's Idea of the Good in the *Republic* as the unparticipated ground of all Being and Knowing beyond any distinction between Being and Becoming, Pure Forms and the physical world. A divinity that transcends all oppositional contrasts between kinds is to be indicated by talk of the 'One' as the unitary, simple and undifferentiated ground of all mind and being. Such talk points to what is strictly nameless, given that human language inevitably suggests particulars differing from one another in virtue of determinate natures. Such talk is therefore to suggest what is beyond both form and formlessness, simplicity and multiplicity, unity and diversity.

Plotinus' actual use of terms predicated of divinity seems to vacillate, however, between univocal predication and contrastive definition. One might say that Plotinus approximates a genuine non-contrastive transcendence by combining these two types of discourse. The use of both at once is the best he can do to suggest a transcendence of divinity for which neither is appropriate.

Thus Plotinus talks about the procession of beings from the One in the terms of natural processes – the effulgence of light, water streaming from its source – that suggest the univocity of participation language. In an order of apparently shared essences, like comes from like: the One brings forth Nous, a realm of both being and intelligence, which is, in an incipiently differentiated and multiple form, *what the One is* without differentiation or division. 'We call [Nous] the image of the One. . . . It is its image because that which is begotten by the One must possess many of its characteristics and resemble it as light resembles the sun.'[8] Thought and Being which proceed ultimately from the One participate in the unity and simplicity which the One itself is to the degree appropriate to diverse natures.[9]

Notwithstanding this language of univocity, Plotinus says the One is not to be identified with any *determinate* particulars or with the *multiple* totality of which it is the source or principle. The One is a simple, undifferentiated unity; as such, it simply *is not* what everything else *specifically is* in virtue of a determinate character, difference from others, and divisibility. Direct contrasts oppose in this way the simplicity of the One to the composite character of what proceeds from it, the unity of the One to multiplicity, its indeterminacy to determinate natures. Plotinus's explicit statements to the contrary, terms predicated of divinity are *used* by him in a manner that suggests God's transcendence is a matter of an oppositional contrast.

Plotinus' emanationist account of divine influence confirms this. A non-contrastive characterization of divine transcendence does not promote a cosmology like that of Plotinus in which the origination of what is from the One takes the form of a serially self-proceeding chain; a contrastive definition will. This connection between the account of transcendence and cosmology follows from a principle that Plotinus himself formulates: if divinity is to be the source of all, and not just the world's organizing principle, it cannot be properly characterized in terms of the differences that hold among entities originating in dependence upon it. Only what is beyond identification with any one side of the logical contrasts applicable to finite beings may be the source of all such differences making for particularity and multiplicity.

Plotinus' cosmology does conform partially to the sort of cosmology to be expected from a non-contrastive account of divine transcendence according to this principle. In Plotinus' emanationist scheme, the One is indeed the source of the whole hierarchy of being. The One is, however, only the *ultimate* source of that hierarchy according to Plotinus; it is simply first in a line of sequentially productive agencies. The immediate influence of the One is restricted. The One gives rise directly to only the next productive agency in line (Nous); every other member of the chain is brought about through the combined influence of the One and intermediate agencies. Without the help of subsequent members of the hierarchy, the generative powers of the One are insufficient for every effect but one.

A contrastive characterization of divine transcendence infiltrates Plotinus' cosmology to produce these results. A non-contrastive definition of transcendence, according to Plotinus' principle, should suggest that the divine source of being is not in a serially proceeding chain of being at all, either as beginning or as part: divinity that is non-contrastively characterized may be related in the same direct fashion to every link in the chain, as the productive agent for the whole. A contrastive definition makes God's productive involvement problematic in every case in which what is to be produced is not like itself: a direct productive relation with those sorts of beings threatens God's transcendence when that is defined in an oppositional manner.

The account of God's productive agency therefore splits for Plotinus into two: one account to cover cases in which divinity produces its like. On the first account, divinity directly produces its effects but tends to lose its transcendence with respect to them: a univocal characterization of cause and effect, like from like, holds in such cases. They are kept to a minimum in order to stress the transcendence of God. Thus in Plotinus' cosmology the direct productive agency of the One is restricted to what the One is most like, to a single emanation of a particular kind (Nous). The One's production of the rest of the hierarchy of being conforms to a second account in which the One exercises its productive agency indirectly and thereby maintains a transcendence by contrast to its effects: only through Nous and succeeding emanations does the One produce what it is not – genuine multiplicity and diversity.

A contrastive definition of divine transcendence shows its influence again in Plotinus' account of the presence and absence of the One to all that arises from it. In Plotinus' contrastive characterization, the One is indeed said to be present to everything that is: the One cannot be other and therefore absent to anything, since it is just differentiation and diversity which the One is not. This means in effect, however, that *nothing* (except perhaps Nous) is present to the One in so far as it is what it is, nothing is present to the One in the multiplicity, division and specific diversity that constitute finite being as such. 'As the One does not contain any difference, it is always present, [but] we are present to it [not in our being composite, not in being other than what we know, not in our specific diversity from others] as soon as we contain no more difference.'[10]

Our treatment of Hellenistic cosmologies is now complete. How does it help us to understand and get beyond potential problems of coherence in Christian talk about God and world? Let us assume that Christianity wants to claim that God is involved in the world: a basic claim of its creeds is the much stronger one that God is the creator of all that is. Let us assume, further, that Christianity wants to maintain the transcendence of God: the God who gives rise to the world must be in some sense beyond it. Our description of Hellenistic cosmologies suggests that claims of this sort may not go together very well. God's involvement with the world is unproblematic when God does not transcend the world; the greater the transcendence, however, the greater the difficulty in understanding that involvement. At the extreme, God's transcendence seems to separate God from the world in an isolated inefficacy; at best, God's influence is widely felt but usually indirect: secondary agencies make up for what God cannot do at once.

Our distinction between contrastive and non-contrastive accounts of divine transcendence allows us to diagnose the problem: God's transcendence and involvement with the world vary inversely in this way only when God's transcendence is defined contrastively. That sort of definition itself suggests a divine involvement with the world that is limited in both extent and mode. God's involvement with the world will appear to lessen, therefore, as claims for that sort of transcendence are strengthened.

We can understand this connection between a contrastive transcendence and a limited divine agency in the following way. Divinity characterized in terms of a direct contrast with certain sorts of being or with the world of non-divine being as a whole is brought down to the level of the world and the beings within it in virtue of that very opposition: God becomes one being among others within a single order. Such talk suggests that God exists alongside the non-divine, that God is limited by what is opposed to it, that God is as finite as the non-divine beings with which it is directly contrasted. A cosmology influenced by such suggestions will characterize a divine agency in the terms appropriate for a finite one. Like that of a finite agent, God's infuence will be of a limited sort: it may not extend to everything, it may presuppose what it does not produce, it may require the intervening agencies of others.

This diagnosis suggests a solution in line with the Plotinian principle we discussed earlier.[11] Far from appearing to be incompatible with it, a non-contrastive transcendence of God suggests an extreme of divine involvement with the world – a divine involvement in the form of a productive agency extending to everything that is in an equally direct manner. Divine involvement with the world need be neither partial, nor mediate, nor simply formative: if divinity is not characterized by contrast with any sort of being, it may be the immediate source of being of every sort.

Such an extreme of divine involvement requires, one could say, an extreme of divine transcendence. A contrastive definition is not radical enough to allow a direct creative involvement of God with the world in its entirety. A contrastive definition does not work through the implications of divine transcendence to the end: a God who transcends the world must also, as we saw, transcend the distinctions by contrast appropriate there. A God who genuinely transcends the world must not be characterized, therefore, by a direct contrast with it. A contrastive definition will show its failure to follow through consistently on divine transcendence by inevitably bringing God down to the level of the non-divine to which it is opposed, in the manner outlined earlier.

The Christian theologian therefore needs to radicalize claims about both God's transcendence and involvement with the world if the two are to work for rather than against one another. Primary Christian practice already includes apparently extreme assertions of the latter sort in talk of God as the creator of the world in its entirety, in talk of God as the source of all that is. If Christians make such affirmations and do not want to identify God with any part or whole of the world, they must radicalize their claims for that divine transcendence, as well, in a non-contrastive direction.

Only that sort of transcendence prevents God's transcendence and creative agency from becoming competitive. If Christians presume that God is somehow beyond this world and is therefore not to be identified with it in part or as a whole, the theologian in the interest of Christian coherence adds that this non-identity must not amount to a simple contrast. This insistence upon a non-contrastive characterization of God's transcendence forces, in turn, Christian talk of God's creative agency to be worked out in a genuinely radical way: God must be directly productive of everything that is in every aspect of its existence. Anything short of that supposes, I have argued, a diminished divine transcendence. Apparent problems of incompatibility are resolved in this manner – not at the cost of either claim but in taking both to their genuine extremes.

Christian theologians elaborate in certain ruled ways, then, the presumptions of Christian practice concerning God's transcendence and creative agency; in that way they ensure the coherence of Christian discourse. The theologian determines what the Christian can and cannot go on to say if Christian talk about a transcendent God who creates the world is to be coherent.

From the preceding discussion we can specify two such rules. First, a rule for speaking of God as transcendent vis-à-vis the world: avoid both a simple univocal attribution of predicates to God and world and a simple contrast of divine and non-divine predicates. In the case of univocity, God is not really transcendent at all. In the case of a simple contrast, God's transcendence is not radical enough. We can call this first rule a rule for talk of God's transcendence beyond both identity and opposition with the non-divine. The second rule is as follows: avoid in talk about God's creative agency all suggestions of limitation in scope or manner. The second rule prescribes talk of God's creative agency as immediate and universally extensive.[12]

Christian theology takes up the task that Plotinus set for himself but failed to actualize in his discourse. It succeeds in that task by actually abiding by a rule that prohibits a simple contrast between divine and non-divine predicates when talking of God's agency. If the theologian's discourse conforms to that rule for talking of God as transcendent, God's agency will be radicalized beyond that envisioned by Plotinus's emanationist cosmology. God will become the genuine source of everything that is, *in* all its diversity, multiplicity and particularity, without the need for any indirection. It is to the Christian performance of this task that we now turn.

ANALYSING THEOLOGICAL CASES

How do Christian theologians manage to follow a rule for discourse about the radical transcendence of God so that they are able to talk coherently of that God's immediate creative agency with respect to all that is? A variety of means are employed in disparate forms of theology. The examples to follow specify some of the options. Each example helps to make concrete the rules we have just formulated for talk about God as transcendent and the creator of the world. Each example helps to fill out, furthermore, our argument for the logical interdependence of assertions about God's transcendence and creative agency when those assertions are constructed according to such rules. Finally, the differences among the cases studied will reveal the way in which these rules are formal directives rather than material proposals.

Preliminary questions

We have argued for the coherence of Christian talk about a transcendent God who is directly involved with the world as its creator, should that talk conform to the rules for discourse we have specified. We are now looking for those rules at work in actual historical cases of Christian theology. Before we start this analysis of cases, it is perhaps wise to tackle several preliminary questions. What might be the relation between *our* formulation of the rules in the last section and what the theologians we study say? With what right do we claim that our rules are adequate to account for the manner in which particular theologians formulate their statements? Since we will be treating a rather large number of theological cases in a compressed space, our arguments will inevitably suggest something of a *fait accompli*. It is appropriate for us to say a bit here about the process of uncovering rules at work that lies behind the results we will give.

To the first question. Formulation of the rules is not the special privilege of a discourse distinct from any to be found in the theologies we study. It is not the prerogative of *our* discourse as analysts of theological language.

The discussion of logical systems in the last chapter might have suggested this. The symbolic logics we mentioned there did not have the capacity to express in their own terms the basic rules they followed in formulating their principles. We expressed the meta-level logical rules of non-contradiction and excluded middle in English, not in the technical notation specific to any logical system abiding by them.

A theologian's language gives him or her, however, a capacity for meta-level talk, for talk about the rules that govern the formation of the theologian's own statements. Theological language is like a non-technical natural language (e.g., English) in this respect: it permits reflection upon the rules of its own operation. If in the last section we formulated rules for theological discourse in terms that would not suggest any particular theologian or theological school, this was to facilitate the recognition that these rules have a general purchase – they may be operative in theologies of very different sorts.

Although a theologian has the linguistic artillery to talk about the rules that govern his or her discursive practice, rules are not often expressed *as such*. Because rules for theological talk fall within the purview of a theologian's language, they can be found within particular theological schemes expressed in the same terms used to make the first-order statements peculiar to them. Often, indeed, nothing about such a statement itself will signal its status as a rule. The same statement may function in a dual capacity: as a first-order claim about God and world in certain contexts (particularly ones of confession and proclamation), or as a rule for the ordering of such first-order claims.[13] Function is the discriminating factor.

The statement 'God is transcendent', for instance, is expressed in a material mode; it appears to be a first-order statement about the nature of God and not a directive for linguistic behaviours. The statement could at least *work*, in addition, as a shorthand for a rule about talk of God in relation to the world of the sort specified in the last section: it would be invoked in that case to head off any inclination to talk of God as simply identical or opposed to what is said of the creature. The statement 'God is the creator of the world' could be used referentially by a theologian; it could also be a reminder not to suggest limitations on the manner or scope of God's agency when talking about the created order.

Statements in a first-order mode that work as rules are often instantiations or applications of rules for discourse; they work as rules by becoming paradigmatic instances of a rule's use. 'God is Being itself' might work, for example, in a certain theological tradition as a paradigmatic instantiation of the rule of divine transcendence; 'God is first cause' might do the same thing for the rule for talk of God as creator. Examples will figure in our discussion of theological cases.

Ian Ramsey, Bernard Lonergan and most recently George Lindbeck have argued that, despite their expression as first-order claims, the trinitarian and Christological creedal formulas of the early church function in this fashion as rules for linguistic practice.[14] The Christological formula of two natures in one person seems to make an ontological claim about the man Jesus. It becomes normative for the church as a model instance of the rule that divine and human predicates are to be attributed to the one subject Jesus Christ.[15] Similarly, talk of the trinity as three persons in the one substance of God becomes a paradigm application of the sort of rule that Athanasius formulated as such: in talking of the Father and Son (for example), whatever is said of the Father is to be said of the Son but the Son is not to be called the Father ('*eadem de Filio quae de Patre dicuntur excepto Patris nomine*')[16]

Our task of finding rules for coherent talk at work in theologies would be easier if theologians did not only use the rules in forming first-order statements about God and the world but also mentioned what they were by the means we have just discussed: by explicitly meta-level talk ('It is appropriate to say. . . It is not appropriate to say. . .'), by first-order claims that indicate rules as shorthands or reminders, by first-order statements that instantiate a rule and therefore pose as models of the process. Our claim that a theologian's discourse is rule-governed would be confirmed by a theologian's own talk about how to formulate statements or by the theologian's own use of certain statements in a first-order mode to direct the formation of further statements.

One could expect an explicit account of rules for discourse from theologians with a heightened selfconsciousness about language use. The cultural milieu or a theologian's personal proclivities might be factors affecting that selfconsciousness. From our first chapter we could expect historical situations of controversy and suspected error to prompt it. The following circumstance of theological discourse formation may also play a role.

Statements of rules as rules often occur where theological discourse incorporates terminology without clearly established prior senses. In case key theological terms have no customary employment in non-theological contexts, they bring along with them no usage rules for a theology to work with. As a result, theological statements including those terms suggest nothing much in themselves about how to go on; the theologian has to provide from the very beginning some indication of rules being followed. Any intelligibility that the body of statements making up such a theology may exhibit is the product solely of rules created from the bottom up for a specifically theological use; those rules must be explicit if a theology is to appear at all coherent.

Lonergan and Ramsey have suggested that terms without established non-theological uses are prominent in the Christology and trinitarian theology of the Christian tradition. Arguments these two make about the use of those terms confirm our point about the need in theologies where this happens for the explicit statement of rules for discourse. According to Lonergan and Ramsey, terms like '*hypostasis*' and '*physis*' in Christology and '*homoousion*' and '*hypostasis*' in trinitarian theology work as undefined heuristic devices (Lonergan) or 'model-less' mnemonics (Ramsey).[17] The classic Christian formulas in which these terms figure become, thereby, rules for discourse. Remaining undefined, the terms work as placeholders, in a manner not unlike variables in mathematical formulae: they stand in for whatever sort of talk is to be regulated.

Very often, however, rules are used and not mentioned by a theologian. If he or she abides by the rules we have formulated, that will only become apparent in the body of the statements about God and the world he or she makes. Several precautions are necessary to ensure an accurate portrayal of a theologian's linguistic habits in that case.

First, one must hold in abeyance the linguistic expectations one brings with one from non-theological linguistic spheres. A priori analysis of the meaning of theological statements is illegitimate: such an analysis will tend to overlook specifically theological restrictions placed on language in favour of apparent senses established elsewhere. One must wait to observe, rather than presume to know ahead of time, the import of a theological statement since that will be settled only in the way a theologian works with it. One cannot know what does or does not follow from a theological statement – what it implies, what it presupposes, the statements with which it is associated or held to be consistent or inconsistent – without waiting to see what a theologian does with it.

A focus on isolated theological statements is improper for the same reason. To determine the rules that govern it, one must attend to the overall 'logical geography' of a theological statement in context – to use Gilbert Ryle's phrase.[18] Taking statements out of context is no way to establish the rules actually at work in their formulation. One must not make a fetish of theological statement and act as if a statement's sense could be read off from it without considering its operation within wider linguistic and historical contexts.

In sum, avoid a priori and abstract analyses. This prerequisite for an accurate accounting of rules at work in a theology implies a positive directive: keeping conclusions in constant correspondence with the evidence at hand, make an in-depth and exhaustive investigation of the manner in which theological statements are actually used.

Attention to the linguistic context that frames a theological statement may not be enough: the historical context of a statement's formulation may be the only thing that establishes what does or does not follow from it. Whether apparent implications are permitted or restricted may become clear, in other words, not from what a theologian goes on to say, but from the historical opponents a statement is used to combat. Thus, apparent implications necessary for a historical objective are clearly permitted whether or not they find an explicit place within the body of statements a theologian makes. Explicit statement of permitted implications may simply be superfluous when the situation of a statement's formulation makes them obvious. Apparent implications that would conflict with a historical aim are not permitted even when their denial is not explicit: the absence of explicit statement to that effect may simply indicate that no one has yet thought to draw such illicit inferences. A thorough historical treatment of a theologian's use of statements becomes the more important, therefore, the more a theologian's permission and restriction of apparent implications of statements is determined solely by situation. Should apparent implications be neither admitted nor restricted by explicit statement and historical contexts provide no help, questions of this sort must be left undecided. To the extent that formulating rules appropriate to a theology depends upon answering them, the formulation must remain indeterminate.

Finding the rules at work even in a single theologian's talk threatens to become in this way an unmanageably complex task, requiring a potentially interminable and therefore futile pursuit after comprehensiveness. The complexity of the task is reduced, however, by our choosing theological cases in which there are ample linguistic indications of rules at work. In the theological cases we will discuss, permission or restriction of a statement's apparent implications tends to be explicit in further statements made, rather than merely implicit in the historically variant purposes a theology serves.

The possibility that rules at work in a theology might never be established conclusively from the evidence at hand is not especially threatening to our project. We are not *deriving* rules for coherent Christian talk from cases of theological language. Rules are arrived at by an argument about what would make Christian talk about God and the world coherent; the analysis of historical cases is designed, as I said, simply to confirm that those rules operate in fact within the Christian theological tradition. Whether or not the evidence in any particular case would be enough by itself to suggest that just those rules are at work, we can rest content if the evidence available simply supports them.

A problem remains, however. Even if we limit investigation to linguistic evidence, the requirement of a painstaking thoroughness in the observation of what a theologian goes on to say seems to make practically unfeasible the task of demonstrating in a short space that a tradition of coherent Christian discourse according to such rules exists. Is there any short cut to help us justify our claim that the theologies we discuss abide by these rules?

A short cut becomes clear when we remember that the circumstance of theological discourse formation is very often different from the one mentioned above. We said in the first chapter that theologians frequently incorporate terminology with established uses outside a theological context. They form their own usage rules for those expressions by skewing ones appropriate elsewhere.

Theologies in this circumstance do not have the same need for an explicit statement of rules that theologies incorporating terminology without previously established senses have. A statement of rules is not necessary to convince the reader, to begin with, that some order among theological statements exists. In virtue of its extra-theological use, the terminology of theological statements will already suggest something of how to go on. Such suggestions will be confirmed at least partially by what a theologian in fact goes on to say, since previous usage rules are skewed but not inoperative. The more that statements suggested by non-theological rules match those permitted in theology, the greater a theology's apparent intelligibility, the more readily, that is, a theology's coherence seems exhibited in the very manner in which its statements follow from other statements, apart from any explicit formulation of rules.

One can say theologies that appropriate terminology with established uses elsewhere have an added dimension of intelligibility from that which would accrue to a theology simply as a ruled use of language. The latter sort of intelligibility is all that a theology will have should it lay out from scratch rules for a technical theological vocabulary. An intelligibility of rhetorical force is added when a theology plays upon the linguistic expectations of an audience. To the extent theological usage matches those expectations, the familiarity of ways of speaking in another context comes to be transferred to theological discourse.

The theologian's play upon previously established usage rules is what gives us our clue for a short cut. The usage rules that a theologian establishes are neither the same as nor entirely different from the usage rules that prevail in the contexts from which a theologian's terminology is borrowed. The theologian establishes an analogical use of terms.[19] What a theologian does with them – the implications, associations etc. a theologian draws from statements that include them – should be suggested in part by rules in use elsewhere. Some of these suggestions will be blocked, however; it is in that manner that a specifically theological use is set up.

To support the claim that our rules for coherent Christian talk are at work in a theology, we should first consider any peculiar linguistic potential of the terminology a theologian employs. Especially if cultural and philosophical circumstances are at all pluralistic, it is reasonable to assume that there is *something* about the non-theological use of a conceptuality that grounds its appropriation in particular within a theological context. The linguistic potential of such a form of speech as established in a non-theological context (i.e., what it allows you to say and the relations among the statements permitted) should make it relatively fit somehow for exhibiting our rules for coherent theological discourse.[20]

The modifications of that use in a theological context should correspond to what our rules for coherent discourse would require. As a second step, then, one should carefully observe when expectations, derived from familiarity with the non-theological use of a conceptuality, are blocked by theological discourse. Here again a theologian's own meta-level talk ('One should not say. . .') becomes important. It is important this time, in context, as a secondary tool necessary to restrict the inappropriate implications of rules pressed into theological service; for us, as a means for demarcating theological rules from non-theological ones. Once certain apparent implications are blocked by the outright denial that they follow, or by such indirect means as odd qualifier words or peculiar grammatical constructions, we should be left with modified usage rules that correspond to our rules for coherent Christian discourse.

In subsequent discussion, we will have the opportunity to look at the peculiar linguistic resources and characteristic theological modifications of (1) Platonic talk about Forms; (2) Aristotelian metaphysical terminology; (3) personalist language of intentionality (e.g., talk of knowing and willing); and (4) Kantian categories for talk about transcendental structures of consciousness.

Examples

I turn now to the discussion of theological cases. Some simply use the rules; others mention them. We will look at theological expressions that signal linguistic prohibitions, statements that illustrate rules in a paradigmatic fashion, theologians drawing out the implications of their statements to conform to our rules, choices of conceptuality that are somehow isomorphic with the rules of coherence we have specified. The theological loci of our discussion will vary: we will look at treatments of God's nature and of God's agency.

Let us start with some theologians of the early church and the rule of divine transcendence. Irenaeus (died c.200) talks about God's nature using terms typically employed in Greek cosmologies to contrast divine and non-divine – God is ingenerate, impassible, simple etc. The predicates he applies to God are apparently the opposite of those appropriate for talk about the world; and nothing about the way Irenaeus uses those terms to talk about God's nature disabuses one of that impression. Irenaeus shows that he does not use the terms to oppose divine and non-divine by denying the implications such a contrastive use would have for an acount of divine agency.

Irenaeus' Gnostic opponents assume the need for mediating agencies between God and the world because of the contrast between a simple, impassible, ingenerate God and a world of change, multiplicity and what comes to be. Irenaeus in the second book of *Against Heresies* argues that this Gnostic limitation on God's power and presence does not follow from the characterization of divinity in such terms. Applying terms of this sort to God suggests to Irenaeus, instead, a principle of universal and immediate divine agency. It is this connection that shows Irenaeus' non-contrastive use of apparently contrastive terms. For Irenaeus, what makes God radically different from every creature – the Fullness without limits of eternal and ingenerate unity – is exactly what assures God's direct and intimate relation with every creature *in the entirety* of its physical and particular being.[21] Because divine transcendence exceeds all oppositional contrasts characteristic of the relations among finite beings – including that of presence and absence – divine transcendence, according to Irenaeus, does not exclude but rather allows for the immanent presence to creatures of God in his otherness.

In a similar fashion, the non-contrastive role of apparently contrastive terms applied to divinity is made clear by Tertullian (died c.220) in combating the Docetic Christology of Marcion.[22] Tertullian also deploys the typical terms of Hellenistic cosmologies that seem to contrast the natures of God and the world; Tertullian shows he does not use those terms to make a simple contrast by denying the implications such a use would have for talk of the incarnation.

If the divine nature were simply changeless (for example) in opposition to a changing world, it would become difficult to understand how God could be intimately one with the human in Christ. If the incarnation is to be intelligible, God's distinction from creatures must not, therfore, be one of simple opposition to change, which excludes intimate relation with what changes. God's distinction from creatures, Tertullian argues, should be understood so as to allow for God's entering into relation with the creature under all possible circumstances without danger of compromising the divine nature. To suppose otherwise and attempt to secure God against a direct relation with creation is to suggest that God is finite, on the same level with things that can be altered by interaction and conditioned by external circumstance.

Besides denying the implications a contrastive use would have for talk about God's involvement with the world, a theologian might illustrate our rule prohibiting a contrastive use of predicates applied to God in the way he or she identifies the divine nature. The theologian in such a case attempts to identify divinity in its uniqueness so as not to suggest that God's nature simply *differs* from that of created beings. Finite beings within the world are specifically identified in virtue of the particular qualities which characterize them and by which they differ from other beings. God, as transcendent, is beyond those relations of identity or opposition, and is therefore not to be characterized in terms of particular natures in contrast to others. It is common to say, instead, that God is radically distinct from the non-divine simply through 'himself'.

In this connection, Christian theologians often remark that God was free to create or not. God did not need to create the world, because the perfection of the divine nature would not have been altered or diminished had God not done so. Such affirmations express in a material mode a prohibition against identifying divinity through terms that refer, by comparison or contrast, to the nature of the non-divine.

Christian theologians often attempt to specify uniquely the nature of God through an odd substantive use of predicates. In talk about ordinary things, the extension of predicates of quality always exceeds the particular subject of discourse (Peter is human but cannot be identical with humanity per se). Where God is the subject of a statement, and only then, the subject God may be *identified* with its predicates. Those predicates are therefore used as substantives. What is an 'is' of predication for creatures becomes an 'is' of identity for God.[23]

In this manner our rule for talk about God as transcendent finds an illustration. God's nature is clearly not being directly opposed to that of things of this world since God is talked about as being simply identical with what is asserted predicatively of those creatures. If a man is righteous, God is righteousness. God is not, however, what created reality is, because in the creature's cases such terms are only asserted predicatively and not substantively. The creature may be said to be righteous but not, in any serious sense, righteousness per se.

Expressed in the material mode of a metaphysical claim, this point about predication could be made by saying that God's essence is identical with God's act of existence. In the modified Aristotelianism of Thomistic metaphysics it would make sense to say that God *is* what creatures only *have* because of a real distinction between their essences and existence. In Karl Barth's way of making this point for twentieth-century Protestant theology, God *is* what characterizes God in act and therefore the meaning of the predicates applied to divinity in virtue of divine acts *ad extra* is exhausted in their attribution to the divine subject.[24] The result of such forms of talk is that God may be other than creatures without differing from them in respect to quality.

A substantive use of predicates is probably executed most often in Christian theology by following a form–itself schema – God is love, goodness, justice . . . itself:[25] the predicate with which God is identified is an abstract noun referring to some perfection. Statements of this sort become paradigmatic illustrations of the rule of divine transcendence in talk of God's nature. God is uniquely specified without opposition to the non-divine by a very peculiar use of an abstract predicate nominative with an 'is' of identity: an abstract noun is used substantively to identify what subsists, and not, as would ordinarily be the case, for purposes of affirming an equivalence on the level of concepts.

The peculiarity of this use is frequently pointed out by the theologian; the theologian indicates in some fashion that these statements are not to be taken in an ordinary manner to affirm an equivalence on the level of concepts. This might be done by prohibiting the reversal of subject and predicate ordinarily allowed in cases where an identification is made with an abstract noun. As Karl Barth was fond of saying, though God is love, one cannot say that love is God. The same point is often made through a complementary use of the adjectival forms of abstract nouns. God is called just, good etc., in addition to being identified with justice or goodness . . . itself. Since adjectival forms are ordinarily predicated of subsisting things, the first set of statements suggests that in the second set God is *subsistent* justice, goodness . . . itself. The first set is used together with the second to show that the latter supposes the concrete existence of God in the same fashion as does ordinary language of predication with respect to finite being.[26]

The form-itself schema had its origin in Hellenistic participation theories of divinity. The 'form' in the scheme was a Platonic Form. The scheme suggested that God is the existence itself of certain qualitative perfections that characterize beings within the world of time and change. In virtue of this non-Christian association, the form-itself schema was an especially effective device in Christian theology for countering characterizations of divinity that oppose divine and non-divine. It was a particularly good instrument for illustrating the 'not opposed' part of the rule for talk of God as transcendent. It was not as useful for the 'not identical' part of the rule. The schema needed to be modified in Christian use to prohibit suggestions of univocity of predication that reduce the transcendence of God in a Hellenistic participation theory of the relation between divinity and the world. The form-itself structure of discourse had to be used in a way that would prevent divinity from being characterized directly within the order of common essences predicated of finite beings. The Christian theologian could not suggest what the Platonic philosopher would affirm: that God simply *is* the subsistence itself of certain determinate kinds, shared by some and contrasted with others in the manner usual within the created order. How might that be done?

Suggestions of univocity were cut off by centring discussion of the divine nature on a peculiar choice of terms to be substituted in the form-itself schema. God is assuredly not being identified with certain qualities that specify the determinate natures of things in the world, if focal terms substituted in the scheme are not the names of particular qualities by which finite beings are determined in distinction from others. They may be terms instead that suggest a lack of formed particularity (limitlessness, infinity, simplicity, fullness). Or they may be terms that in common parlance or technical philosophical discussion are applied universally and indiscriminately to whatever falls within the universe of discourse concerned with finite entities, terms that are applied, that is, without regard for distinctions among particular natures (e.g., Being, Act of Existence, other Transcendentals).

Examples of both these sorts of strategy for prohibiting implications of univocity in a form-itself schema abound in the history of Christian theology. With his claim that God's essence and existence are identical, the thirteenth-century theologian Thomas Aquinas provides a particularly interesting example of the latter sort of strategy. According to Thomas, the formal essence of God, God's nature, is to be identified with God's *esse* or act of existence. God has no additional nature of a determinate kind, but is simply identical with that Act of Existence itself in virtue of which any and all determinate kinds are. Putting this in a formal mode, we can say that the terms of the form-itself schema are not to be filled with any descriptive predicates; the 'to be' ordinarily supposed in any predication is to be substituted in the schema all by itself.[27] God's identity with what is affirmed only predicatively of finite beings now takes the doubly odd form of a substantive use of 'to be'.

In addition to these single statements, like 'God is *Ipsum Esse*', which are model exemplifications through the combined effects of grammatical and term substitution oddities, the rule for talk about God as transcendent might be indicated in explicitly meta-level discourse. First order discourse that apparently describes the nature of God – no matter how odd its formulation – tends to give the impression that terms applied to God refer either to characteristics shared by some things of this world and not by others, or to characteristics that things of this world simply lack. If theological discourse is shifted from talk about God to a meta-level discussion of that talk itself, God's transcendent nature can be identified with reference to the very peculiarity of rules for talk about it. An attempt is not made to delimit the divine nature by saying something about it, by descriptive characterization of some odd sort. Instead, divinity is specified in its uniqueness through the very prohibition of such a descriptive attempt. God is identified by rules for discourse that announce the general inadequacy of the language we use for talk about the world.

Terms attributed to divinity in apparently first-order discourse would be chosen in this case for their usefulness in signalling the proscription of descriptive language with its suggestions of either univocal or contrastive predication. Simplicity instead of compositeness would be chosen, for instance, simply as a heuristic device, to indicate the general structural inadequacy of the language we use to talk about the world. We describe things of this world in language *composed* of subject and predicate; talk of God as simple would therefore indicate, as talk of God as composite could not, the inappropriateness of such language in talk about God. Immutability would be chosen, similarly, not to suggest that God is at rest rather than in motion, or that God is fixed and simply opposed to change – God as the transcendent source of all being is presumably beyond the contrasts by which finite beings are distinguished and differentiated. This choice would indicate, as the contrary terms could not, that all our language, supposing as it does a world in process, is inappropriate. David Burrell, in his *Aquinas* and *Exercises in Religious Understanding*, argues that Thomas Aquinas, for one, is engaged in just such a meta-level articulation of radical transcendence in the first thirteen questions of the *Summa Theologica*.[28]

Whether the linguistic prohibitions that constitute our rules for discourse are mentioned by a theologian or not, those prohibitions may inform the body of a theologian's statements about God and the world. In that case, it is the complex of ruled relations among those statements, the structure of such talk, that will display, e.g., our rule for talk of God as transcendent. If our argument in the preceding section is correct, that rule will be worked out not just in talk of God's nature vis-à-vis the world but in an account of divine agency that follows a rule prescribing its immediacy and universal scope. We now need to investigate, then, Christian strategies for forming a body of statements about both God's nature and agency in conformity with our rules.

I said above that the general strategy is to choose for theological employment a form of speech whose usage rules match as closely as possible those for coherent Christian talk. In practice that strategy encompasses two options: the form of speech chosen may be paticularly suited to exhibit either the rule for talk about God as transcendent or the rule for talk about God as a creative agent.

In the first case, the theologian often incorporates talk about productive principles found in some metaphysical or epistemological theory. We will discuss several examples in a moment. If it is to serve principally as a means for structuring discourse that accords with our rule for talk of divine agency as immediate and universally extensive, talk of such productive principles will have to suggest their primacy over the range of all other principles, causes or ontological components. Talk of this sort will have to have, secondarily, a complex enough linguistic structure to show in theological discourse the prohibition against univocity or simple opposition in talk of God as transcendent. Such forms of speech will presumably, however, be in more serious need of explicit modifications in order to prevent violations of that rule. Talk of God in the terms of primary productive principles found within the created order could easily suggest, on the one hand, God's simple identity with those principles, or, on the other, the sort of contrastive opposition between a productive principle and what it grounds that holds within the created order.

In the second case, where a form of speech is chosen primarily for its usefulness in structuring discourse according to our rule for talk of God as transcendent, its ordinary use must be somehow conducive to talk of God that neither identifies nor opposes divine and created attributes. Examples will follow. One would suppose such language to be most in need of modification in order to conform to the rule for talk of God's immediate and universal creative agency.

Thomas's use of a basically Aristotelian metaphysics provides an example of the first option for exhibiting our rules in the body of theological statements. Theological discourse about divine agency is structured by incorporating metaphysical talk about primary productive principles – in this case the principles of efficient causality and act of existence (*esse*). When talk of those principles is suitably modified, talk of divine agency follows our rule for it.

On Thomas's account of Aristotelian causes, the mutually conditioned exercise of material, formal, efficient and final causes within the created order occurs by the absolute primacy of the third of these – efficient causality. An efficient cause acts for the sake of an end (final cause). An efficient cause can bring about the existence of a thing with a particular nature only through form (formal cause) which actualizes otherwise non-existent matter (material cause) by determining it to be of such and such a kind. Nevertheless, the end exists only in virtue of efficient causality and exerts an influence as final cause only because of the act of an efficient cause tending towards it. Similarly, a formal cause achieves actuality, in determining matter to be a particular kind, only through efficient causality. All other orders of causality as Thomas understands them are in potency, therefore, vis-à-vis the founding acts of efficient causes.

The will, as an instance of efficient causality in deliberate agency, has the same sort of primacy among human faculties. The will is always determined in the end to which it wills and the specification of what it wills by an object presented to it by the intellect. Yet it retains an absolute priority over the intellect (and all other faculties) in so far as the will is what determines the intellect to act at all.[29]

This absolute priority of efficient causality presupposes and is made sense of for Thomas, in terms of the metaphysical priority of act of existence (*esse*). In the order of becoming, of generation and alteration, a thing's act of existence is derived from form, following the Platonic equation of form and reality and the Aristotelian identification of form with act. *Forma dat esse* in the sense that form constitutes, with or without matter, the essence of created reality, and only that which has an essence (i.e., which is something determinate) exists. Nonetheless, for Thomas the act of existence or *esse* retains primacy: substantial and accidental forms and all other aspects of being are in potency with respect to it. The actuality of form and of matter through form, and all secondary acts of a composite being or subsistent form, occur through the reception of *esse*. *Esse* therefore immediately embraces all distinctions within the order of essence – form and matter, substance and accident.[30] In this way Thomas extends Aristotle's distinction between act and potency so that a form/matter distinction between act and potency is included under the broader one of *esse*/essence.

Thomas talks of God's agency by extending still further this talk of a distinction between act and potency. The broadest distinction between act and potency within the created order, that of *esse* and essence, is now said to fall under an even broader one that holds between God and the world. God is said to be the non-created *esse* with respect to which the whole of the orders of created *esse* and essence are in potency. Thomas talks about God as the Pure Act of Existence, and therefore as the very first will-ful, efficient cause of the world in all its metaphysical aspects.

Metaphysical talk of the relation between act of existence and essential distinctions, between efficient causality and all other causal principles, between the will and all other human faculties, is in this way taken up and mirrored by talk of the relation between God and creatures. The result is a body of statements that meets the requirements of our rule for talk of God as an agent. The primacy of *esse* in metaphysical talk about the created order is radicalized in structurally isomorphic theological talk: God has the same sort of intensive primacy but now with respect to *all* created being, including all acts of existence and efficient and will-ful agencies within the created order.

The transcendence of God is also suggested by such talk. Metaphysical categories which, in their ontological and causal primacy, extend over the range of kinds of cause and distinction within the order of essence are used in talk of God to suggest the way in which God transcends in a non-contrastive fashion all distinctions that hold within the created order – even the distinction between the created orders of *esse* and essence. Although the material mode of theological language (e.g., 'God is Pure Act of Existence') might suggest it, God is not being identified with created act of existence or created efficient agency in simple contrast to created formal essence. God's agency is simply talked about, even with respect to created *esse* and efficient causality, and therefore with respect to everything over which they have primacy, in the terms of primacy ordinarily ascribed to them within the created order.

Let us move to the nineteenth and twentieth centuries for a very different example of language suitable for exhibiting our rule for talk of God's agency. After Kant's critique of an 'objectivist' metaphysics, philosophical discussion of primary founding agencies shifts to a transcendental analysis of subjective structures of consciousness. Structures of consciousness are said to be the transcendental preconditions for all experience of objects; structures of consciousness supply, in other words, an interpretive frame that must be presupposed in all qualitative distinctions and assertions of existence concerning objects as they appear to us. Immediate preconceptual apprehension of self is such a transcendental condition: it must accompany all contents of consciousness and all thematic knowledge of the self as determined by these contents. Following Fichte, this pre-thematic 'I think' of transcendental apperception becomes the primary ground for all other transcendental structures of consciousness.[31]

Such talk became the intellectual currency of theology in Germany. The nineteenth-century Protestant theologian Friedrich Schleiermacher, and the twentieth-century Roman Catholic theologian Karl Rahner, are notable cases in point. Schleiermacher deploys such talk as it filters through nineteenth-century German Romanticism; Rahner, as it works its way through German Idealism and the early writings of Martin Heidegger.

Both theologians talk of God's agency in relation to all that is, in a way that is structurally isomorphic with the relation between the transcendental ground of human knowledge and its categorical determinations. God is said, first of all, to be the transcendental ground and never simply a particular object of consciousness. As such, God is immediately associated with transcendental self-consciousness. Thus for Schleiermacher, God is present in our abiding pre-thematic awareness of self which persists unaltered through the diversity of all empirical determinations of consciousness and all knowledge of ourselves as so determined. For Rahner, God is present as the term and principle of our dynamic self-possession; an unthematic awareness of God in the human subject's dynamism towards the transcendent is the backdrop against which the human subject achieves selfconsciousness.

The primacy of transcendental selfconsciousness vis-à-vis categorical determinations of consciousness is then radicalized in talk about God in relation to the whole created order of physical objects and human subjects. Talk of God's agency in these terms exhibits our rule for it. God is said to be the transcendental precondition for both human selfconsciousness and the objects of experience which that selfconsciousness conditions. The whole world, made up of both human knowers and the objects they know, can therefore be talked about as immediately and totally dependent upon God.

Let us see in more detail how this works. First, human selfconsciousness is said to have God-consciousness for its transcendental condition. It can therefore be said to owe its existence to God. God-consciousness in the transcendental immediacy of our self-consciousness is the feeling of our absolute dependence upon God (Schleiermacher). Transcendental selfconsciousness, as dynamically oriented in its transcendence by the pre-apprehension of the absolute being of God, is a preconceptual awareness of self as grounded and disposed by holy mystery (Rahner).

According to transcendental philosophy, this transcendental selfconsciousness is the precondition for all our experience of objects. Because God-consciousness is its precondition in turn, our theologians can say, in the second place, that the world in its entirety exists in dependence upon God. The world cannot exist for us at all apart from the a priori structure of human subjectivity which is itself a dynamic transcendence towards God.[32] Since transcendental self-presence essentially involves a pre-thematic awareness of dependence upon God, the whole of reality as it appears to human subjectivity is experienced as grounded absolutely in God.[33] The immediate selfconsciousness in which the self is aware of its absolute dependence upon God accompanies all consciousness of oneself as determined diversely by the empirical contents of consciousness. That totality of being comprehended in consciousness is therefore experienced as absolutely dependent on God as well.[34] The immediate selfconsciousness of our absolute dependence upon God is expanded in this way into an experience of the creatureliness of the world in general.[35]

This theological use of the language of transcendental self-consciousness may also produce a body of statements that exhibits our rule for talk of God as transcendent. A transcendence beyond relations of identity or simple contrast is conveyed by the complexity of the relation that holds between transcendental precondition and the variety of categorical determinations it grounds. Divinity is not what the beings it grounds are. The transcendental ground of the world, since it is the rule or limit or horizon by which all else appears, cannot be identified with any part or the whole of the categorical objects it grounds. The difference between God and the world as the difference between transcendental ground and the categorical world of objects grounded is indeed the original distinction, the precondition required for any possibility of specifying objects in their distinction from others at all.[36] As such, however, it is a unique distinction, one that cannot be captured in terms of identifications and contrasts appropriate for the categorical world of objects it makes possible. The difference between God and the world is an unnameable difference since, as the transcendental precondition for the possibility of all categorized distinctions, it is not itself specifiable by those same modes of distinction.[37]

Since talk of divine transcendence in terms of a unique, nameless distinction between transcendental and categorical does not simply contrast divine and non-divine, a theology of this sort will not go on in an account of divine agency to separate God from the world, restrict the scope of divine agency, or seal the world off in any respect from divine influence. Our rule for talk of divine agency as universal and direct will not be violated in any of these ways. Instead, the unique difference between God and the world talked about in terms of a distinction between transcendental and categorical is said to be the difference in which God and the world are united and present to each other. The nameless differentiation between transcendental ground and all else as grounded is precisely the difference in which divinity is intimately present in its founding agency to the world: God is present to the world in the relation whereby God and the world are distinguished since in that relation the world rests in the entirety of its being upon God.[38] The use of the language of transcendental selfconsciousness in Christian theology allows the theologian to say that the very difference between God and world ensures God's presence to the world as its constantly accompanying condition, and to say that in this unity of presence the difference remains. The oppositional implications, which this language may have in a philosophical context, are thereby restricted in theological use. It becomes incorrect to say in an account of divine agency what a direct contrast between ground and grounded might imply: God as transcendental ground of the world does not stand on one side, with the world God grounds on the other; God does not leave the world alone in serving as its ground. God as the transcendental condition for a created order does not merely supply conditions of *possibility* for that world; God does not just make the world possible so that what categorically exists may have its own self-created actuality of being and agency independent of any immediate founding influence of God.[39]

So far we have been looking at cases where metaphysical principles are chosen for use in theology because their primacy within the created order helps to suggest the radical character of God's creative agency. I said before, however, that a conceptuality might be incorporated in talk about divine agency because the complex of statements formed through its use conforms more easily to our rule for talk of God as transcendent. This is the second general way I said a body of theological statements may be constructed so as to exhibit rules for Christian coherence. A striking case of this latter sort is the Christian theologian's use of terms of rational volition in talk of God's involvement with the world.

Christians frequently talk of God using personalist language; they speak of God's acting according to reason and will. Such talk has a biblical basis. Some have suggested it reflects a psychological disposition to appeal in worship to what is like oneself.[40] The theologian's choice of personalist language suggests a specifically theological point.

Let us surmise such language is a useful tool for coherent Christian talk about God as a creative agent. With which rule would discourse structured along those lines most easily conform? Personalist categories are arguably the most frequently employed categories in Christian theology for talk about God as an agent. It is unlikely that over the centuries of this theological employment categories of personal agency always suggested a productive principle of greater primacy than could be had using other available categories. Let us suppose, therefore, that personalist categories are more helpful in forming discourse that accords with our rule for talk of God as transcendent. Their use by theologians of very different philosophical persuasions hints that the theologian's preference for them is based upon their grammatical features or linguistic capabilities in a non technical extra-theological use.

Something as 'simple' as the following grammatical fact about personalist language gives it the capacity to structure discourse about God as an agent so that such talk has the complexity necessary to exhibit our rule for talk of God as transcendent. 'Intentional' language (talk of knowing, willing, thinking, intending, etc.) is peculiar in that every statement of that sort has for its grammatical object, at least implicitly, a 'that' clause and not a single term.[41] Two consequences of this prove important for theological purposes.

First, since it is a clause, the grammatical object of intentional language has to include at least two terms (subject and verb). It may also include more than one substantive or verb depending on the grammatical complexity of the clause. The subject of intentional verbs like 'know' and 'will' is at the very least, then, not determined to a single object of a simple sort. The number of terms in any object-clause may indeed be extended indefinitely; a single grammatical object-clause may have embedded within it a potentially endless number of further clauses.

This first grammatical consequence of a 'that' clause structure is useful for forming discourse according to our rule for talk of God's agency. Because the terms of an object clause are indefinitely extendable, talk of God's creating by knowing and willing enables one to talk of all that is in all its intricacy as immediately encompassed by God's creative intention. Language of knowing and willing is therefore structurally suitable for displaying our rule for talk and God's direct and universal agency.

A second grammatical consequence of a 'that' clause structure makes intentional language highly unusual. It is this feature that makes it especially suitable in talk of God's agency as a means for constructing discourse according to our rule for talk of God as transcendent. Terms in the object-clauses of intentional statements may be referentially opaque. Instead of referring transparently to their objects, these terms incorporate particular descriptions of those objects in referring to them. One might say the sense of these terms becomes at least a part of their reference.

In the hope of making this clear, an appeal to mental acts or attitudes might tempt the ontologically inclined. The referential opacity of intentional language could be explained by saying that such statements have to do with the subjective states of human beings. Particular descriptions are included in referring terms when those terms concern not just what is the case but what human beings think and feel about it. Referential opacity follows from the fact that intentional statements have to do with the 'mental life' of human beings.

Let us be content to show how referential opacity works itself out in certain peculiar logical rules for the use of intentional statements. First of all, the truth of intentional statements is not necessarily retained when the substantive terms of their clauses are replaced by others with the same reference but different senses. For example, the intentional statement 'John thinks his little sister is dead' may be true, while the statement 'John thinks the Queen of Sheba is dead' may be false, even when John's little sister and the Queen of Sheba are one and the same person. The truth of the first statement is not retained with the substitution 'Queen of Sheba' in case it is proper to go on to say that John does not know his sister's identity as the queen.

Second, predicates of logic that concern the truth, existence, modality or quantity of intentional statements need not be applicable as well to the terms of their object-clauses. This is the grammatical consequence of referential opacity that is theologically useful. If such logical predicates apply to an intentional statement as a whole, that says nothing, positively or negatively, about their application to the terms of that statement's object-clause.

This is simply an abstract formulation of an everyday habit. To use an unproblematic example: it may be true (or possible or necessary etc.) that John thinks his sister is dead. On the basis of such a statement one can make no necessary inferences about the truth (possibility, necessity, etc.) of John's sister's death.

Talk of deliberate agency, talk about intentional courses of action, exhibits this same complexity of predication since, like 'think' language, object-clauses specifying what is intentionally willed may be taken to be referentially opaque. Such talk will therefore block necessary relations of either identity or contrast between predicates applies to the terms of an object-clause (predicates that characterize what is deliberately willed) and predicates applied to a statement of deliberate agency as a whole (predicates that characterize the agent's intention to act).

This makes talk about God's creating the world by deliberate agency suitable for exhibiting our rule for talk of God as transcendent. In theological discourse constructed according to this grammatical feature of intentional language, the character of God's deliberate agency will bear no necessary relation of identity or contrast with the character of what God deliberately wills. God will be talked about as beyond relations of either identity or direct contrast with the world God creates when God's agency is talked about using intentional language. Bringing this theological consequence of intentional language together with the first one, we can conclude that the use of intentional language promotes the idea of an overarching divine agency, comprehensive of the whole and without essential relation to its effects by either simple identity or opposition.

Thomas Aquinas works out these implications of personalist language for theological discourse and extends them in certain ways through his use of metaphysical principles and logical categories appropriate to the thirteenth century. Let us begin by looking at his metaphysical account. The linguistic resources of intentional language are expressed by Thomas in a material mode according to a basically Aristotelian account of the difference between natural processes and intentional agency. Natural causes are the foil for understanding what is at stake in talk about action by knowing and willing. A metaphysical distinction between natural causes and deliberate agents makes clear why God's creating the world should be discussed in the latter terms.

A natural cause, according to Thomas, necessarily acts in conformity with its mode of being so as to bring forth one sort of effect. A natural cause, whenever circumstances permit, acts according to a particular principle of action, and no other, which specifies the character of its effects. Talk about God's creative powers in those terms would suggest that God can only produce one kind of effect and therefore cannot be responsible for diversity.[42]

The class into which the effects of a natural cause fall is one, moreover, like itself; a natural cause always produces something of its own nature unless hindered by defect or external influences. Natural causes are univocal causes since their effects belong to the same class of beings as themselves and are, therefore, categorized together under the same name (univocally).

Employing this simple structure of univocity when characterizing the cause and proper effect of God's agency suggests either of two things. It suggests that what God directly effects is the equal of divinity.[43] If those effects are not talked about in terms appropriate to divinity, it suggests that God's agency is mediated or influenced from the outside by circumstances or other agents in the way the proper causal efficacy of any natural cause is modified.

In general, then, talk of God as a creator in terms of natural processes either reduces divine transcendence or restricts the range of God's direct creative influence. Thomas believed such forces to be at work in the Arabic Neo-Platonic Aristotelianism of his day.

A being that acts by rational volition, on the other hand, is not determined to bring about effects of a single kind like itself. A rational agent acts according to what it knows and not according to what it is; its effects may be various, therefore, and none of them need bear any necessary relation of identity or contrast with its own nature. A being acting deliberately is not a univocal cause, in other words; it need not act so as to produce a simple univocal relation between its effects and itself.

The language of rational agency in talk about God as a creator will therefore suggest, contrary to the implications of the language of natural processes, that (1) God may bring about a simple or complex effect, and (2) those effects may or may not resemble as a whole or in part the God upon whom they depend. God whose being is characterized in terms of eternality may, for example, bring about by rational volition a world that either begins to be or that exists for an eternal duration in dependence upon God.[44] God whose being is necessary may produce deliberately a world of creatures that are either necesary or contingent on the supposition of other things willed by God. An immutable God may create by knowledge and will beings that are either corruptible (e.g., composite substances) or incorruptible (e.g., immaterial substances) in their being in dependence upon God.[45]

Because a more complex predication relation holds between cause and effect where action is deliberate, talk of deliberate divine agency can circumvent the immediate reduction of divine transcendence that follows from talk of God as a univocal cause: God and the world need not be talked about in the same terms. It can do so without, on the other hand, suggesting that the transcendence of divinity requires a relation of simple contrast between divine and creaturely predicates: the creature may be talked about in terms used of God, in virtue of certain properties it exhibits within the order of the world, within limits imposed by its dependence upon God.

Thomas complicates his account of deliberate agency by distinguishing between the will of the agent and the content willed, and by claiming for them the same complex predication relation we have just discussed. The complex predication relation that holds between the being of the agent and its effects holds between the very will of the agent and its object. A rational agent acts by joining its will to what the intellect conceives; because the intellect intervenes to propose an object for the will, the character of what is willed bears no necessary relation of either identity or contrast with the character of the will itself. Thomas can therefore say that the divine will is simple and invariable while willing what is complex and changing.[46] In this way, what Thomas says once again follows our rule for talk of God as transcendent. Thereby, Thomas's discourse also accords with our rule for talk of God's universal agency. The characteristics of the divine will say nothing about the sorts of things that God can will; they therefore put no constraints on the scope of the divine intention.

This distinction between will and content willed allows Thomas to say at the same time that the effects of God's agency do have a necessary relation with what God wills. The created effects of God's will have a necessary relation with the content of the conception God inclines his will to enact. The character of those effects necessarily corresponds to what God wills even though the character of neither of them has to correspond to that of the divine will itself.[47] The divine will is radically transcendent, in other words, but necessarily efficacious: what God wills has to happen. Because the will of God is without defect and cannot be hindered by circumstances or forces outside its control, what God brings about is always exactly what God intended.

Thomas appeals explicitly to the logical features of intentional language to explain this distinction between will and content willed and the complex predication relations it involves. In the terms of medieval logic, statements about deliberate agency permit predication either *de dicto* or *de re*. Modal categories or adverbial phrases that characterize the will of an agent are applied, as second-order predicates, to statements that concern that agent's will; they apply *de dicto*. They cover the grammatical object-clauses that express what the agent wills in so far as those clauses are included in such statements; they apply to an object-clause in its composed sense. A grammatical object-clause can also be considered in itself, i.e., in a divided sense, as if it were not included in a statement of that sort. Predicates applied *de dicto* do not also apply as a matter of course to clauses taken in that sense: doing so would mean attributing those predicates *de re*, to the ontological constitution of the particular things discussed there. Predicates used *de re* with respect to the object-clause and predicates applied *de dicto* to the statement as a whole need not correspond. The predication relations that hold between will and content willed must respect, in other words, the difference between meta-level predicates (predicates applied *de dicto*) and object-language predicates (predicates *de re*): predicates characterizing a statement as a whole in logically relevant respects (a metalinguistic use of predicates) do not imply anything about the material application of the same predicates to what is talked about in a statement's grammatical object-clause (an object-language use of predicates).

Applying Thomas's grammatical remarks about intentional language to talk of divine agency one gets the following consequence. Used *de dicto* to cover statements about divine agency as wholes, adverbial phrases characterize God's will for the world. Since object-clauses that concern the world willed by God are included in those statements, adverbial phrases used *de dicto* also characterize the world's relation as a whole to God's will. The same predicates need not apply *de re* to what is discussed in the object-clauses, to the world itself, its particulars, or the relations among them, considered in abstraction from the relation to divine creative agency discussed in the proposition as a whole. The over-arching agency of a transcendent God beyond necessary relations of either identity or direct contrast with the world is suggested by talk of divine agency that follows in this way the structure of predication in intentional language: what qualifies divine agency, and is therefore predicated over any proposition as a whole discussing God's creative willing of the world, need not be predicated of what God brings about considered in itself.

Thomas uses other grammatical remarks to support his right to claim a necessary correspondence between what God wills and what God effects while maintaining that neither of the two necessarily corresponds to the character of God's will. This might not seem a consistent position. A necessary correspondence between what God wills and what God effects means, we said before, that God's will is necessarily efficacious, infallibly effective. Should not that sort of necessity of will require the effects of God's will to be necessary? If what God wills has to happen, should not what happens be necessary too? If so, the character of what exists by God's will must match the character of the divine will itself in at least this one respect. Our rule for talk of God as transcendent would be thereby violated.

To show the consistency of his position, Thomas talks about God's agency in bringing about the world God wills in the way it is customary to talk about logical relations of implication between statements. Specifically, the character of God's agency in bringing about what God wills is talked about in terms of the logical relation of implication that holds between a statement of God's agency, 'God wills that x exist', and the statement of the object-clause as a fact, 'x exists'. The statement of God's agency as a whole becomes an antecedent proposition (p), its object-clause a consequent proposition (q) in the conditional 'If God wills that x exist, then x exists' $(p > q)$. The necessity with which the world's existence follows from God's willing it, the necessity of God's infallible will, is then talked about as a necessity of logical implication ($\square$) that holds between the antecedent proposition 'God wills that the world exist' (p) and the consequent proposition 'the world exists' (q) in such a conditional. In symbols, $\square$ $(p > q)$.

According to logical rules for statements of this sort, modalities (e.g., necessity, possibility, impossibility) can characterize a conditional relation of implication without characterizing its consequent. The necessity ($\square$) of a conditional statement $(p > q)$ does not imply, therefore, the necessity of the simple consequent proposition (q). In short, $\square$ $(p > q) > \square$ q is not a valid proposition. Substituting our theological statements for the ps and qs, one can conclude from this rule of modal logic that the necessity of the world's existence, the necessity of q, is not a valid inference to draw from the necessity with which the world's existence follows from God's willing it, $\square$ $p > q$.

This logical rule for the modal term 'necessity' in particular is just a consequence of the general fact that logical relations of necessity hold in deductive arguments irrespective of the contingency or necessity of what those arguments concern. From the statement 'Socrates remains seated' it follows necessarily that 'Socrates sits.' But that necessity of implication says nothing about the necessity or contingency of Socrates' sedentary ways at any particular moment. If one talks, then, about the necessary efficaciousness of the divine will in terms of the necessity of a logical implication, nothing follows concerning the ontological contingency or necessity of what God effects.

Only if God *had to will* what God in fact wills, only if the statement 'God wills that the world exist' (*p*) were itself necessary, would Thomas be inconsistent in claiming that the world's necessity does not follow from the necessary efficaciousness of God's will. If God had to will that the world exist, and what God wills has to happen, the existence of the world itself would be necessary. The following proposition of modal logic is a valid one: $\Box p > \Box (p > q) > \Box q$. In words, if *p* ('God wills that the world exist') is necessary, and *p*'s implication of *q* is necessary ('the world exists' necessarily follows from 'God wills that the world exist'), then *q* ('the world exists') is itself a necessary proposition.

Thomas denies, however, that God has to will the world. God would have to will the world only in case an inclination in that direction were a necessary implication of the divine nature. Thomas is trying to block such a necessary relation of implication by talk about God as a deliberate agent. What God is does not form the principle of God's action; God inclines to a course of action, we said, according to what God knows and not according to what God is.

This does seem to block any immediate assumption of a necessary relation of implication between God's nature and God's inclination to enact a created world. Even so, might it not be the case that God's will has to incline to some objects that God's intellect proposes? According to Thomas, a rational agent necessarily inclines only towards an absolute good proposed by the intellect. God alone is that absolute good. God does not have to will, therefore, any object that includes the non-divine.

Further discussion of the intricacies of Thomas's theology would lead us rather far afield. Let us turn now to another example of a theology that uses personalist language – a twentieth-century example of a far different theological and philosophical background. The Protestant theologian Karl Barth structures his discourse in a way that accords with our rule for talk of God as transcendent by talking of God as a personal subject whose activities are self-expressive and whose freedom is a matter of autonomous self-determination. Barth uses this account of God as a personal subject to prescribe certain rules for discourse; those rules make clear that God's transcendence is compatible with the most intimate involvement of God with the world.

Barth talks of God as a self-expressive subject whose identity persists throughout the living diversity of its acts and their effects. Barth does so to suggest that God is not bound inflexibly to a certain mode of action proceeding uniformly from him: God's constancy as an agent is

> not the constancy of a supreme natural law or mechanism. The fact that he is one and the same does not mean that he is bound to be and say and do only one and the same thing, so that all the distinctions of his being, speaking and acting are only a semblance, only the various refractions of a beam of light which are eternally the same.[48]

The created effects of such a divine agency may be of the widest possible range, of such a potential diversity that no simple comparison or contrast can hold between them and God.

Barth says, furthermore, that God is a freely self-determining subject. It makes sense to say on that basis that the acts in which divinity expresses itself properly reflect the divine nature. God's agency, as that of a subject with the power of free self-determination, is not limited or distorted by external circumstance; it is not channelled, as our finite agency is, by conditions ultimately outside its control. The character of divine acts *ad extra* is therefore truly revelatory of the divine being. Barth expresses the import of such a statement in the form of a rule for theological discussion: the apparent character of God's activity in the world is not to be overlooked or trivialized by privileging general a priori notions of what God must be like.[49]

Though the divine nature is properly characterized, therefore, in terms appropriate to its acts, it also follows that a God who is freely self-determining may not be resolved into or exhaustively reduced to them. Doing so would make the divine subject appear rigidly determined by, rather than self-determining with respect to, the predicates representative of its own acts. Divinity, in the language Barth likes to use, is not the 'prisoner' of the character of its acts, but 'sovereign Lord' of its own attributes in all their specific appropriateness.[50] Divinity is a self-determining subject even with respect to its own proper predicates.

If so, a second rule for discourse follows: predicates that are properly applied to divinity on the a posteriori basis of its revealed character in act must not be understood in a general way apart from their ascription to this particular subject. 'As the Subject of His works God is so decisively characteristic for their nature and understanding that without this Subject they would be something quite different from what they are in accordance with God's Word, and on the basis of the Word of God we can necessarily recognize and understand them only together with their Subject.'[51] The statement that divinity sovereignly self-determines its own predicates justifies, therefore, a recommendation not to work out the sense of those predicates along the fixed lines of previously established uses. If God is a free subject, all that one attributes to God as acting subject can take on a revised meaning – a meaning not rigidly bound by what those predicates suggest when applied to the activity of non-divine subjects.[52]

In ordinary application, certain predicates are the direct antitheses of others. This is part of the general sense of predicates that Barth says must be open to modification when the particular subject is God. The linguistic prohibition we have just discussed issues in a more specific one, therefore: predicates applied to divinity should not be rigidly identified with one side or another of an exclusive contrast. Divinity must not be 'drawn into the dialectic of the world's antitheses' by a method of predication, like that in ordinary use, that requires a negative relation of exclusion between abstract contraries. Divine infinity must not be simply contrasted with the finite; divine eternality must not be simply opposed to temporality etc.[53] We have our rule for a non-contrastive characterization of God as transcendent.

Let us see how this rule may be suggested directly from the nature of God as a self-determining subject. If divinity is a freely self-determining subject, God's transcendence must be freely self-determined too. As such, it cannot be determined by even a negative relation to the world; a transcendence dependent upon an opposition with the non-divine would not be a self-determined one. A genuinely self-determined transcendence can only be one grounded positively and properly in the divine subject itself, beyond and above any direct contrast with a reality that is not divine.[54] Divine reality is indeed distinguished from the non-divine precisely in that the latter always is what it is over and against others. Divine reality is radically transcendent in a manner beyond the reach of created beings: created beings can never be themselves in utter independence of the beings with which they exist in essential contrast.

Because it is not based essentially on an opposition with the non-divine, this radical transcendence of God can be exercised in both God's otherness over and against the world and God's immanent presence within it.[55] A self-determined transcendence does not limit God's relation with the world to one of distance. A radical transcendence does not exclude God's positive fellowship with the world or presence within it.[56] Only created beings, which remain themselves over and against others, risk the distinctness of their own natures by entering into intimate relations with another.[57] God's transcendence alone is one that may be properly exercised in the radical immanence by which God is said to be nearer to us than we are to ourselves.[58]

God's transcendence over and against the world and God's immanent presence within it become non-exclusive possibilities, then, when God's primary transcendence is a self-determined transcendence essentially independent of a contrast with the non-divine. The ordinarily mutually exclusive predicates 'transcendence' and 'immanence' may both be applied to one and the same self-determining divine subject. The apparent mutual exclusiveness of those terms has to give way before a God who is freely self-determining.

It is the mutual exclusiveness of *all* apparent antitheses, not just that of transcendence and immanence, which must give way before such a God. This means that God must not be identified with one side of an exclusive contrast, the world with the other. It means, moreover, that when one side of a contrast is applied to God, the other may be also: it must be possible to say that God is infinite, eternal and non-spatial in such a manner that 'the antithesis and mutual exclusiveness of infinite and finite, non-spatiality and timelessness, on the one hand, and spatiality and temporality, on the other, do not enclose and imprison Him.'[59]

The apparent mutual exclusiveness of terms will, however, 'imprison' divinity if the import of each is unfolded separately, if each predicate is considered abstractly in its general sense apart from its contrary. Such a procedure will prohibit the ascription of both terms to one and the same subject, requiring instead a division of the divine subject (i.e., a sharp distinction between God in 'himself' and God for us) or the identification of divinity with one term to the exclusion of the other. The attribution of ordinarily exclusive terms to the same divine subject requires, instead, a mutual modification of the proper meaning of both terms in the course of a theological use that assumes the appropriate predication of both to the same God in the same respects.

In the case of concern to us, predicates affirming the free transcendence of God should be used to characterize God in the very same respects as predicates affirming loving intimacy. One must say, across the range of predicates that suggest either free transcendence or intimate involvement with the world, that God is loving in the exercise of divine freedom and free in the exercise of divine love.[60] The body of statements that result will display the radical transcendence of God appropriate to a self-determining divine subject, and exhibit, in the process, the compatibility of divine transcendence and divine involvement with the world.

We have completed our argument for this chapter. I have shown that Christian discourse about a transcendent God who creates the world is coherent in virtue of certain rules for discourse, and I have shown how those rules are at work to form a variegated tradition of Christian discourse. How might the discussion of this chapter help us to determine the coherence of Christian talk in which God is said to create beings with their own powers and efficacy? It is to this topic that I now turn.

3

God and the Efficacy of Creatures
The Basic Structure of Christian Discourse II

It is only a miserable and wordly picture of the dialectic of power to say that it becomes greater in proportion as it can compel and make things dependent. Socrates knew better; the art of using power is to make free. But between men that can never happen . . . only omnipotence can do so. If, therefore, man had even the least independent existence . . . God would not be able to make him free . . . If in order to create man God had lost any of his power, then he could not have made man independent.

Søren Kierkegaard, *Journals*, 1846[1]

Let us review the results of the last chapter. Talk in Christian theology about God as a transcendent creator was shown to conform to two rules: (1) for talk of God as transcendent beyond necessary relations of identity or difference with the non–divine, and (2) for talk of God's agency as immediate and universally extensive. Theological positions of widely different sorts were successfully analysed in terms of these same rules for talk. A cumulative case was thereby made for the existence of a basic structure of Christian discourse recognizable in terms of second-order rules for the regulation of theological language.

I argued that Christian discourse about a transcendent God who creates the world hangs together intelligibly when so structured. A distinction between consistent and coherent discourse can be introduced in this connection. It is not simply that Christian statements about God as transcendent and about God's creative involvement with the world do not contradict one another when constructed according to our rules; statements of these sorts are not merely logically consistent. They *imply* one another and therefore meet requirements for a stronger kind of intelligibility, systematic coherence.[2] Let us summarize this argument for the mutual implication of Christian statements about God's transcendence and God's creative involvement with the world.

The rule for talk of God as transcendent requires that divine agency with respect to the non-divine be possible. Talk of God as transcendent beyond opposition with the non-divine precludes any a priori separation of divine and non-divine and therefore implies at least the compatibility of divine transcendence and the involvement of God with the world.

Should Christians affirm that involvement, the rule for talk of God as transcendent requires talk of it as a universally extensive and immediate agency. God must not be said to be at work to a limited extent on or with what pre-exists it. God must not be talked about as only indirectly efficacious of the whole in virtue of intermediate agencies. In either case God would take on the character of a finite agent; the rule for talk of God as transcendent would thereby be violated. According to our rules, then, statements about God's transcendence imply statements about a direct and comprehensive creative agency of God.

The reverse holds as well. When Christian discourse conforms to our rules, statements about God's creative agency imply statements about the radical transcendence of God. God may be talked about as a creative agent, immediately effecting every non-divine being in every respect by which it may be likened to or distinguished from other finite beings; but only if God's nature as a transcendent being cannot be captured by any characterization in the same terms of similarity and difference. Talk of that sort about God's creative agency makes sense only if Christian statements about God as transcendent conform to our rule.

This chapter continues our analysis of rules in Christian talk. I will consider whether Christian discourse according to our rules remains coherent when the world a transcendent God creates is said to include creatures with their own powers and efficacy. Christians want to say that people in particular genuinely effect changes within the created order. They share these sorts of affirmations with non-Christians in the modern West. A person's responsibility for a moral life according to divine mandate seems to require such a supposition. When Christians talk about their acts against the will of God as sinners and about their loving service to God and neighbour as saved, they seem to presume that men and women can be genuine agents. Are statements of the creature's power and efficacy consistent with those that affirm the transcendence and creative agency of God? How, in particular, can there be room for talk of created agents if our rule for talk of God's agency requires the theologian to avoid any suggestions of intermediary created causes and to maintain that God's creative agency is at work everywhere?

In the first section of this chapter I argue that talk about a transcendent God's creative agency is compatible with talk about the creature's own powers when Christian discourse is structured according to our two rules. The same rules that render statements of God's transcendence and creative agency compatible ensure the coherence of Christian talk about that God in relation to a world where creatures exercise their own efficacious powers. In a second section I derive a subsidiary body of rules for Christian discourse on this specific topic. The arguments of both sections are supplemented by illustrations from different cases of theological discourse, to support the point once again that these rules delimit a variegated historical tradition. Karl Barth and Thomas Aquinas will be favourite examples – the first as a representative of Protestant concerns, the second as an authority for Roman Catholic theology – in an attempt to highlight the inclusiveness of such a tradition of coherent Christian talk.

The third section will mark a shift in my argument. Prior to that point my agenda will have been to establish that a host of different theologies do much the same thing: by different means they show the coherence of Christian talk about God and creation. For all their differences, they are functional equivalents, to use the language of the first chapter. Now, in section three I argue that differences behind historical factionalism in Christian theology are not ultimate. I hope to show that the body of rules we will have formulated by then are resources for complexity in Christian theology. The rules may be divided into two sets depending upon whether statements formulated according to the rules in question highlight God's gifts to the creature or the sovereignty of the divine agent who gives them. The same rules may therefore be used with a diversity of emphases. The theologies that result are thereby functional complements, to use again the language of the first chapter. Factors that affect a theologian's emphasis in the use of these rules include, we shall see, a theologian's metaphysical commitments, methodology and particular theological priorities.

The Coherence of Christian Talk about the Creature's Power and Efficacy

Some unpacking of the rule for talk of God's creative agency is necessary in order to see how, together with the rule for talk of God as transcendent, it allows the theologian to affirm the genuine power and efficacy of created beings. We need to see first of all the relevance of that rule for talk about the creature.

If God's agency must be talked about as universal and immediate, then, conversely, everything non-divine must be talked about as existing in a relation of total and immediate dependence upon God. Non-divine being must be talked about as always and in every respect *constituted* by, and therefore *nothing apart from*, an immediate relation with the founding agency of God. The rule for talk about God as an agent becomes a rule for talk about creatures in relation to God's agency.

Statements in a material mode that illustrate this rule take a variety of forms in Christian theology. A theologian influenced by the participationist language of Platonism might express the rule by saying that created being exists only as communicated form in essential dependence upon Pure Form. In the modified participationist language that Thomas uses, the rule might be expressed by saying that created being, formed of a distinction between *esse* and essence, simply *is* what exists in a relation of dependence upon that which is essentially *esse*. A dynamic metaphysics like that of transcendental Thomism might instantiate such a rule by affirming that created being is intrinsically determined as the dynamism it is by a tendency towards God as final end. A theology availing itself of an event-centred ontology might do much the same thing by saying that created being *is* the history of its acts in obedient response to God's action in Christ.[3]

This rule for talk of the creature in relation to God's agency issues in a more specific directive. It requires the theologian to maintain a direct rather than inverse proportion between what the creature has, on the one hand, and the extent and influence of God's agency, on the other. One must say created being becomes what it is and this all the more fully, not by way of separation or neutrality from God, but within the intimacy of a relationship to divinity as its total ground. The more one talks of the realization and perfection of created beings, the more must one be willing to talk of God's immediate creative working. One must not assume that talk of God's working takes away from what the creature has; talk of the creature's stature does not take away from God's but magnifies it.

In a way that exemplifies this principle of a direct proportion, Karl Barth uses the unity of God and humanity in Jesus Christ as a rule: whatever is affirmed of humanity's exaltation in Christ must be said to be nothing but a perfect and total following directly upon the will of God. For the Roman Catholic theologian Karl Rahner, it is axiomatic for a Christian account of the relationship between divine and non-divine that the non-divine have its own being in all its proper autonomy, integrity and worth only in the degree to which it is totally and immediately grounded in the creative agency of God.[4]

If power and efficacy are perfections, the principle of direct proportion requires that creatures be said to gain those qualities, not in the degree God's agency is restricted, but in the degree God's creative agency is extended to them. Talk of the creature's power and efficacy is compatible with talk about God's universal and immediate agency if the theologian follows a rule according to which divinity is said to exercise its power in founding rather than suppressing created being, and created being is said to maintain and fulfil itself, not independently of such agency, but in essential dependence upon it.

The same conclusion of compatibility seems to follow simply from substituting 'created power and efficacy' as instances of the sort of being to be talked about according to our rule for discourse concerning the creature in relation to divine agency. Created power and efficacy just become cases of created being existing in a total and immediate dependence upon the God who brings it to be.

This sort of substitution seems appropriate since according to our rule for talk of God as an agent God's creative powers must be said to extend to all created existence, including presumably any power or efficacy that created beings themselves have. God's creative agency must be said to found created being in whatever mechanical causality, animate working or self-determining agency it might evidence. A created cause can be said to bring about a certain created effect by its own power, or a created agency can be talked about as freely intending the object of its rational volition, only if God is said to found that causality or agency directly and *in toto* – in power, exercise, manner of activity and effect.

A Christian theologian would be mistaken, therefore, if he or she denied that created powers and efficacy exist, simply because God's agency must have a universal range. Such a denial of the compatibility of divine agency and created efficacy is a theological occasionalism that refuses to the creature the ability to act or produce effects by its own proper power, in order to ensure the sovereignty of divine agency. On that account the creature is not the genuine cause of subsequent effects in the created order. What the creature does is simply the occasion for God's own creative action in bringing to be what happens next. The creature becomes the empty shell for an exercise of divine power.

From the perspective of a proper employment of the rule for talk of divine agency, it makes as much sense to deny there are created powers and efficacy because God brings about all that is, as to deny there is a creation because there is a creator.[5] It makes no sense at all, for the same reason in both cases – one would be denying the existence of an effect because of the existence of a cause.

If that were the principle behind theological occasionalism, a theologian of that ilk should be led to deny the very existence of the creature. A consistent theological occasionalist should affirm that nothing but God exists: either God creates nothing, or the world God does create must participate in divinity. If the former, a basic affirmation of Christian practice is denied. If the latter, our rule for talk of God as transcendent is violated.

A theologian would be equally mistaken if he or she affirmed the existence of created operations and efficacy but denied that God's creative agency extended directly to them because of the same sort of belief in their incompatibility. In this case the theologian would espouse a deistic naturalism like that prevalent in the Enlightenment: God sets the world in existence and then leaves the creature alone to run according to its own laws.

From the standpoint of our rule for talk about the creature in relation to divine agency, such a position would proclaim the existence of an effect while denying its cause. Some aspect of non–divine reality would be talked about as existing independently of that relation of dependence upon divinity that constitutes created being as such. The rule for talk of the creature would thereby be violated. Creatures would be talked about as absolutely self-generating in respect of their operations and efficacy. Creatures would no longer be talked about *as* creatures in those respects.

The theological occasionalist might respond to our charges by claiming to abide by our rules for talk of God's creative agency and the creature. 'Created efficacy', the theological occasionalist would argue, is just not a possible substitution instance in those rules. The theological occasionalist may suggest it is improper to say that both God and created beings bring about effects in the created order: genuine efficacy cannot be predicated of both God and the creature.

Such a claim of impropriety conflicts, however, with our rule for talk of God as transcendent. That rule does exclude any a priori identity of predicates applied to God and creature. If God is said to have power and be efficacious, that does not *require* the conclusion that God communicates to creatures a power and efficacy appropriate to them. The rule also prohibits an a priori opposition between divine and created predicates that would absolutely *prevent* such a communication. The theological occasionalist forgets this.

To exclude genuine created efficacy as a possible direct effect of God's agency is to misunderstand, then, the nature of the transcendence implied by the supremacy, sovereignty and holiness of God. In the Christian tradition, God's greatness does not require any denial of the creature whose being is constituted in dependence upon 'him'.[6] The Protestant theologian Karl Barth makes this point eloquently: God's sovereign right over creation may be exercised by

> conceding to this existence a reality side by side with His own, and fulfilling His will towards this other in such a way that He

does not suspend and destroy it as this other but accompanies and sustains it and allows it to develop in freedom.[7]

It is at once apparent that the formula 'God everything and man nothing'. . . is . . . pure nonsense . . . In the giving of His Son . . . God is indeed everything but only in order that man may not be nothing, in order that he may be His man, in order that as such he, too, may be everything in his own place, on his own level and within his own limits.[8]

The God who Himself became a creature in Jesus Christ . . . is not exalted in the suppression of the creature. He does not find His triumph in the creature's lack of freedom or power compared with His own unconditional and irresistible lordship. He does not work alone even when he works in all.[9]

The deist might argue against us that our rules for talk of God's agency and the creature must be violated since there exists an aspect of non-divine reality that cannot be a substitution instance in those rules. The particular character of genuine non-divine efficacy conflicts with talk of its existing in a relation of dependence upon God. The theological occasionalist could take heart from this argument as well; if non-divine efficacy would involve such a conflict then it must not exist.

What would prevent such a substitution? Our rule for talk of the creature in relation to God's agency restricts the substitution of only those predicates that conflict with the very relation of essential dependence upon divinity that constitutes the rule itself. Does talk of a creature's acting and bringing about effects by his own power present such a conflict? Must the particular character of created efficacy be incompatible with what has to be said of any substitution instance in our rule for talk of the creature?

To assume so is to misapprehend the *formal* character of talk about utter dependence upon divinity. Talk about what is as existing in a relation of dependence upon God can be extended universally to cover any material account of the particular natures of non-divine beings.[10] This is what our rule for talk of God as transcendent requires.

We saw in the last chapter that an account of divine agency that accords with our rule for talk of God as transcendent must claim for divine agency an a priori indeterminate complexity of possible mode of effect. The particular characteristics of the created beings God brings about cannot be determined in advance simply on the basis of what is said about the nature of God's being and will. The transcendent character of God's agency makes it impossible to deduce from it the specific natures of the creatures God produces. The nature of God's agency puts no strictures of itself on the sorts of beings that may come to be.

This means conversely that no particular characterization of the natures of non-divine beings is required for talk about them as utterly dependent upon God. Because of the a priori indeterminacy of the possible modes of God's effects, God's creative agency can be said to extend to non-divine beings of any empirical character – even those with their own power and efficacy within the created world. There is no reason to suppose that God's creative powers are exercised more easily or more thoroughly for inert natures, constrained in total passivity by other created forces, then they are for creatures with their own powers of action.

If 'created efficacy' is not a proper substitution instance in our rules it must conflict, then, with the formal theological requirement according to which created beings of every material description are said to exist in dependence upon God. The deist must be assuming that any genuine created agent or cause operates independently and to the exclusion of divine creative agency for it. This, however, is not an empirical judgement. It is a theological remark concerning a particular kind of non-divine being's relation to God. Our rule for talk about the creature does not run aground, then, as the deist asserts, upon the fact of an aspect of non-divine reality that cannot be substituted in it. The deist simply makes, as we initially charged, a theological judgement that violates our rules.

Substituting 'created power and efficacy' within our rule for talk of the creature results in discourse that highlights the very rule for talk of God as transcendent that makes such a substitution possible. The theologian talks of an ordered nexus of created causes and effects in a relation of total and immediate dependence upon divine agency. Two different orders of efficacy become evident: along a 'horizontal' plane, an order of created causes and effects; along a 'vertical' plane, the order whereby God founds the former. Predicates applied to created beings may concern what happens within the created order; they can be understood to hold simply within the horizontal plane of relations among created beings. Predicates of that sort say nothing about the vertical relation of a creature's dependence upon God. Ascribing them to created beings cannot run contrary, then, to our rules for talk of God's agency and the creature.

Take, for example, freedom and contingency as attributes of the creature that might suggest a conflict with the theological formality of a creature's complete determination by God's creative agency. These predicates may simply concern the nature of the relation between created beings and their created effects. To be free, a person must be master, one might suppose, of that which conditions choice on the created level. To be contingent, a created cause must have a non-necessary logical relation with its created effects. Freedom or contingency of such a sort says nothing about a creature's freedom or contingency with respect to the divine agent who creatively founds the whole of created beings and their effects and their mode of relation. There need be no contradiction in saying relations that are free or contingent along the horizontal axis of a created order are determined to be so in a vertical relation of absolute dependence upon divine agency.

Talk of two orders of predication goes some way, then, towards countering a more narrowly circumscribed deistic position: one that objects only to 'free agents' as substitution instances in our rules. Again, the theological formality required by our rules would be compatible with any empirical or metaphysical description of freedom – however extreme – so long as it did not require the further theological judgement that the creature's freedom is a freedom from God.[11]

RULES FOR TALK ABOUT GOD'S AGENCY AND CREATED EFFICACY

I have argued that our rule for talk of the creature can apply in talk about the powers and operations of non-divine beings. From that application I will now derive a number of general and particular rules for talking specifically about divine agency and created efficacy.

If we are right that our rule for talk of the creature holds in talk about non-divine efficacy, talk of God's agency according to our rules and talk of created efficacy are compatible. The rules we are to derive represent, then, a set of immediate linguistic directives that must be followed if talk of that sort is to be coherent. This secondary set of rules warrants for that reason a careful analysis. The detail of it will also help us understand the often quite subtle modifications of these rules in modern times, to be discussed in the next chapter.

The most general rule for talk about created efficacy is as follows. It is simply a specification of our rule for discourse about the creature. The theologian should talk of created efficacy as immediately and entirely grounded in the creative agency of God. If a theologian's discourse conforms to our rule for talk of God's agency, he or she should say that divine agency is required for any power, operation and efficacy of created beings; conversely, created beings should be said to have power, to operate and produce created effects only as God's agency extends to them in those respects.

The theologian who conforms his or her discourse to this general rule for talk of created efficacy should ask rhetorically with Barth, then, 'Where or when could the creature accomplish or perform even the slightest act without this also taking place, without God being with it in this act of lordship?'[12] Nothing prevents the theologian from affirming that genuine created activities, natural powers and free human decision exist within the created order. In Barth's words, 'Alongside [God's] activity there is a place for that of the creature. We even dare and indeed have to make the . . . assertion that He cooperates with the creature, meaning that as He Himself works He allows the creature to also be active in its freedom.'[13] The existence of this genuine created causal efficacy must be said, however, to follow only from the direct founding agency of God for it. 'It is not of itself', Barth says, 'that it can exist and work side by side with Him; it is always . . . the gift of God.'[14] Wherever created activity occurs it is 'in virtue of [God's] directly effective will to preserve, under His direct and superior cooperation and according to His immediate direction'.[15]

Thomas illustrates this rule for talk of created efficacy in statements about two orders of causality. Created causes are *secondary* causes with respect to the *primary* creative agency of God.[16] God as a creative agent must be said to will any order among things that created causes carry out; created causes are therefore subordinate to God's own agency.

Thomas says in this vein that created causes possess a principle of operation for created effects so as to be the executors of the created causal order God ordains. This does not mean that created causes simply take their marching orders from God. The all-encompassing creative agency of God directly founds and sustains a created being in its power, operations and actual production of created effects.[17] Created beings are the executors of the order for the world that God ordains but only as God's creative agency is at work every step of the way by which such an order is produced.

Should the created cause of an effect be sufficient for it within the created order our general rule becomes a more specific one: what we can call, following Thomas, a rule for talk of two total subordinated causes.[18] According to our general rule for talk of created efficacy, God's creative agency must be said to found a created cause in the very operations by which it proves sufficient to produce an effect within the created order. The whole of a created effect must be said, therefore, to depend both on divine agency and its created cause.

Thomas illustrates the rule in the following statement: the same effect 'is wholly done by both [a natural cause and divine power], according to a different way, just as the same effect is wholly attributed to the instrument and also wholly to the principal agency'.[19] In other words, a created effect can be attributed in its entirety both to its created cause and to divine agency since the created cause is totally subordinated to the God who creatively founds it. Bernard of Clairvaux (died 1274) provides a fine illustration of the rule's application to the special case of the relation between God's cooperating grace and human free will: 'Free will accomplishes the entire work and grace performs the entire work; in such a way, however, that the entire work is in the will precisely because the entire work is from grace.'[20]

A number of more specific rules follow from this rule for talk of two total subordinated causes. Bernard says in the same context I have quoted, 'Not grace separately, nor free will separately, but rather both, each by its own activity, accomplish the entire work.'

Generalizing from this, we have a first series of more specific rules, formed by violating in a systematic fashion our expectations for talk of sufficient causes.

Ordinarily, when discussion is limited to created causes, talk of two sufficient causes working for the same effect makes no sense. Perhaps the causes are not really two. But Bernard says 'each by its own activity'. According to our rule for talk of God as transcendent, we cannot identify God's working with our own. Perhaps the one cause works in cases where the other does not. If both are genuinely sufficient causes, each is separately sufficient and the other is superfluous while it works. But Bernard prohibits talk of separate sufficiency. Where created causes are operative, it is improper to claim that God's work is separately sufficient for a created effect to the exclusion of created causes. Such a statement is not well formed since God's creative intention includes in this instance the founding of created causes.[21] It is also not correct to hold a sufficient created cause is independent of divine agency: created causes that are sufficient within the created order for certain effects are only such through God's creative agency for them.[22]

Perhaps what are called sufficient causes are not really so: each cause is sufficient for only a part of the entire created effect. But according to Bernard, 'each accomplishes the entire work.' And Thomas: 'The same effect is not attributed to a natural cause and to divine power in such a way that it is partly done by God and partly by the natural agent; rather it is wholly done by both.'[23] God's agency is always sufficient: God's creative working according to our rule for talk about it must be said to be universally extensive. In a sense the created cause is not a sufficient cause: every aspect of its efficacy depends upon God's creative agency for it. But nothing prohibits a created cause from being genuinely sufficient within the created order: in such cases no aspect of a created effect may be isolated for which a created cause is not responsible.

A number of other rules put restrictions on the way God is said simply to work with the creature. Divine *concursus*, God's working with creatures who work, should first of all not be talked about as a concord, a convergence of independent lines of divine and created agencies productive of a single created effect. God's transcendence prohibits talk of God's working with created causality in any way that implies the parity of divine agency and created causality within a common causal nexus or plane. According to the rule for talk of God's agency, God can be said to work with created causes only in the sense that God creatively establishes ʰhat causality to have its place within a created order directly established as a whole by God. It cannot mean that God works with created operations that are not themselves directly dependent upon this same divine working.

Since divine agency is necessary for any action of the creature at all, it cannot be proper to say that God's activity is *added on to* the creature's. As Barth says,

> In the rule of God we do not have to do first with a creaturely action and then – somewhere above or behind, but quite distinct from it, like a hidden meaning and content – with an operation of God Himself. To describe *concursus divinis* we cannot use the mathematical picture of two parallel lines. But creaturely events take place as God Himself acts.[24]

A rule restricts talk of composition. The *activity* of the creature cannot be talked about as composed of a divine and a created operation; the created *effect* of God and a created cause should not be spoken of as a composition of distinct created and divine effects. For example, the created effects of divine power should not be confined to an indifferent or general substratum, specified or particularized by created causes. God as *universalis causa essendi* does not creatively found only what is common in being, leaving to secondary causes the determination of particular natures.[25] Statements of the first sort that concern composite created activities suggest that God is brought down within the created order as a part of it. Statements of both the first and second sort, concerning composite created effects, suggest that God's creative agency does not extend as far as the creature's own work as an active cause.

To sum up this second set of derivative rules, having to do with talk of a divine *concursus*: God's agency is not to be talked about as partial, or as composed or mixed with created causality. None of that is proper since God is said to be at work as a transcendent agent founding created causality as a whole.

In the third place, prohibitions extend to talk about the influence of divine agency as any sort of *working on* created operations already in act. The efficacy of divine agency with respect to created causes cannot amount to an after-the-fact determination of already constituted created operations. Since the entirety of created being is conferred by divine agency, created beings have no domain of operations independent of God's agency. God's influence in the created order is therefore not properly said to be a secondary interference or conditioning, affecting the outcome of created operations from without by force or contraint or even persuasion.

God does not influence the actions of others in the manner of non-creative, finite agents. God does not work on created beings already inclined in a direction contrary to the divine will in order to reorient them. God may indeed *change* the customary direction of created operations but God does so by a creative working that brings created operations to be with a new direction. Created agents can only *affect* the operations of other creatures to bring them in line with their own wishes; God alone can be said to *effect* the actions of others by a creative operation that brings creatures to be in accord with God's intention for them.

One might say that God brings forth the operations of created causes by working interiorly, in their depths. A transcendent God can be said to have such an extraordinary immanence of operation when discussion of God's agency accords with our rule for talk of God as transcendent. Following our rule for talk of God's agency as immediate, one can say that God operates from within created causes, in the very place from which their operations arise.

As a result, God's agency may extend without violence to created causes whose movements are self-initiated.[26] Thus Thomas says, rather quaintly, that although 'the action of an angel does have some effect on man's choice by way of persuasion, and. . . the corporeal impressions of celestial bodies on our bodies give a disposition to certain choices', 'God alone directly [effects] the choice made by man' as the very cause of its being.[27] Because God is not working from without, it seems right to say that 'God [can] cause a movement of the will in us without prejudice to freedom of the will.'[28] More cautiously, the act is at least voluntary; we are not constrained against our will.[29] The point might be made within the more mystical tradition of an introspective spirituality, which seeks God's presence where the human soul draws its own substantiality immediately from God: 'God then does not work in us from the outside, violently imposing Himself on us, binding and determining us to do what is good. As Creator, He stands at the wellspring of our existence, at the point where it flows uninterruptedly from His creative hand. He alone can reach our freedom at its source and yet do it no violence.'[30]

In the fourth place, rules restrict talk about created causes influencing God or God's agency. By our general rule for talk of created efficacy, one must say that any ordering among things arising from created causes is itself included under the immediate creative agency of God.[31] No created cause can therefore be said to influence God or God's agency in a strong sense requiring the operation of those causes outside a direct determination by God.[32] As Barth expresses this point in the technical Thomistic language of two orders,

> [God] cannot encounter any limits in the creaturely sphere which can and must compel Him to conform, differentiating and adjusting and orientating Himself according to the activity of the creature . . . He is absolutely sovereign in relation to all the different possibilities of the creature, for there is not one of them which was not preceded by His own long before it ever existed or was free to lay hold of any possibilities.[33]

Such a prohibition does not, however, exclude talk of an influence of the creature on God in a weak sense supposing the prior extension of God's creative agency for that influence. In the personalistic language of intentionality discussed in the previous chapter, the complex creative intention of God would have to be said to include in that case the very influence of the creature on God. By its own creative intention, divinity would be determining itself to be determined by the creature in certain respects. Divinity would not, then, be conditioned or altered by created reality operating in independence of, or effective opposition to, its own creative will; any influence of the creature on God would arise only because, and in the manner and extent to which, God creatively willed it to do so. In Barth's words, 'There is no creaturely freedom which can limit or compete with the sole sovereignty and efficacy of God. But permitted by God, and indeed willed and created by Him, there is the freedom of the friends of God concerning whom He has determined that without abandoning the helm for one moment He will still allow Himself to be determined by them.'[34] In sum, it is proper to say that God is directly affected or determined by what the creature does; but only so long as the creature's effect on God is part of the complex creative intention by which God determines himself.

This rule prohibiting talk of the creature's independent conditioning of God does cut off, however, talk of the creature's influence on God's very agency. A created cause cannot influence God's own agency without being really independent of it, but it is just this independence that our general rule for talk of created efficacy rules out. According to that rule, created causes are always the result of God's agency; they can never have an existence before it to condition it. Making the same point in the personalist language of intentionality: God's creative intention of the whole of what happens cannot be conditioned by any created cause since created causes only come to be as a consequence of that intention.

More specific still, created causes for created effects cannot be said to condition God's creative will for those effects.[35] A created effect may exist because of a particular created cause, but it is not proper to say that God brings that created effect into existence *because* that created cause exists. The created cause exists only because God wills into existence a created causal order that includes it. God's will for the whole of the created order is primary: the existence of any particular created cause is a consequence of it. To underscore that God's intentions for the created order are not conditioned by created causes, one might even say that God wills their existence simply to be the means for the created effects God wants. There is an order to the divine intention and it reverses the order by which created causes execute it.[36]

Christians do say, however, that God responds to the prayers of the faithful. Are there not, then, exceptional cases where God's agency for created effects is determined by what the creature does? We have to say that a statement like 'God grants petitions' holds, not because God's agency is itself altered by prayer, but because prayer is according to God's will a necessary created condition in particular cases for a created effect or for the alteration of the usual order of created cause and effect.[37] To say that God makes up for the deficiency of created causes to produce the effect for which a person prays is to say, according to our account, that God's creative intention includes the effect and the prayer as its condition but not adequate secondary causes.

Could one say instead that God creatively intends his own agency to be conditioned by prayer? If one could, one would avoid talk of the creature's influencing or altering divine agency in any strong sense. Such statements can only collapse, however, into the ones we have just recommended, if our rules for talk of the creature's influence on God are correct. According to those rules, it is appropriate to say things like 'God hears our prayers'; God's creative intention may be said to include 'himself' as genuinely affected by creatures. One cannot talk in the same way to suggest the conditioning of God's very agency by creatures; the divine agency forming a creative intention cannot be included in any real sense within it.

All the rules we have looked at so far concern talk of God and the created order where created causes are said to be sufficient or at least operative. What rules hold where created causes are said to be inoperative or insufficient to produce created effects?

First it should be noted it is possible for God to create a world without sufficient created causes for what happens. We saw that our rules do not forbid talk of created beings with their own powers and efficacy. We shall see now that the rules also do not require such talk: God may be said to create a world in which created efficacy is partially or totally absent.

This possibility may be derived from our rules for talk of God as transcendent. If no a priori relations of identity hold between the characterizations of God and created beings, talk of God's power and efficacy does not require their conferral upon creatures.

God's creating a world without sufficient created causes for what happens is also a possibility according to our rule for talk of God's agency as immediate. In a certain sense God never works with created causes; in a certain sense God always brings about the created effects of divine agency without the help of created causes.

Secondary created causes never intervene in the creative operation by which God brings the non-divine in its entirety to be; no created causes work to bring about that relation of dependence upon divinity that constitutes created beings in their entirety. God's creative agency extends *immediately* to every created being in every respect; the creature's relation of dependence upon divinity is one of *immediate* dependence.

It is never appropriate, then, to bring in created causes when talking about the very constitution of the creature in its relation of dependence upon divinity. Created causes can never be said to be responsible in any degree for the *fact that* the world is created and preserved, ruled and saved in the way it is by God. It is appropriate to try to give an account of *what* God effects in terms of created causes, but one must not try to include in such an account the relation of dependence upon God by which any of those effects exists.

The sort of immediacy we have been discussing holds whether or not the world God creates is said to include creatures with power and efficacy. Even when God brings a created causal order to be, God immediately establishes each element and aspect of that order: created causes and effects and the power, operations and efficacy by which the later follow from the former. God's agency extends to what happens no less directly when created causes for those happenings exist than when they do not. Barth makes the point in this way: 'If the ruling of God consists first and foremost in His subordinating all things to Himself, this means that without prejudice to their mutual relations he deals with each one in a direct and immediate encounter and relationship with Himself.'[38]

Created causes that do exist are not the intermediaries, then, for God's creative establishing of their created effects. God's efficacy with respect to what happens in the world does not require, therefore, their existence. Only if God were to create with the aid of created causes would God be unable to do without them. We have our rule: one is permitted to talk of God's bringing to be created effects without sufficient created causes for them.

This rule allows Christian discourse to proceed in the face of metaphysical or empirical claims that certain happenings either exceed the capacities of any being within the natural order, or cannot be adequately explained by the causes actually at work in a particular case. The rule permits, in other words, talk of miracles, although it implies nothing about whether or not they do in fact occur. Thomas says,

> Without a doubt God can work in creatures independently of created causes, just as he works in all created causes; and by working independently of created causes he can produce the same effects and in the same order as he produces them by their means; or even other effects and in a different order so that he is able to do something contrary to the common and customary course of nature.[39]

Because of the immediacy of God's agency in any case, God can effect without created causes what ordinarily happens with them (e.g., conception without a male's contribution). God can also do what exceeds created power in general (e.g., the revivification of the dead); God can do what is impossible within the created order but not absolutely impossible.[40] When it comes to our salvation, the rule allows the theologian to say God effects what is discontinuous with our prior sinful inclinations or what exceeds altogether the created capabilities of human beings. The rule can also accommodate a metaphysical occasionalism (of the sort found, for instance, in some followers of Descartes), although, again, it does not imply or require any such occasionalism. God could be said to create a world in which events always happen without sufficient created causes.

Rules for talk specifically about God and a created order without sufficient created causes do not quite conform to those discussed earlier. Most significantly, talk of composition, though dangerous, is not so rigidly restricted. If created causes are insufficient to produce created effects, the theologian may use synergistic language: divine agency may be said to remedy by addition or intervention the deficiencies of created causes. If created causes are allegedly inoperative, either in general or in particular cases, the theologian may say that a creature acts by the infusion of a divine power – the creature acts not by its own power but by the power of God. Divine operations take the place of created ones. In all these cases talk of the created causal order suggests a composition of the divine and the non-divine.

Such statements are nevertheless proper if they can avoid implying a distinction within the created order between what is and is not the direct effect of divine agency. Were one to say God's production of a particular created effect is joined with the creature's production of another to produce a composite whole, this would indeed be the implication. It would seem that God is directly efficacious of this particular created effect but not of the creature's own efficacy. If one says God acts to remedy the deficiencies of a created cause or acts in its place this need not be the implication. Such statements may simply be a way of saying that God produces certain created effects without creating sufficient causes for them. The latter affirmation has no such worrisome implications. If the theologian's statements can be translated in this fashion, the theologian in talking the way he or she does may be assuming the total-working agency of God. Indeed, the theologian's own form of statement gives us no reason to conclude that God is not directly behind both the created effect and the created beings that are without sufficient power to produce the effect. These forms of expression highlight a created cause's direct dependence upon God.

A theologian's further statements may show if he or she is assuming the total-working agency of God in talk about God's action supplementing powers of the creature that are inadequate within the created order. The theologian should go on to violate certain rules for discourse formation that hold when the actions of beings within the world are said to supplement one another. There, the statement that one being's action is inadequate without the aid of another's implies the converse: the latter's action should be inadequate as well without the help of the former. The theologian cuts off, however, the converse of statements requiring divine aid if the creature is to produce created effects. God helps the creature to attain effects that would otherwise be beyond its capabilities; but the creature's activites are not, in the process, making up for any deficiencies in God's own agency. God's agency is a total-working creative agency; the created efforts that God aids are not independent of God's creative agency for them. Augustine makes the point:

if we may rightly say 'it is not of man that willeth, but of God that showeth mercy', because the will of man is not enough,

why may we not also rightly put it in the converse way: 'it is
not of God that showeth mercy, but of man that willeth',
because the mercy of God by itself does not suffice? Surely, if
no Christian will dare to say this . . . it follows that the true
interpretation of the [first] saying . . . is that the whole work
belongs to God.[41]

Might not talk of the creature acting by the power of God or
talk of divine operations taking the place of created causes imply
that God's agency in these respects is enclosed within the created
sphere? God's power and operations become a part of the created
order; God becomes one agent among others. This would clearly
violate our rule for talk of God as transcendent. Such talk has no
such implication if, once again, it is simply a way of saying God's
agency does not extend to the establishment of created causes.

Talk of God's remedying the deficiencies of created causes or
taking their place will violate neither our rule for talk of God as
transcendent nor our rule for talk of God's creative agency, if it
abides, then, by such a translation rule. The rule in this case is just
an instance of a more general one: predicates that diversify divine
agency should be able to be ascribed to only the effects of divine
agency. Saying that divine agency is indirect, for example, means
that God establishes created causal media for created effects;
saying that divine agency continues in preserving creatures means
that God founds created reality in its duration; saying that God
moves the creature means that God establishes created being in
motion; saying that God modifies created being means that God
founds created being in differences of quality across time. In the
same way, saying that God's agency *supplements* or *replaces* secondary causality is simply to say that divine agency founds created
effects without sufficient created causes.

Intentional language in talk of God's agency is particularly
suitable for exhibiting this linguistic rule because of the complex
predication relations it allows between attributes of the agent
intending and the effects intended. Expressions with an ambiguous placement in a sentence might qualify the subject intending or
the objects intended. Such statements can be disambiguated by
linguistic transpositions of the sort we have just discussed – by
moving those qualifiers to the object–clause. Once moved, the

qualifiers say nothing any longer about divine agency because of the complex predication relations that hold in statements of intentionality. Qualifiers that seemed to diversify divine agency may indicate only a real difference in that agency's effects: the operation of divine agency remains constant – simple and undifferentiated.

Such a linguistic rule might be a way of formulating in a formal mode the Thomistic dictum that divine agency is logically but not really related to its created effects.[42] The claim amounts to the rule that talk in which the character of divine agency varies with its effects be able to be reduced without remainder to talk about the self-same divine will having different created effects. Divine agency would be logically and not really related to its created effects in the sense that, according to this rule, (whatever the variety of things said about it) the character of divine agency does not really change with the diversity of things it brings about.

Fear of composition language in talk about insufficient or inoperative created causes need not prompt, therefore, the extreme reaction of prohibiting this language altogether. One should not claim that divine agency cannot work without sufficient secondary causes within the created order, in order to effect such a prohibition. This happens in Roman Catholic polemics, to combat Protestant claims of total human depravity and a Protestant preference for an account of the effects of grace that stresses the creature's changed relationship with God rather than the transformation of the creature's own powers of action.[43] If God must establish created causes sufficient for the created effects God wills, Protestant theologians cannot say the saving action of God works a good of which human beings in their depravity are utterly incapable. Nor can they say human beings as saved do the good through God's power and not their own. The same strategy for prohibiting composition talk figures in Protestant theology, too. Here, it may represent an accommodation by theology to a modern scientific worldview's emphasis on natural uniformity. It may also be a means of opposing a form of theology known as rationalistic supernaturalism where miracles tend to become the exclusive locus of direct divine influence on the world.[44] Whatever the case, this method of preventing talk of composition is in irremediable conflict with our rules for talk of God's creative agency and transcendence. According to those rules, the theologian must be able to say that God can bring about created effects without establishing created causes for them.

RULES AS RESOURCES OF COMPLEXITY

To sum up: in the first section I argued from the rule for talk of God as transcendent that God can be said to create non-divine beings with their own powers and operations productive of created effects. Assuming such an extension of God's creative agency, we saw in the second place that the rule for talk of God's agency becomes a rule requiring talk of God's direct establishment of every aspect of created efficacy. Passively understood as a rule for talk of created efficacy, it requires that created powers and operations productive of created effects be said to exist only in a relation of immediate and total dependence upon God. From the rules for talk of God's agency and transcendence we also derived a second general rule: divine agency may be said to extend to created effects without establishing created powers or operations for those effects. Finally, we derived a number of more specific rules concerning talk of the relation between divine agency and created efficacy in terms of either composition and supplementation, or alteration and counter-influence.

In this section, this subsidiary body of rules will be shown to permit, and even to suggest, the possibility of very different theological emphases to be determined specifically by a number of theological and extra-theological variables. Major divergent theological strands within the Christian tradition will be considered as functional complements in virtue of such differences of emphasis in their utilization of the same basic rules for coherent Christian discourse.

My contention that the rules proposed accurately capture a structure basic to Christian theology will be supported by this argument: I will show the rules are adequate to account for theological differences more serious than those based on the sort of variations in conceptuality we looked at in chapter 2. Historical examples will be mentioned for illustrative purposes in this section but the discussion will remain in a hypothetical mode since it is

not possible – or necessary for my argument – to engage here in
the historical arguments that would be required to support claims
of the proper classification and analysis of the examples under the
rubrics discussed below.

The two-sided character of the rules

The rules we have specified are a force for theological diversity
because they have two sides. They include both positive and
negative rules and versions of rules. On the positive side: we can
say that the creature is everything with God; that God grants us
our own powers and in that sense works with us; that our doing
may be a necessary moment of the created order God wills. On
the negative side: we must say that we are nothing without God;
that God's will is not constrained by anything we do; that God can
work without us by creating a world that does not include
creatures with power. The positive side of the rules structures
theological discourse so that it stresses the creature's capacities and
God's creative agency as a bestowal of such gifts. The negative
side of the rules forms theological discourse that emphasizes
divine sovereignty, the unconditioned primacy and unqualified
supremacy of God's power.

Our rules for talk of the creature and created efficacy specifically
have a similar dual capacity. The rule for talk of the creature as
directly dependent in its entirety upon God can be used either to
highlight what the creature has in dependence upon God or to
underscore the very relation of dependence by which the creature
has it. The first use promotes theological discussion of the creature
in itself, its own value and dignity. Created reality takes on a
certain opacity; it can be considered in itself apart from an
immediate reference to the God who brings it to be. The second
use fosters discourse that subordinates the creature to God.
Created reality becomes a transparent reference to the God upon
whom it depends.

When the rule for talk of the creature is extended to the case of
created efficacy, the same dual capacity for discourse is accen-
tuated. The theologian can always make a thematic reference to
the creature's dependence upon God and will be assuming it in any
case. But the creature can be described in terms of its relations

with others within a created causal nexus, without any explicit mention of God.

The positive side of the rules is aligned with discourse that focuses on the creature in itself. For instance, the rule for talk of two total subordinated causes suggests that empirically sufficient descriptions of created beings can be given by a theologian apart from a reference to divine agency. There can be an adequate explanation for a created effect in terms of created causes; it will not include a reference to God's agency although the created causes mentioned are established in their sufficiency by God.

The negative side of the rules is aligned with theological discourse that focuses on the creature's relation of dependence upon God. The negative force of our rule for talk of the creature, 'the creature is nothing without God', requires, for example, an immediate reference to God when discussing created reality. The negative rule that God may be said to work without sufficient created causes has the same effect: it highlights the immediacy of the creature's relation of dependence upon God. If God can do without them, created causes, even where they exist, become of little account. Where the rule applies because one cannot give an adequate explanation of a created effect in terms of created causes, talk of what happens will require a direct reference to God's own agency. If there appear to be sufficient created causes, the rule can still be invoked to claim that those causes work not by their own power but by the power of God. This use of the rule guarantees that talk of the activities of the creature remains inextricably bound up with talk of God's creative agency.

Factors influencing the side of the rules emphasized

A number of different factors may converge to bring a theologian to emphasize a certain side of the rules. Let us isolate several of these factors now.

First, the particular philosophical milieu may help channel theological discussion in one direction or another. Take, for example, Platonic metaphysics. The qualities that distinguish beings within the world are referred immediately to transcendent forms by a vertical relation of participation or imitation. A theology that incorporates the vocabulary and thought-forms of

Platonism tends, therefore, to consider created beings and their relations, not in themselves, but always in their reference to God. Bonaventure's *Itinerarium Mentis in Deum* (1259) provides a classic example: created things become signs and symbols of divinity; ideally, one is to see God directly in them, as one would see a reflection in a mirror.

A more 'horizontal' metaphysics, like Aristotle's, in which the ontological components of existing things have their primary locus within the worldly order, might prompt a theologian to discuss created beings in themselves. There would be something to say about them in intra-mundane terms, apart from any reference to God. A description of particular created natures would not have to incorporate a discussion of the creature's relation to God. Such a discussion would surely precede or follow but would in any case form a separate theme. The theologian's discourse might come to include as a result a moment of what looks like straightforward philosophical description. The reason and point of it would be, nevertheless, theological; the world would come in for treatment because it is God's creature, for the ultimate purpose of suggesting something about the one who created it.[45]

Emphasis on the negative or positive side of the rules may vary depending upon the reluctance of a theologian's philosophical milieu to admit occult created powers or the reality of created relations. Thus, nominalist or rigidly empiricist philosophies, à la Ockam or Hume, in which such a reluctance is strongly felt, may influence a theologian to refer any causal order to divine power and stress the nothingness of created relations apart from God's plan. So long as these nominalist or empiricist philosophical judgements concern the fact of what God has done and do not constrain the theologian to deny God's ability to create beings with their own powers and efficacy, the theologian's discourse will not violate our rules.

Differences in the metaphysical accounts that are influential in theology may have a relatively circumscribed effect on the sort of rules brought to bear in particular theological loci. If the topic is of central enough importance for a theologian, the result may be a general favouring of either negative or positive rules. Different rules or aspects of the rules may come to the fore within Roman

Catholic treatments of providence, for example, depending upon whether they incorporate a Thomistic or a Suarezian metaphysical account of the movement of a power to act. According to Suarez's but not to Thomas's account, movement to act is within the capacities of a created power.[46] One would therefore expect Thomas, and not Suarez, to talk of the creature's actualization of its potential under divine rule so as to stress the 'immediate dependence' side of our rules for talk of the creature and the negative rule that allows talk of God's working without the creature.[47] In a similar way, the metaphysical commitments of theological schools may play a role in determining which rules apply in talk of human works under God's saving grace. Thomas, for instance – in contrast to Peter Lombard, much of the Protestant tradition and theologies which stress sanctification as an immediate union with God[48] – does not avail himself of the negative rule permitting talk of God's operation without secondary causes and say that we do good works by the power of God. He employs instead the positive rule for talk of two total subordinated causes and speaks of created habits, powers or dispositions for good in human persons under God's grace. This may be due at least in small part to the influence of a metaphysical theory that makes it difficult to understand how the actions specific to a human being can proceed apart from an internal principle of operation. If human action under grace remains that appropriate to a human being, God's grace must be received and accommodated to that nature to produce a new internal principle for action.[49]

Besides the influence of metaphysical conclusions, very general differences in thought-structure or conceptuality often lead to variations in the side of the rules emphasized. A theology whose conceptuality is predominantly shaped by categories of personal relation – perhaps as a way of approximating biblical language – may focus, for instance, on the relation between creatures and God while eschewing any ontological/anthropological account of created things and human persons in themselves. Reformation treatments of salvation might be interpreted in this way, as simple descriptions of a new life under God's favour, completely devoid of concern for any metaphysical illumination of human nature and action under these conditions. Theologies informed by the language of personal relationship would be naturally inclined towards a constantly practical, existential view of human persons *coram Deo*, standing before God. The creature's own powers, operations and efficacy would become of utter insignificance from that perspective and therefore the negative side of our rules would tend to be emphasized.

A theological conceptuality that is not predominantly relational, but informed, say, by a more 'substantialist' ontology like that found in Aristotle's division of categories, might not promote the same degree of concentration on the creature's relation of dependence upon God. Talk of essences and accidents, of acts and potencies for action, would be relatively difficult to use in talk of the creature's relation of dependence upon God; relatively easy to use in talk of the created natures and operations which are the immediate effects of such a relation. A metaphysics that highlights categories of relationality might also, of course, be used by the theologian to give an account of the natures of creatures per se; the nature of a particular created being would be explicated in terms of its relations with others. But a relational account of the creature could easily comprise nothing more than an account of the creature's relation of dependence upon God: the relations that constitute creatures are their relations with God. Thereby, the material account of the nature of created reality would merely reflect the formal theological description of it as essentially determined by a relation of dependence upon divinity. Once again, the result would be the elimination of any consideration of the creature itself apart from a direct reference to its being under God. Gerhard Ebeling and Karl Barth in Protestant theology, Karl Rahner and the tradition of 'la nouvelle theologie' in Roman Catholicism, provide examples of this.[50] For Rahner, for instance, the immanent operations of the human subject cannot be discussed intelligibly apart from the orientation of the subject towards the transcendent. For Barth, there is nothing to say about human beings in themselves apart from their history with God, centred on Christ.

Theological method is another general factor influencing the stress of discourse that conforms to our rules. A theology that does not engage in systematic analysis or exposition according to an abstract ordering is not very likely to direct attention to the creature in itself apart from explicit reference to the God upon whom the creature depends. The creature never *really* exists apart from a relation of dependence upon divinity; it may simply be *considered* thus. A theologian therefore needs to stray in thought from the real order of things in order to consider the creature in itself; he or she must consider the creature abstractly, i.e., abstracting from the relation of dependence upon God by which it really exists. Should a theology be organized according to the logical distinctions necessary for precise definition, a consideration of created reality apart from a thematic reference to divinity may take place. The theologian in such cases is simply engaged in a process of concept formation and is not making any judgement thereby that the creature really exists independently of divinity.

An abstract consideration of the creature in itself would be particularly unproblematic in cases like that of Thomas's *Summa Theologica* where the principle in accordance with which every topic is understood and ordered itself involves a necessary reference to God.[51] Theological exposition proceeds, Thomas claims, in the light of divine revelation. A logically ordered body of sacred doctrine is formed thereby. On the basis of revealed principles, the theologian attempts to approximate the divine science itself (i.e., the very order which things have in God's own knowledge). Everything that theology treats is arranged according to the principle of *omnia sub ratione Dei*. Nothing becomes a topic for theological discussion unless it has a reference to God; the principle in accordance with which the system is organized requires all things under theological discussion to find their beginning and end in God. Creatures may come up for independent discussion, therefore; but only in so far as the placement of that discussion in the system shows them to be the result of divine agency and to be on their way back to God. Thomas can concentrate, then, on human persons and created things without a thematic reminder of their actual subordination to God; a reference to divinity is the constant presupposition of his theological system even where they may be no thematic reference to divinity in the treatment of a specific subject matter.

A theology does not, however, have to be organized in this way. It may be focused, either systematically or unsystematically, on a theme considered of paramount importance (e.g., the salvation of the sinner in Christ). In that case the theologian's exposition tends to follow strictly a real rather than abstract order. Theological concern will tend to centre on the actual relations that hold between what is being discussed – e.g., what must be assumed about divine power and human beings from the fact that God saved us in Christ. Formal requirements of theoretical precision will not prompt a consideration of people apart from a reference, in this case, to the real relation that connects them with the saving work of Christ. If a reference to divinity is to have central importance in a theology of this sort, that reference can be absolutely assured only by preventing creatures or human beings in themselves from becoming a distinct theme in Christian theology.[52]

Apart from these very general considerations of how theological exposition is organized, the particular topics and issues that have priority for a theologian may play an important role. A stress on one side of the rules might be a general feature of a theology if that side is predominant or the only one applicable in talk about what is of central importance for it. Especially where a theologian is pastorally or existentially rather than speculatively inclined, the side of the rules suitable for topics of focal importance tends to become the norm for talk on all topics.

Take, for example, Martin Luther's concentration on God's gracious justification of the sinner in Christ as his choice for the central topic of theology. If God's own agency as the justifier of the sinner is under consideration, there are no created causes for this; negative rules apply that prohibit talk of the creature conditioning God's agency. The creature's capacities must be said to have no efficacy in this regard; talk about them is pointless unless it is to make clear their inadequacy. The negative version of the rule for talk of the creature seems peculiarly appropriate: the creature must be said to be nothing without God.

Luther and his followers tend to extend these rules where others do not, in talking generally about created being and activity and specifically about what God's saving agency effects. In every case, a direct reference to divine agency is a part of the account of created being and activity; in every case the creature's own power, value and efficacy are played down. These theologians stress the human being's lack of created powers, even as saved, and its continuing dependence, therefore, upon God *alone* for all that God effects whether as Creator or Saviour. They shy away, in particular, from saying that God's grace issues in new created powers which are themselves evocative of a transformed life of reconciliation with God. Talk about the effects of grace in terms of a changed relationship with God highlights the creature's dependence. A Reformation Protestant emphasis on the pervasive effects of sin along with suggestions of a general divine determinism, Lutheran accounts of extrospective faith, alien righteousness, and the *simul justus et peccator* status of the faithful, could all be understood along these lines. They are attempts to extend as far as possible the application of the negative side of rules appropriate for talk about the very saving agency of God.

Take as another example a theology whose thematic focus is less directly soteriological; one in which, let us say, the doctrine of creation figures more prominently. A theology of that sort may tend to emphasize those claims of Christian soteriology that can be directly accommodated to the positive side of the rules since those are particularly appropriate in talk about God's creation and providential rule of the world. There is some precedent for viewing the theology of Thomas and his followers from this perspective.[53]

In the doctrine of creation God's agency is viewed primarily as issuing in created effects, the world in all its respects. If the God who justifies and sanctifies human persons is considered under the perspective of a doctrine of God as Creator, then it is quite natural to stress the created effects in which God's saving agency issues, to talk of God's grace in its efficacy as created grace. Human beings must not be said to be responsible for their salvation – there are no created causes for God's own agency – but this does not take away from a stress on God's agency as an agency that bestows. The God who in loving the world becomes the creative ground of genuine being and value in dependence upon 'him' is assumed to be again, in saving us, immediately effective for our good within the created order. The transformative effects of God's grace are assumed to include genuine created dispositions for good works under God's direction; in this way the account of our salvation accords with the doctrine of creation in which divine agency is said to establish created beings in the created powers whereby they exercise their own operations and efficacy. Created beings by their own movements and activities attain what they are providentially ordained to attain by God. In the same way, created dispositions, which are the created effects of God's grace, become genuine secondary causes for the very increase or growth of grace in our own lives that God effects. A Roman Catholic account of merit follows, then, the positive rule for talk of two total subordinated causes which generally holds in talk of a created causal order.

Finally and most importantly for our overall project in this book, the side of the rules emphasized by a theologian may follow his or her estimation of the relative importance of claims about either divine sovereignty or the integrity of the created order. That judgement may depend in turn upon the particular practical agenda of a theologian. The sort of claims a theologian favours, and therefore the side of the rules he or she emphasizes, may depend upon the sort of behaviours the theologian wishes to encourage or counteract.

It is to be expected from our account in chapter 1 of the close connection between theological speculation and Christian practice that theologians often make assertions of fact with the practical intent of either warranting or countermanding certain attitudes and forms of comportment. The theologian's statements affirm in the former case what those attitudes or forms of comportment suppose about God and the world; in the latter case, they contradict them.

Let us see how a theologian's stress on either God's sovereignty or the integrity of the creature's capacities, in talk according to the negative side of the rules in the former case and the positive side in the latter, might express a positive vision of a Christian form of life. Let us take affirmations of divine sovereignty first. Statements to the effect that we are nothing without God, which follow the negative version of our rule for talk of the creature, encourage Christian humility. Talk of God at work everywhere and even without us prompts the Christian 'to glorify God and magnify his name'. Talk of the unconditioned agency of God according to our rules that restrict talk of the creature's influence on God may promote a hope in God's saving power despite our moral failings, a trust that God will fulfil what has been promised, patience and confidence in the face of adversity. Luther says 'Now that God has taken my salvation out of [my] control . . . and put it under . . . His, and promised to save me . . . I have the comfortable certainty that He is faithful and will not lie to me . . . that He is [so] great and powerful . . . that no . . . opposition can break Him or pluck me from Him.'[54] John Calvin maintains that despite the innumerable evils that beset human life, despite the innumerable deaths that imperil it, a knowledge of God's sovereign rule gives the godly an 'immeasurable felicity'.[55]

How might talk of the creature's capacities according to the positive side of our rules express a different vision of Christian life? Created capacities seem a presupposition of moral injunctions to do right and avoid evil. Such talk promotes thanksgiving, a loving respect and praise for God's munificence.

The sort of claim we have been discussing may be designed, however, only to undercut forms of behaviour and attitude that are viewed as unchristian. Advocacies of the two different sorts of claim do not represent, then, alternative visions of what makes a Christian form of life; they represent different estimations of the dangers to it.

The theologian stresses divine sovereignty to avoid unchristian attitudes and behaviours that might find a warrant in a theologian's claims for created capacities. Talk of the creature's capacities could promote a preoccupation with self that dishonours the pre-eminence of God. It might foster a kind of self-reliance that indicates distrust of God. In the face of human achievement such talk might prompt a prideful, self-satisfied smugness. In the face of human failings, it could undergird anxiety about the future. In cases where human effort always seems to fall short, it might produce a feeling of hopeless despair. Finally, an emphasis on the creature's capacities might lead to an attitude of ingratitude to God; one does not recognize that what one has is a gift.

A theologian might stress created capacities, on the other hand, to avoid untoward consequences for Christian behaviour of talk about divine sovereignty. Talk of God's ability to work without created causes may provide a warrant for moral torpor. Talk of God's unconditioned agency may raise suspicions of divine injustice and indifference; it may foster a fear of God tinged with resentment. Talk of the sovereignty of God's agency that fails to mention God's gifts may lead to a lack of love on the Christian's part. It may promote ingratitude; one assumes one has nothing to be thankful for.

In each case, unchristian behaviours and attitudes are the results of illicit inferences from claims about divine sovereignty or the integrity of the creature's own capacities. Statements of either sort must be unpacked in ways that violate our rules for talk if they are to provide a warrant for the forms of comportment our theologians want to avoid. Some examples may make this clear.

For talk of the creature in itself to promote a self-centred pride that dishonours God, it must be taken to suggest the creature's real independence of God. For human failing to provoke anxiety and despair, one must infer from talk of created causes that God never works without them. Moral laxity results from talk of God's working without created causes only if one infers from such statements that God's creative will cannot include creatures who act. Hostility and ingratitude are the behavioural consequences of talk of God's sovereignty should one assume from that an inverse proportion between what we have and God's working; claims that we are nothing without God must be taken to imply that we are nothing even *with* God; one must infer from talk about God's unconditioned agency that God cannot grant the creature its own powers.

Theologians form statements about the creature's capacities, then, to head off illicit implications of talk about divine sovereignty. Theologians form statements about divine sovereignty to counter improper inferences from talk about the creature's capacities. In doing so, they further their own practical agendas while ensuring that talk of God and the world conform to our rules for coherence.

A number of factors may enter into the theologian's determination of which sort of statement poses the greater danger for a Christian form of life. By implication these factors decide the relative dangers of emphasizing one side or the other of the rules. Theologians may simply disagree about how essential certain behaviours and attitudes are to a Christian form of life. Short of that, their reasoning will take into account the particular audience they address. Which sort of statement is that audience more likely to misconstrue?

Theologians may decide this question according to their general account of the nature of sin. An audience is likely to interpret a theological remark to conform to its interests. Sinful interests lead to illicit inferences.

Different accounts of the nature of sin tend to produce, then, different emphases with respect to claims about divine sovereignty and the creature's own capacities. A theologian who views sin, for example, as an attempt at some sort of self-referential isolation over against God will avoid discourse that focuses on created being and its powers in themselves. The theologian fears that people's sinful interest will prompt them to infer the real independence of the creature from talk of its existence and powers that makes no explicit mention of their dependence upon God. Such an inference will warrant their self-satisfied pride in their own persons and achievements, or their desperate attempts after an ever-elusive self-justification. The theologian will stress, instead, the negative side of the rules in talk about the unconditioned agency of God. In that way he or she can humble self-aggrandizing arrogance or comfort terrified consciences. Such concerns one could argue are behind the *sola gratia* and *sola fide* traditions in Christian theology, respectively. A theologian who considers sin to be primarily a lack of love and gratitude toward God is likely to stress the other, positive side of the rules in talk of God's beneficence and the creature's God-given capacities. If sin is viewed as a failure to abide by divine law, the theologian stresses the same side of the rules to talk of creatures empowered by God and operating in fulfilment of the divine will; in that way human beings can be exhorted to struggle on in their pursuit of good works.

Whatever a theologian's general account of the nature of sin may lead him or her to expect, relative dangers of misapprehension may be decided by historical circumstance. The sort of misapprehension a theologian is most concerned to avoid must match the actual dangers that a particular time and place present. As Luther put it: 'If I profess with the loudest voice and clearest exposition every portion of the truth of God except that little point which the world and the devil at that moment are attacking, I am not confessing Christ . . . Where the battle rages there the loyalty of the soldier is proved.'[56]

Take, for example, a theologian who generally employs the rules in their negative force in conformity with an account of sin as pride. He or she will need to use the rules in their positive force if the historical situation no longer reflects expected claims for human self-sufficiency but reveals instead a quietistic or antinomian shirking of responsibility for the doing of good works in obedience to Christian law. St Augustine's concerns in his 214th and 215th epistles and 'On Grace and Free Will' can be understood in this fashion. John Calvin's tempering of his usual stress on the negative rules as he attempts to consolidate Protestantism as an institution may present a similar case. A preoccupation with the positive formation of human behaviours, which is appropriate for that particular historical circumstance, leads Calvin away from the negative side of the rules he otherwise likes to employ for the purpose of promoting Christian humility under God's sovereign rule. In the next chapter, we will have the occasion to ask whether a modern circumstance presents any particular dangers of misapprehension: which side of the rules, which sort of claim, is more prone to misconstrual in modern times?

A theologian's assessment of the dangers of misconstrual in a particular historical circumstance may be based upon a judgement of how the philosophical commonplaces of the day may skew the responses of the persons he or she addresses. In reaction, for example, to a predominantly Hellenistic cultural or philosophical climate a theologian may emphasize the positive side of the rules in talk about both the creature's power, integrity, and freely effective agency, and God's creative bestowal of being and value. The theologian fears that the cosmic fatalism of that climate will prompt improper inferences from talk of God's sovereign power: one might assume creatures have no powers of their own to effect what happens within the created order. Its denigration of the body, along with Gnostic suspicions about the goodness of God and world, might lead one to assume that God's sovereignty implies the suppression and devaluation of what is not divine. The theological impulses of the early Greek Fathers on this score may provide a case in point.[57]

Another theologian may fear that Platonic/Aristotelian cosmologies, which restrict the domain of God's direct agency and attenuate the distinction between divine and non-divine, may lead a Christian audience educated on that material to similar inferences. A theologian with such a fear may tend to apply whenever possible the positive rule for talk of two total subordinated causes, in order to prevent any suggestion of a divinization of the creature and consequent loss of the creature's own integrity. Additionally, he or she may shy away from talk of created beings operated by the power of God, in order to block any implication that divine agency does not directly determine the whole of created being. Such reasons may be behind Thomas's insistence, for example, that God's saving agency directly issues in a new created *habitus*: an infused created habit sufficient for further increases in the gifts of God's grace heads off the idea that God's power becomes the creature's own, and makes clear that human free will unrevised by grace is not a principle factor in God's salvation of us.[58] In the next chapter I will provide my own assessment of how philosophical commonplaces in a modern era might result in the misconstrual of theological claims.

We can end this chapter by turning back to a notion mentioned in the first chapter. I have tried to show here how theologies emphasizing either divine sovereignty or created capacities, and one side or the other of our rules, may be functional complements. In the first place, theologies of the one sort may assume what theologies of the other sort make explicit; together they may represent, therefore, the whole of legitimate Christian claims on the topic of God and creation and the rules by which they can be made. The theologies we have analysed are complementary as well because they function to cut off possible misconstruals of one another. Theological discourse that emphasizes the negative force of the rules serves as a corrective for theological discourse that stresses their positive force. It prevents specifically the latter's abstract consideration of created being per se from becoming a real separation of created being from divine efficacy, and the latter's stress on the rules for talk about God's working with creatures from becoming an a priori requirement of sufficient secondary causes. A theology that emphasizes the positive force of the rules rectifies, on the other hand, any tendency for an emphasis on their negative force to result in a denigration of the being and value of the creature, an a priori denial of secondary created causality in particular, or a general failure to appreciate that the power of God may be lovingly manifested in the extent and depth of God's gifts to the creature.

In the next chapter I will analyse certain typical forms of subverted theological discourse in modern times. I will argue that a tendency for misconstrual afflicts both sorts of claims; all the rules for coherent Christian discourse are prone to violation. Such a situation cannot be remedied by rhetorical shifts in the sort of claim emphasized and the side of the rules employed.

4

The Modern Breakdown of Theological Discourse

'Tis all in peeces, all cohaerence gone
John Donne, 'An Anatomy of the World: The First
Anniversary', 1611

In the last section of the preceding chapter we tried to show how the rules we specified can be used in different ways. The rules have a positive and negative side. Some theologians emphasize the negative side, some the positive, depending upon the intellectual climate, their method of exposition, the theological topics of special importance to them, and their practical agendas.

In connection with the last factor influencing how the rules are used, the question of their rhetorical effects was raised. To further a practical agenda, the theologian, we saw, has to assess likely audience reaction to certain forms of assertion about God and the world. Specifically, to discourage unchristian attitudes and behaviours that are especially threatening to a Christian form of life at a particular place and time, the theologian must determine the sorts of claim that are especially prone to misinterpretation in those circumstances. Is it more dangerous to talk of divine sovereignty, according to the negative side of our rules, or about the creature's capacities, according to the positive side? Consideration of audience reaction in a particular historical context is therefore fundamental to the formation of practical objectives of this sort because it is crucial generally for determining how to talk about God and the world so as not to be misunderstood. Apparent implications of statements vary with the historical context, from audience to audience. The theologian has to consider the likely illicit inferences of the particular audience addressed, if he or she is to take adequate precautions against them.

Rhetorical conditions are therefore placed upon a theologian's faithfulness to the rules. It is not enough simply to follow the rules; one must do so in a way suitable to a particular time and place. One must know which sorts of rule to use when. Rules, unlike simple statements of fact, have circumstantial conditions of applicability.

Let us be clear about this. Statements that are formed according to our rules are correct as they stand whatever the historical circumstances. Sometimes, however, some forms of those statements are especially dangerous: what they *suggest* to a particular audience will be incorrect. If the theologian neglects likely audience reaction, it might very well be the case that he or she abides by our rules for coherent Christian discourse without doing so effectively. The theologian may make statements that are quite prone to misinterpretation, and provide no adequate counter.

This question of meeting the challenge set by a particular historical context figures centrally in arguments to follow. I will contend in this chapter that modern theologies are generally not successful in holding at bay the untoward influences of a modern historical context. In the last section of the chapter I will begin to consider how they might do so.

Some description of a modern nexus of ideas and methods of approach is necessary in order to assess the influence of a modern cultural context on theology. Such a description is presented in the first section. Generalizations are always dangerous; the broader the generalizations, the more vapid they tend to become, the more they tend to smooth over important distinctions. The warrant for the description I offer lies in what can be done with it, its usefulness in forming an incisive commentary on certain modern trends in theology.

On the basis of this description, I will argue that a modern context has two general sorts of effect. First, common claims made for human beings and the natural order in modern times encourage improper inferences from theological statements associated with the positive side of our rules: talk of the creature's power and freedom suggests a power and freedom viv-à-vis God's own agency. Second, modern methods of analysis promote the distortion of both sides of the rules. Talk of the creature's capacities moves in a Pelagian direction while talk of God's sovereignty approaches an advocacy of divine tyranny. When both sides of the rules are distorted in this way, statements affirming the creature's capacities seem to conflict with statements upholding the traditional rights of divine sovereignty. Theological positions of the sort I talked about at the end of the last chapter, theologies that are complementary on our rules, become mutually exclusive alternatives. Christian talk that maintains both sorts of claims becomes incoherent.

My argument concerns not just the shape of likely misinterpretations of theological statements: I am not simply specifying the manner in which a modern audience is liable to misconstrue theological statements that accord with our rules. I am arguing that modern theologians tend to *form* their statements about God and the world in violation of our rules. The modern theologian's own attempt to take up the tradition of Christian discourse and continue it in a form appropriate for a contemporary audience is skewed by improper inferences that a modern cultural context promotes. These theologians may make the traditional claims about God and the world – God has an unconditioned sovereign power; we have our own powers, including some sort of capacity for free self-determination – but they no longer follow our rules for discourse on those topics. Such talk becomes generally incoherent as a result; the two sorts of claim no longer hang together intelligibly.

I am not arguing that every theologian in a modern context makes the sort of mis-steps I will recount. I have illustrated our rules for coherent Christian discourse with reference to a number of post-sixteenth-century theologians. I am not arguing that these mis-steps have never been taken before. The fourth-century Pelagius will come immediately to mind as a theologian who formed improper inferences from statements associated with the positive side of our rules in the way I argue a modern context promotes. What is new to a modern circumstance is, first of all, the pervasiveness of that mis-step. It becomes a commonplace of modern theology. Those who draw Pelagian inferences from traditional theological talk of the creature's capacities are no longer countered by a general Christian witness to proper theological discourse; no consensus of 'competent speakers' of Christian discourse opposes them. Those theologians who do object become one faction in what appears to be, at best, an irresolvable dispute. Where victory is declared, the Pelagian contingent is the more likely to receive the laurels. Pelagianism of some sort becomes arguably the dominant motif in modern theology. When it seems one can hold on to traditional claims for divine sovereignty only at the cost of the creature's own integrity, most theologians, with good reason, choose not to do so.

What is new to modern times, in the second place, is the general deformation of the rules – both positive and negative sides of the rules are skewed. As a result, a proper rhetorical posture is insufficient to avert the dangers of a modern cultural context. A theologian may affirm the unconditioned sovereignty of God in an effort to counter improper inferences from statements associated with the positive side of the rules. In doing so, however, he or she tends to draw the illicit inferences of an emphasis on the negative side. The theologian who emphasizes God's sovereignty cedes discourse according to the positive side of the rules to the improper use modernity suggests. God's sovereignty excludes talk of the creature's own power and freedom. Thereby, we shall see, the original intention to counter Pelagianism falters.

We need to make our charges concrete by looking at cases. After the description of modernity in the first section I examine historical examples of theological discourse, for the distortions of the rules I have mentioned. Because we will be concerned with often subtle modifications in the use of statements, each case requires an in-depth analysis. I will consider therefore only a few. I propose them, however, as paradigms of modern developments in the use of certain sorts of traditional statement. A third section generalizes the results of these historical analyses. By means of a purely conceptual argument, I deduce what one could expect from theology that conforms to a modern cultural context; our historical examples are shown to match those expectations. The account in this section of the ways in which a modern framework distorts Christian discourse is the basis for a discussion in the next section of how that distortion might be circumvented.

A Modern Framework for Discourse

The nature of a transition to distinctively modern forms of discourse is discussed in this section in very general terms. I cannot pretend in such short compass to cover with any degree of adequacy the complex and subtle question of the nature of modernity. Relying on the work of others, I hope only to sketch those oft-mentioned features of a modern outlook that prove particularly illuminating of changes in the use of traditional theological language to be documented in the next section.[1] The historical accuracy of the presentation is basically assumed here, without a great deal of argument. If the description can be successfully correlated with changes in the early modern use of theological language, we will have provided it with at least some historical confirmation.

First, what might be called a drive towards 'decontextualization' typifies methods of inquiry in the transition to distinctively modern forms of discourse. Inquiry is 'decontextualized' in accord with the assumption that truth is to be sought by holding in abeyance the prejudices of place, the traditions of the past, and the authority of books. One must retire to search for the truth, as the rationalist Descartes contends, suspending belief in what one has heard and read before and giving oneself over to a reflection on the naked ideas of one's own mind.[2] Idols of the Tribe which prejudice judgement to conform to common tendencies of human thought and affection, Idols of the Cave formed by the education and environment of individuals, Idols of the Theatre represented by philosophical dogmas and received systems, and Idols of the Marketplace where words form a merely self-referential nexus of disputation or cobweb of textual commentary – all these, according to the empiricist Francis Bacon, must be eschewed in favour of a method that proceeds directly to nature.[3]

A decontextualized method of inquiry has its effect on an understanding of human beings. A modern sensibility no longer views persons in a broad context of social, cosmic and divine relationships. Persons are no longer essentially parts of a whole society, no longer reflections of a world formed by repeated patterns of resemblance. They are typically set over against their situations, as individuals whose identities are distinguished, without regard for objectively given norms and the external constraints of tradition or circumstance, through autonomous powers of separate self-constitution.[4] It is common to affirm with Pico della Mirandola in his *Oration on the Dignity of Man* (1496) that humans possess the place which they give themselves only as a consequence of their own free activity. Their identities are not determined by what they have received but by what they make of themselves and their world through the essential human power of active self-assertion.

The world viewed apart from conventional discourse, from the tradition of textual commentary and from the opinions of authorities, has its own peculiarly modern appearance. It meets the modern investigator as a 'brute fact'. The world is to appear for once as it is 'in itself', independent of any context supplied by traditional belief, independent in particular of any religious reference to God. For the modern interpreter, what one gets when one strips away those contexts is not an abstraction, the world viewed apart from its real relations with divinity and a community of human knowers. One is left with the world as it is in its own integrity as an already constituted fact. This world in itself is not considered merely the result of an analysis of a more concrete appearance; it is what one starts with, a given, to which a religious interpretation, like any other, may be appended. Thus it is that a man like Petrarch feels a need for God only at the end of his life: it takes some time for a sense of lack to arise within the experience of a world initially not defined in relation to God.[5]

The world finds a new locus of intelligibility. The world viewed in ideally 'suppositionless' freedom from traditional belief is to be understood no longer according to the fanciful connections formed by the word play of the book-learned, nor primarily by association with a transcendent realm affirmed by a religious tradition. The reason of the world is, instead, the reason within things, the reason of immanent law. Explanation of what exists proceeds not by way of a transcendent reference but with reference only to what is also in and of the world according to principles manifested by the visible intra-worldly connections of proximate and particular causes.

The complex and multifarious connections that phenomena of the natural and human world exhibit within a context tend to be dissolved. A modern preoccupation with certainty, clarity and linear order sets these aside. The Moderns quarrel with the Ancients because of what now seems to be the latter's intolerable and offensive penchant for the dark density of ambiguous and polysemous discourse, for the concentric circularity and random inclusiveness of orderings according to resemblance. In the search for truth, the modern investigator must favour, on the contrary, the simple and transparently unequivocal, those clear distinctions of identity and difference which can be made linearly syntactic along a single horizontal plane. The task of the new philosophy is to shear through with quick, clean strokes the 'cunning cobweb contextures' which traditional learning spins, circle inside circle.[6] The endless to and fro of verbal disputations according to the vagaries of conventional discourse should be banished by recourse to 'clear and settled significations'.[7] The ancient encyclopaedic thinker for whom nothing is irrelevant, distracted by the impertinent in gathering up and going over the thick, diverse aggregate of the accidental and the external, is to be replaced by the 'abstemious' modern investigator who cares only for that pure 'internal centre of nature's abstruse and occult operations' by which connections among things in nature may be fixed according to definite ruled relations.[8] In place of an endless drawing of things together, a constructive compiling which follows the always ultimately mysterious interplay of similitudes, analogies and affinities, modern discourse substitutes the quest for a universal language of perfect referential and analytic accuracy. Assuming the initial exteriority of sign, world and reason, the modern thinker nevertheless aims to produce an artifical language whose clear and distinct signs transparently offer simple worldly referents, and whose syntactic structure coincides with both the logical ordering of reason and the structural connection of things in the world.[9]

The priority placed upon human self-assertion dovetails with abstractive tendencies of modern methods of inquiry. The modern project of human self-assertion, in which 'man posits his existence in a historical situation and indicates to himself how he is going to deal with the reality surrounding him and what use he will make of the possibilities that are open to him',[10] requires in the first place an abstractive 'unitizing' analysis. In that way the phenomena of nature become 'manageable'.

One starts the process by isolating discrete natural phenomena in the bare factuality of their existence. One supposes the world offers for analysis fixed objects which can be known quite independently of the discourse contexts in which human beings through the course of their everyday lives speak and think about them. These concrete phenomena of perception are then divided up into the simplest isolable elements or units – the clear and distinct ideas of the mind (e.g., Descartes) or the immediate data of the inward and outward senses (e.g., Locke) – by abstracting from the complex inter-relationships and sensory richness which the phenomena initially present. The multifariously interconnected and superimposed elements making up the world of facts are to be separated by an intellectual, often explicitly mathematical analysis. These elements are then susceptible of empirical confirmation through experiments which make them singly visible and permit their individual activities to be traced.

In proceeding in this fashion, a modern method investigation – whether it be mathematical, mechanistic, or empirical – is following the general directive of Descartes:

> [One] divide[s] into as many parts as possible . . . in order that, by commencing with objects the simplest and easiest to know, [one] might ascend little by little, and, as it were, step by step, to the knowledge of the more complex; assigning in thought a certain order even to those objects which in their own nature do not stand in a relation of antecedence and sequence.[11]

In other words, the investigator is to engage in a process of reductive resolution and subsequent composition. Like algebraic analysis, in which every number is broken down into prime factors and represented as their product, the phenomena of nature are to be reduced to their most elemental constituents and reformulated according to orderly, set rules of combination.[12]

A modern concern for reliable predication and control of natural events demands a generality of principle. That sort of generality is not, however, overtly discernible from either the concrete context of natural phenomena or their particular characters. To specify the regularities of a natural order one must leave behind, first of all, the fleeting specificities of particular circumstance. Uniform laws will not become apparent by strictly observing phenomena *in situ*. One requires the '*mente concipio*' of Galileo, the construction of ideal cases in which things are assumed to exist independently of their actual situations, so that they may be projected into a variety of others, real or merely imaginable. Furthermore, after concrete phenomena are reductively analysed by thought and experiment into simple elements, attention must be given only to those elements that can be effectively 'decontextualized' from the specific circumstances in which they happen to be placed. Thereby one attains constants for generalizations about the serial ordering of phenomena which can hold under as many different concrete conditions as possible.

The uniquely characteristic or the variable qualities of concrete phenomena that are conditioned by particular circumstance become in this way irrelevant. Discrete units to which whole phenomena are reduced have importance for modern methods of inquiry only to the extent they have, instead, the colourless anonymity and self-contained monad-like 'in-itselfness' that permit their substitution as interchangeable bits in any number of ruled regularities that apply regardless of context. One must distinguish, in short, primary from secondary qualities. By sharply separating fact from interpretation, particulars are denuded of their special characteristics and contextually conditioned qualities. They can then be externally related in terms of universal principles. Like the algebraic formalizations of arithmetic in which variables stand impartially for any number and functions of one or more variables may be applied without limitation to particular cases, the modern method of inquiry proceeds by overlooking specificity in order to find ruled relations that hold between any entities whatever in any circumstance.

Modern methods of inquiry 'work over', then, concrete phenomena. A blueprint or framework of assumptions determines in advance what sort of thing may count as suitable data or results for purposes of calculation and control.[13] The origin of this framework as a kind of selective emphasis for particular purposes tends to be occulted, however.[14] A modern framework of assumptions is not considered a historically conditioned feature of a particular context of inquiry. To back up that contention and occlude the interests behind its operation, a modern framework repudiates any hint of opacity or mediatedness in the instruments of inquiry. The discourse of modern methods of inquiry is claimed to have the transparency of the telescope, or to be formed of only 'neutral counters' so that it resembles nothing so much as 'pure, clear water with no taste',[15] Abstract distinctions drawn in fact for the promotion of certain interests are not recognized as the products of a particular method of human inquiry; they are promoted instead as the already given features of reality itself which need only to be discovered by 'direct grasp and envisagement'.[16]

Distinctions in thought, which denote differences of functional status, are consequently taken to represent fundamentally different kinds of existence.[17] What is important for purposes of calculation and control becomes the really real, the substance and core of particular natures, to which are optionally and externally appended those qualities of value and enjoyment which are not similarly serviceable. The ideal, intellectual ordering of discrete elements in lawful series is privileged to replace the world that was initially assumed before abstractive analyses. By the 'fallacy of misplaced concreteness', reality is assumed to be actually exhaustively reducible to those elemental constants and serial orderings that result from modern methods of inquiry.[18] On this assumption, the world is made up simply of physical units – characterized only by those real properties of, say, mass, velocity and spatio-temporal location, interconnected by a few basic laws which hold with absolute generality, each existing nevertheless in essential independence of relations with any others.

Philosophical problems endemic to modern times have been linked with this sort of reification of abstract distinctions.[19] It is not unreasonable, then, for us to look for similar problems in theological discourse. The philosophical conundrums of modern times (scepticism, mind/body dualism, the fact/value split, the alienation of free human subjects in a depersonalized world, the problem of free will) are said to result from the tendency of modern methods of inquiry to hypostatize severally, as real and essentially independent 'things', those logical aspects of concrete phenomena which have been discriminated from certain perspectives for certain purposes. Let us review the basic shape of these arguments before beginning the next section.

The analytic discriminations by which modern modes of inquiry divide up the concrete phenomena of sense could be easily harmonized, if they were viewed as the results of approaching phenomena from different perspectives, with different purposes; the distinctions would simply refer to different aspects of concrete entities. Once such distinctions are reified, however, the world comes to have a 'stratigraphic' configuration – the first fundamental layer, the substance of the real, characterized by those properties most important for universally applicable generalizations (e.g., matter, mass); the second, more 'external' accidental layer of immediate sensory qualities (e.g., colour and shape); and a third 'outermost' layer, the optional clothing of valuation or customary attributions. Different aspects of the same concrete phenomena become separate sorts of thing, exclusive of one another and, therefore, difficult to hold together. A 'Humpty-Dumpty syndrome' befalls modern discourse: once the egg breaks, the king's men cannot quite get everything to go back together again.[20] Intractable problems arise concerning the possibility of interrelating fundamentally independent and antithetical spheres of being. Description and appreciation tend to fall apart in disjoined levels of discourse.

Since the real substance of things is, moreover, being identified with what is of the greatest importance for the purposes of calculation and control, the immediate enjoyment of the world and its valuational or customary significance for people become accretions difficult to ground with reference to the real. Problems connecting up the outer layers with the inner come at the expense, therefore, of the former. Those aspects of concrete phenomena that are conditioned by the sense organs, spatial position or social circumstances of humans, and which are, therefore, unserviceable as constants for universally applicable generalizations, are left hanging loose from the real being of things. They are derogatorily termed 'appearances'; and since they, nevertheless, have to 'be' somewhere, they become the 'things' of the mind, which is assumed, in keeping with the same modern tendency to reify, to be itself a sort of thing with which to contain them. Mind is given its own separate space with special 'furniture' (Locke).

Mind and Matter are themselves stratified with independent spheres of operation that become notoriously hard to inter-relate. Questions arise as to how the mind can know anything at all in light of the mysterious difficulties that surround the outer world's influence on inner mind or the mind's grasp of objects that are its antithesis. Given this setup – the world as a realm of constants and rules useful for purposes of control, the mind as the realm containing everything else – one can only either accept their separation and be a dualist, or become one or another variety of monist, putting mind inside matter or matter inside mind.[21] If one resigns oneself to the dualistic implications of stratification, the real object of experience tends to become an elusive 'thing-in-itself'; the mind always directly apprehends reality from the place of human subjectivity where the bodies of nature are clothed with sensory qualities, interpretations and values that do not really belong to them.

The human qualities of experience – all those affectional and volitional elements that characterize human beings – find refuge in a psychic sphere, isolated and alienated against the blind run of a 'disenchanted' material world. Too intimate a connection with such a world seems, indeed, to endanger the peculiar prerogatives of the psychic sphere. For example, where psychic operations are tied too closely to one's own body or material objects within the world, deterministic explanations lurk.

Even when the human subject is the focus of distinctively 'humanistic' descriptions, the structure of modern methods of inquiry infiltrates to form what Gilbert Ryle calls a counterpart 'para-mechanical' idiom: the same basic structure of discourse recurs, filled now, however, with very special 'stuff' of a mental sort.[22] Different logical or functional aspects of human action become separate, subsequently interconnected things. Thus, the fact that an action could have been otherwise is 'substantialized' in talk of a something or other called free will that precedes an action as its cause.[23] Similar difficulties recur. Talk about a single action done both by choice and with a motive is transformed, for example, into a contest between two things, motive as rigid, choice as flexible, the first coming before the second and threatening to determine it.[24]

With this account of a modern framework of discourse and its problems in mind, let us turn now to our analysis of instances of theological discourse in the transition to modern times.

HISTORICAL EXAMPLES OF THE TRANSFORMATION OF THEOLOGICAL DISCOURSE IN MODERN TIMES

The historical examples of theological discourse in this section are divided in two, to correspond to the two sorts of misuse of the rules mentioned in the introduction of the chapter. The first example concerns a trend in late medieval and early modern theology associated with Gabriel Biel (died 1495): improper inferences are drawn from a stress on the positive side of our rules. The second example concerns the *de Auxiliis* controversies between Dominicans and Jesuits in the sixteenth and seventeenth centuries: the example illustrates the general dynamic by which both sides of our rules are distorted in modern theology. We will be making occasional references to the features of a modern framework of discourse discussed in the previous section; but a full-blown correlation of those features with specific violations of the rules will await the next section.

Example 1

I hope to show how, in the theological trend Gabriel Biel represents, traditional scholastic axioms and distinctions are unselfconsciously used in novel ways to propound the absolute freedom of human beings, an optimistic understanding of human powers of self-assertion apart from divine aid and a generally naturalistic view of being that excludes it dependence upon God's immediate agency. By subtle modifications in the use of these axioms and distinctions, Biel and those like him draw improper inferences from a stress on the positive side of the rules: they assume the real existence of the creature apart from God's agency; they require the existence of sufficient created causes; they suggest, as a result, that God's agency is neither unconditioned nor immediate.

Some qualifications and clarifying remarks are in order before we begin. Although I will be appealing to Gabriel Biel's use of traditional scholastic notions, my argument does not hinge on the historical accuracy of ascribing such things to him in particular. For my purposes it is enough that historical scholarship supports the idea of such a trend in the use of scholastic distinctions and axioms around this time, however inconclusive the arguments that any particular theologian instantiates it.[25] As a matter of fact substantial agreement exists among scholars of historical theology concerning the case of Gabriel Biel.[26]

Note, too, that the fault for their misuse does not lie with the scholastic notions themselves. Our analysis of the mechanism of their misuse should make this evident. The fault also does not lie with the particular philosophical and theological schools with which Biel is associated. The scholastic axioms and distinctions I will mention are found in the work of other Franciscan or nominalist theologians without evidencing the modern trends in their use to be discussed.[27] No doubt the character of late medieval nominalism has something to do with the rise of these trends in their misuse: the nominalistic tendency, for example, to restrict the referents of conceptual distinctions to really separable individual entities fits the description of distinctively modern modes of discourse that I am claiming are behind transformations in theology. Our discussion will make clear, however, that the decisive factors are not nominalistic in any specific, technical sense.

Let us begin the analysis of Biel's theology by looking at his use of the scholastic distinction between God's absolute and ordained power. Talk of God's absolute power works to encourage rather than restrict the illegitimate implications that talk about God's ordained power might suggest. Such a procedure contravenes the traditional use of the distinction.

From the beginning of the scholastic tradition (e.g., Hugh of St Victor) through Thomas Aquinas and at least up until the death of Scotus (the case of Ockham is disputed), talk about God's absolute power functioned as a way of stressing the immediacy of the ordering of all created things to God and the unconditional character of divine agency.[28] It worked, on our terms, as an example of discourse conforming to the negative side of our rules. Talk about God's ordained power, on the other hand, underscored the genuine existence of created beings in dependence upon God, in accord with the positive side of our rules: one talked of an ordained order of created powers and operations under God. When complemented by discourse about God's absolute power, statements concerning God's ordained power could not be misunderstood to imply (1) that created reality exists independently of God's agency for it, (2) that secondary created causes are the necessary, independently operative intermediate agents in the ordering of created being to God, or (3) that an ineluctable created causal order constrains the operation of divine agency. The prominence of talk about the *potentia absoluta* of God in late thirteenth- and fourteenth-century theology can be traced in great part to a heightened urgency to avoid these illicit implications of discourse according to the positive side of our rules, after their explicit condemnation in the Paris Articles of 1277.[29]

Talk of God's absolute power could contravene these implications to the extent that the distinction between God's ordained and absolute power was a way of pointing out two aspects of a single order of divine operation. The reliable order among created beings established by divine agency *de potentia ordinata* appears, nevertheless, in its contingency, relativized under the sovereignty of divine agency, when considered with respect to the absolute power of God to do otherwise. God's absolute power is still in effect with respect to the created order that comes to be according to the ordained power of God; the created order God ordains *de potentia ordinata* remains, therefore, in an immediate relation of total dependence upon God's agency for it. Because what God has ordained *de potentia ordinata* is at the same time the manifestation of the absolute power of God, God's agency cannot be constrained by the immanent causal connections ordained for created things *de potentia ordinata*. God's agency, in respect of its absolute power, retains the capacity to bring into existence created effects without sufficient created causes.

In Biel's use of the distinction, these different aspects of the same agency and operation come to be reified as separate domains in a way that accords with modern tendencies of interpretation. The absolute power of God extends only so far; it is kept out of the created order that divine agency establishes *de potentia ordinata*. A dome is thereby formed, around a self-enclosed created order of causes that proceed *ex puris naturalibus*.[30] Contrary to the traditional use in which God's operation *de potentia ordinata* itself manifests God's absolute power, the absolute power of God now characterizes only the free choice behind God's decision for a certain order of created causes and effects.[31] Although God freely chose to bring about a particular created order with an absolute power unconditioned by any created cause operating independently of it, the same talk of God's agency *de potentia absoluta* is no longer appropriate with respect to the created order so established. God relinquishes absolute power in the decision for a certain created order *de potentia ordinata*.

Thereby created causes and agencies gain for Biel the freedom and dignity of their own self-initiated achievements. The freedom and sovereignty of God's absolute power must recede to an upper hemisphere. The domain of God's freedom and sovereignty must be restricted, in order for the creature to have the capacity for free operations within its own sphere.

Biel seems to assume that without this recourse the unconditioned and necessary efficacy of God's agency would conflict with the creation of free agents. Such a conflict results, however, only if divine and created agencies are included within a single linear order of predication, in violation of our rule for talk of God as transcendent. Within a single order of predication, the necessity or infallibility of divine efficacy must also characterize its created effects. Necessity of consequence would imply the necessity of the thing consequent, to use the scholastic jargon.[32] To circumvent the denial of creaturely freedom that would result from this, Biel stratifies God's absolute and ordained power so that the necessity of consequence or infallibility of divine agency does not extend directly to the action of creatures.

Talk of God's absolute power traditionally comes up in discussing the mercy of God, salvation *sola gratia* and predestination *ante praevisa merita*. Biel's use of such language in all these cases exhibits the same dome structure protecting a basically naturalistic or Pelagian substructure.[33] The negative side of the rules which should be at work in talk of God's absolute power loses its capacity to restrict the illicit implications that are suggested by a stress on the positive side of the rules in talk about the creature.

Thus, God's mercy consists for Biel in the *fact that* God chose freely and without any created condition to require of creatures what is not impossible for them to perform. The order of salvation God wills *de potentia ordinata* constitutes of itself, however, an ineluctable order of *justice*; God does not exercise free and unconditioned mercy within that order. God saves only when the creature meets the conditions God sets.

Similarly, salvation by grace alone pertains exclusively to the free sovereignty God displays before deciding to grant salvation only to those who do their very best, *facere quod in se est*. Predestination *ante praevisa merita* refers simply to the unconstrained decision by which God determines to save those whom God foresees will merit salvation by their good works. God decides *de potentia absoluta* to delegate to people a free power and efficacy for good works apart from the operation of divine agency; God's saving agency *de potentia ordinata* is therefore conditioned by created beings operating independently of it. Persons who do all that they can, do not do so in dependence upon God's gracious agency working to establish them in those created acts. Within an order of salvation that accords with the scholastic maxim *facere quod in se est*, God becomes a debtor, therefore; God owes grace to these persons in a strong sense. Talk about created causes, using the positive side of our rules, is misapplied in this way to cover cases where the very saving agency of God is under consideration.

There are some traditional uses of talk about God's absolute power that make explicit reference to the created order ordained by God *de potentia ordinata*. God's absolute power tends to come up, for example, in connection with the scholastic maxim that whatever God does with a created cause God can do without one. Such cases would clearly seem to run counter to Biel's relegation of God's absolute and ordained power to separate spheres. Biel retains maxims of this sort, however; he simply draws different implications from them. Contrary to their traditional function, they can then be used by Biel to confirm illicit implications of a stress on the positive side of our rules.

Let us take the scholastic maxim that God *de potentia absoluta* can do without a created cause what God ordinarily does with a created cause, as it applies to the case of created grace or the habit of grace, *gratia gratum faciens*. As a formulation of the negative side of the rules, the maxim that God can work without secondary causes should be applied to the case of created grace to underscore the constant immediacy of our dependence upon divine agency. We owe our salvation to God alone, whatever we may be able to do as a result of God's gift of created grace. God operates with unconstrained mercy and graciousness for our salvation, even though it may ordinarily be the case that God rewards those who do their very best with a habit of grace which makes further good works meritorious of eternal life. To Biel, the fact that God may save us apart from the infusion of a created habit of grace and good works done on that basis suggests, on the contrary, that God often does in a supernatural way, by infusion of special habits, what might have been done by the natural power of humans alone.[34] The application of the maxim to created grace suggests to Biel the basic adequacy of created powers to earn salvation naturalistically, apart from God's gift of special or extraordinary created habits and operations.[37] *De facto*, created grace may indeed be necessary to attain salvation in keeping with the actual order of salvation ordained by God *de potentia ordinata*. By applying the maxim that God can work without created causes Biel concludes, however, that this necessity is not based upon any real insufficiency or inability on the part of humans to work their own salvation. Human beings by their natural powers can fulfil *quoad substantiam actus* the no doubt arduous but nevertheless humanly possible requirements for salvation ordained by God.

Talk about human action meriting eternal life by divine ordinance (Thomas) or divine acceptation (Scotus) is similarly skewed to line up with this use of the maxim. Thomas and Duns Scotus appealed to those notions to make the point that eternal life does not come to people by right. For Biel they imply that good works substantially earn eternal life, though *quoad intentionem legislatoris* those good works are accepted by God as having a meritorious status worthy of eternal life only when adorned with the habit of grace.[36] Once again, we see the created order works with fundamental self-sufficiency for its own salvation; God's own agency for specifically salvific effects is set to the side.

So far we have looked at the way Biel uses traditional scholastic notions and axioms to suggest the creature's real independence of God, the inviolability of the created order, and the creature's ability, consequently, to condition divine agency. Notions and axioms that are traditionally associated with the negative side of our rules, and that traditionally work, therefore, to cut off improper implications of discourse according to the positive side, foster those implications instead. The result is an overwhelming stress on the positive side of the rules with all the attendant dangers of that use unchecked – what one might expect from theology should it lose its way in accommodating a modern glorification of human powers of self-constitution and a modern penchant for explanations of natural phenomena that make no reference to what transcends the world. I will make an argument out of this suggestion in the third section.

These developments in theology are helped along by talk about divine and created agencies that hypostatizes and serially orders conceptual distinctions in typically modern fashion as though they referred to really separable things. The general effect of such a hermeneutic on traditional forms of discourse becomes especially evident in the account of salvation. Terms like 'created grace' and 'merit' that concern human operations and powers are used so as to assume their real separability from the activity of God in saving us. As a result, divine and human agencies are conceived as interacting for the salvation of human beings within a single order of consecutive action and reaction.

Created grace, for example, should be construed, according to our rules for discourse, as existing in immediate dependence upon the operation of divine agency for our salvation. Including the word 'grace' in a term that refers to created habits underscores that it is the very saving grace of God in its immediate effect and power within the life of human persons.[37] Created grace is not really separable from God's saving agency even though, as something with its own created reality, it may be discussed apart from any direct reference to that agency. To point out the priority of God's agency and distinguish the variety of God's effects as creator and saviour one can produce a linear exposition: God's agency for essential human capacities, those created effects, God's agency for what heals and exalts the human creature, those salvific effects that include created grace. This is a logical ordering and does not imply the real independence of the creature in a play of action and reaction.

Biel, however, detaches created grace from the saving efficacy of God. It is no longer the created resonance of God's own grace.

As a special human disposition for action it operates and has its own efficacy apart from God's own saving agency for those effects. The referents of a possible linear exposition are reified as actually separate entities so that created grace is distanced from divine agency as either its presupposition or subsequent effect: created grace actually succeeds initial divine favour and actually precedes subsequent divine acceptance in the form of the infusion of the Holy Spirit or uncreated grace.[38]

Created grace, operating independently of the direct influence of God's agency for it, can elicit God's own action. Human acts performed on the basis of the created habit of grace can therefore be said to merit increases in grace and eternal life in a very strong sense. The traditional account of merit is hereby revised.

The notion of merit was traditionally used to articulate the biblical language of reward, so that the personal character of the relationship between God and humans in the work of salvation finds expression.[39] Now it comes to be interpreted by Biel in the primary sense of a legal claim or title. Traditionally, talk of people meriting further graces by the exercise of created grace was understood in terms of the internal teleology of that grace. The exercise of created grace merits further graces in the sense that the active unfolding of that created habit executes an order of secondary created causes and effects ordained in its entirety by God. Merit is simply a part of the order of salvation that results *in toto* from God's direct agency. God's agency for that order has no causes; further graces are therefore just as much pure gifts of grace as they are consequences of the creature's own efforts. For Biel, however, action by created grace is meritorious as the sufficient condition for God's very ordination of a human being's increase in grace towards eternal life and glory. Once divine agency has worked created grace, human works undertaken on that basis are the primary condition for a second, really subsequent divine act in which increase in grace towards eternal life is ordained.[40]

The traditional distinction between congruous and condign merit is also interpreted by Biel in a novel fashion to refer to really different and successive sorts of human operation. The two sorts of merit are distinguished by the degree to which the human agent can do without supplementary divine aid. The distinction marks degrees of human self-sufficiency.

In traditional use (e.g., Thomas), the distinction between congruous and condign merit was a way of considering the same human action performed on the basis of created grace under two different aspects – from the side of human agency on the one hand and divine agency on the other.[41] Human works performed on the basis of created grace may be said to merit salvation *de condigno* to the extent that such works are considered to proceed from the grace of the Holy Spirit and to the extent, therefore, that eternal life appears as the fitting completion of the gift of created grace from the side of the divine agency which works both. When the same human action performed on the basis of created grace is considered on its human side, it is said to merit salvation merely *de congruo*. One can assert this, moreover, only because God is operating as well to complete 'his' own work *de condigno*. Human acts have no claim in themselves to an eternal 'supernatural' life; nevertheless, they may be said to merit salvation *de congruo* to the extent that God out of free mercy rewards 'his' own gifts.

On Biel's use, on the contrary, congruous merit is reified as a form of merit really distinct from condign merit, having its ground in human achievement alone apart from any direct operation of divine agency effective of grace. Congruous merit becomes a naturalistically interpreted preparation for the reception of the habit of grace, proceeding apart from any direct establishment of the relevant human operations by divine saving agency.[42] In technical scholastic language, preparation for the reception of created grace is, according to Biel, essentially performed by human power without being itself established either by the very 'form' of created grace as its appropriate material condition (Thomas) or by *gratia gratis data* or *auxilium Dei speciale*.[43] The traditional scholastic formula *facere quod in se est*, according to which God does not deny grace to those who do what is in them *under the influence of grace*, takes on the character of a self-originating human activity conditioning the divine ordination of grace.[44]

Once the habit of grace has been received on this basis, those who do their best under its influence merit *de condigno* God's acceptance of their good works as worthy of an eternal reward. The habit of grace they have received merely *assists or facilitates* the doing of further good works by essentially sufficient natural human powers. Created grace is simply *added to* good works performed on the basis of natural human capacities to provide them with the *dignitas* required for salvation according to divine decree.[45] Since people who do their best without being aided or elevated by divine grace are able to merit the offer of created grace, condign merit, which accrues to human action when adorned with created grace, no longer has its ground in what is not merited. The ground of condign merit is no longer found in the ordering of God alone who creatively effects humans in their own performance of the good works by which they increase in grace. Condign merit was traditionally based on the free mercy of God who ordains that unmerited created grace should be completed by eternal life; now it comes instead to be attributed at least partially – perhaps even in the main – to the independent efforts of human persons to perform good works. Condign merit no longer expresses the loving largesse of a God who rewards what itself arises only as a free divine gift; it is instead taken to represent the result of the joint co-agency of God and independently operative human beings. Although the human performance of good works cannot effect salvation apart from the divine gift of created grace, a radical autonomy of operation is conferred upon human agency by saying that the divine offer of grace is equally futile without the independent efforts of human persons.[46] God and humans operate with a parity of status within the same causal order, each contributing its necessary but separately insufficient share in the cooperative venture whereby humans gain salvation.

Example 2

The next historical example centres on a dispute that began in the second half of the sixteenth century with Dominic Banez of the Dominican Order and Luis de Molina of the Society of Jesus, the so-called *de Auxiliis* controversy.[47] It is designed to show how in modern times the ruled structure of theological discourse is deformed so as to promote persistent wrangling over traditional Christian affirmations of divine sovereignty and the creature's power and freedom. Theological positions that would otherwise constitute complementary emphases of our rules, according to differing theologial priorities and estimates of historical exigency, turn into mutually exclusive options. Banezian Thomists, who uphold divine sovereignty, and Molinists, who defend the rights of the creature, meet head on, because both violate our rules for coherent discourse in much the same way. The manner in which this violation occurs suggests, moreover, an accord with structural requirements of modern methods of inquiry.

The followers of Banez and Molina are orthodox on the level of affirmation, i.e., each continues at least to assert the traditional claims about both divine sovereignty and human freedom.[48] The conflict between them is never effectively resolved, however, because neither side provides an adequate explanation for the coherent affirmation of both claims together. Each side's primary concern in the framing of theological statements (to ensure divine sovereignty or free human agency) seems logically to exclude its secondary concern not to deny human freedom in affirming divine sovereignty or divine sovereignty in highlighting human freedom. Because of this internal incoherence of primary and secondary claims, endemic to both sides in the dispute, the sides remain irreconcilable even though the one opponent's discourse is just affirming what is the other's own secondary concern.

The *de Auxiliis* controversy occurred within the ranks of the Roman Catholic church after the Council of Trent. I intend the example to be representative, however, of similar disputes throughout sixteenth- and seventeenth-century theology. Arguments focusing on divine sovereignty and the power and freedom of the creature erupt with peculiar prominence and frequency in this period. They include, for example, the controversies over sin and grace at the time of the Reformation, typical Protestant/Roman Catholic polemics afterwards, within Protestant churches the contention between Arminians and conservative Calvinists, Philippists verus Gnesio-Lutherans in the Lutheran Synergist controversy, Lutheran and Calvinist protests against Socinianism, and disputes between Lutheran and Calvinist theologians over predestination.[49]

Our analysis of the *de Auxiliis* controversy in terms of the influence of a modern framework for discourse will allow us to generalize its dynamic. The choice of this intra-Catholic controversy as representative of a common theological tendency has historical grounds. The vocabulary and theological foundations of the *de Auxiliis* disputes found their way, via Francisco Suarez's *Disputationes Metaphysicae* (1597), into the theology of Protestant controversialists addressing both Roman Catholic and Protestant opponents.[50]

A basic structure of shared assumptions for talk about divine agency and created being formed the backdrop for the *de Auxiliis* controversies. A growing 'extrinsicism' in the understanding of nature and grace tended by implication towards a secularistic naturalism. Both sides in the dispute accepted, therefore, what can be called a Pelagian structure of discourse.

Prior to the fifteenth century, especially in the Augustinian and Thomistic traditions, appeals to 'pure nature' involved distinguishing certain aspects and functions of humans who were actually ordained to a supernatural end by the creative agency of God.[51]. One might talk of pure nature to indicate metaphysical principles constituting the essence of human persons, or to incorporate the natural ends of human life discussed by philosophers, or to characterize human persons as they would be apart from sin and ordained to beatitude but without the actual gifts of grace. In all these cases one supposed, however, that pure nature has its reality only in subordination to the supernatural finality for grace and beatitude that characterizes all humans in the concrete. Human beings are created by God to be the sort of being that is fulfilled by God's grace; they never exist apart from that supernatural finality.

After Cardinal Cajetan (died 1534) and his influential commentary on Thomas, the general theological climate of opinion in Catholicism favoured, on the contrary, a two-storey conception of the relation between nature and grace. A really separable self-enclosed natural order (pure nature) precedes and/or runs parallel to a supplementary ordination and elevation to grace. A dualistic structuring of created and divine orders is suggested: created being seems to have its own order of existence in self-sufficient independence of God's will for it.

This development is in keeping with the structural features of modern methods of inquiry, which separately reify and serially order conceptual distinctions. The conceptual distinctions between nature and grace reflect a real difference between the natural and the supernatural; the natural and the supernatural are not the same. After Cajetan, however, the distinction is taken to indicate the real possibility of a separately existing human order. The real reference of 'nature' is capable of a self-contained existence independent of any supernatural finality. The intellectual division between subject and predicate in statements like 'humans receive from God an orientation to a supernatural end' is thought to imply that the subject and predicate can be really dissociated and separately spread out over instances of time. Intellectual division is taken to represent a real separation so that our ordering to grace becomes something really secondary, something only externally added on to an already complete, concrete human personhood.[52]

By means of this two-storey conception of the relation between nature and grace, Roman Catholic theologians tried to meet certain historical exigencies. Protestant pessimism about our corruption after the loss of God's grace could be countered by talk of a human nature with its own integrity and immanent *telos* apart from any consideration of grace and a relation of communion with God. At the same time one could combat the theological position of someone like Baius (condemned by Rome in 1567 and 1580), who naturalizes grace by making its reception a required means to the end of being simply a human being. The supernatural must be purely gratuitous, *pace* Baius, since it is set over against a self-sufficient natural order with its own naturally realizable goals. The gratuity of grace is bought, however, at the price of strongly suggesting its superficiality and superfluity. Ordination to God which is our supernatural finality becomes a superimposed template over what appears to be a properly human order existing in naturalistic independence of God.

If both sides in the *de Auxiliis* controversy assume this naturalistic structure of discourse, they will also share a subversion of our rules for discourse. Once those rules are subverted traditional theological discourse about God's sovereignty and the power and freedom of the creature is no longer coherent. An either/or option between the traditional affirmations about God and human freedom will result: the theologian can affirm the creature's freedom and power at the expense of God's sovereignty or affirm God's sovereignty at the expense of the creature's freedom and power.

On the first option, theological discourse directly accommodates itself to the naturalistic structure of talk about pure nature and extrinsic grace. The Pelagian assumptions of that structure are quite explicit. The theologian's primary concern is to ensure the freedom and power of human persons. Their existence is affirmed by restricting the range of immediate divine agency. The theologian assumes fairly straightforwardly that the freedom of human beings must be a freedom from God. This is the theological option taken by Molinists. Let us work through the details.

In one version of Molinism, the human act of will and what it effects are only mediately influenced by God. An indifferent divine agency simply creates and preserves the power by which humans alone bring about their own acts of will for particular effects.[53] For Molina himself, God works directly for the particular effects that a created cause also works to produce; the act of the human will is still assumed, however, to occur independently of any divine agency for it. God works alongside a human agent as a partial cause of the same created effects on the model of two horses pulling a barge.[54] Human willing is not efficacious without divine agency working with it but human agency is solely responsible for its own action and therefore for that aspect of the created effect it works to bring about.[55] In cooperating with the supernatural acts of the human will, divine agency as a *gratia praeveniens* is indeed directed towards the created will itself in a certain sense: it elevates the will to the power to produce a supernatural act. Such acts take place, however, by the will of the human agent alone. When that happens, divine agency as *gratia adiuvans* simply concurs, once again, with the creature's operation as a simultaneous partial cause of supernatural effects.[56] The human being responds to prevenient grace of its own free will, independent of any divine efficacy for such an act.

In these accounts the existence of the free act of the human will is withdrawn in a theologically inexplicable manner from the direct influence of God's creative agency. Despite this fact, Molinism attempts to maintain the sovereignty of divine agency by instituting a new idiom of theological discourse. Molina talks of a divine *scientia media* or middle knowledge of futuribles, that is, a divine knowledge of what a free agent *would* do in this or that circumstance.

By this device God's knowledge and will are really dissociated. Divine knowledge of free human choices precedes the divine will for these same created effects. God knows free human acts determinately in a middle knowledge before God's free determination of anything.[57]

In Molina's use of the notion, God foresees by *scientia media* who will merit salvation by their actions under the circumstances God has ordained, and predestines to salvation only those. Predestination is properly *post praevisa merita*. God's choice of these circumstances remains, however, *ante praevisa merita*. It is not similarly conditioned by God's foreknowledge of who will merit salvation under those circumstances.[58] Since God knows by *scientia media* that certain gifts of grace will be followed by a human's consent, that grace is, moreover, *in actu primo*, or before the person's consent, infallibly certain to gain it.[59] Nevertheless, the circumstances God gives are only specified in their effects by what the free human will chooses to do independently of divine agency. God's will is, consequently, not of itself entirely efficacious of man's salvation.

In the Congruist form of Molinism (Bellarmine, Suarez),[60] the theological innovation of *scientia media* is used to provide a stronger sense for the unconditional efficacy of the divine will. God's very ordination of persons to glory or damnation is without created conditions in the sense that God does not use foreknowledge of merits by *scientia media* to determine who will or will not be saved. God predestines *ante praevisa merita*. Foreknowledge by *scientia media* is employed by God simply to determine the conditions that must be supplied if the people God wants to save are to accept the offer and those God wants to reprobate are to reject it. God's choice of circumstances is therefore *post praevisa merita*. God uses *scientia media* only to distribute appropriately or congruously the graces that will be efficacious of the ends God has preordained. It remains the case, however, that God's preordaining will is not entirely efficacious of the end willed. The will of God becomes actually efficacious only upon the choice of the free human will. That choice, the Congruist admits, occurs independently of any direct divine agency for it. On their account too, then, not only what the divine will intends but also the divine will itself has created conditions foreseen via the *scientia media*.

The Molinist use of *scientia media* confirms, moreover, our argument in preceding chapters that human freedom cannot be maintained together with traditional affirmations of divine sovereignty without abiding by our rules for talk about divine transcendence and creative agency. Because it violates those rules, the use of *scientia media* to affirm divine sovereignty can only suggest the unreality of human free will. This becomes clear from what a Molinist must say about how God knows futuribles.

If God has an infallible middle knowledge of what the human will would do in any particular circumstance, what is the means of that knowlege? The Molinist cannot say as we can that God knows what a person will do because God knows God's own will for that act of the person. The divine will itself, in its direct universality, does not provide God with the means for that knowledge. The Molinist must say God is able to know what a human agent will do by way of a 'supercomprehension' of either the human agent itself (Suarez)[61] or the created conditions for its act provided by external circumstance (Molina).[62] In the first case, the infallibility of God's middle knowledge would require acts of human agents to be generated in a necessary fashion from the human will itself.[63] In the second case, it would require external circumstances to effect without fail a particular human choice.[64]

Let us turn now to Dominic Banez and his followers. Banezian Thomism reacts against Molinist affirmations of human freedom that restrict the scope of God's immediate agency. Specifically, Banez rejects the classic Molinist tenet that God works for the created effects of human agents by simultaneously concurring with the human will's own independently exercised acts. In opposing this tenet, Banez does not, however, choose to use the language of *divinis concursus* properly, without the illicit supposition that the human will acts apart from the divine will for it. Instead, Banez maintains that divine agency, by means of a physical premotion, works directly *on* the human agent to move it to its own act of some specific sort.[65]

This sounds like a traditional Thomistic denial of the autonomy of the human agent vis-à-vis God: divine agency extends to the free will itself. Such talk of God's working *on* the human agent takes place, however, against the backdrop of assumptions shared with Molinism. Its import is therefore surreptitiously altered.

Banez talks of God's working on the human agent and not with it because according to Banez creatures with apparently self-initiated movements lack the power to move themselves to act. This is not a matter simply of the world God happened to intend, a world where a creature's acts cannot be sufficiently explained in terms of its own powers. The sovereignty of God's agency for such acts is possible only in that sort of world. God is not talked about as simply remedying any deficiency of created causes for extant created effects; God's sovereignty *requires* the inadequacy of created causes.

Banez makes with Molinism the following naturalistic presumption: a human agent's power to move itself to act would necessarily exclude divine agency for that movement. To admit the human will's ability to move itself to act is to suggest that this power can really take effect apart from God's creative will. Banez must therefore insist upon a created defect, that the human agent cannot move itself to its own act of will, in order to maintain the utter dependence of that will upon God's agency for it. If God works directly for the movement of a creature to act there cannot be created causes sufficient for that movement.

This supposition violates our rule for talk of God as transcendent. According to that rule, divine agency may be said to ground the creature's own self-initiated acts. By excluding that possibility, Banez is presupposing along with Molina that created beings and God are included alongside one another in a single order of predication. What characterizes created powers with reference to the created order must also hold of their relation with divine agency. Banez denies the creature any self-initiated movement to act so that it will not be an absolute power, independent of God. Molina, in affirming the creature's capacity for self-initiated action, makes it absolute and therefore exclusive of God's direct creative agency for action of that sort. The one affirms the creature's capacity for self-initiated action, the other disputes it, but because they both violate the rule for talk of God as transcendent they agree about what would happen *if* the creature had the capacity: the creature's action would be self-initiated not just in the sense that it would not be worked by outside created causes but also in the sense that it would not be worked by God.

Because both parties violate the rule for talk of God's transcendence, what might have been a complementary difference of theological priorities turns into a theological conflict. Banez, who wishes to maintain the sovereignty of God's direct and universal agency, is forced to deny the capacity of the creature for self-initiated action. Molina, who wishes to affirm the self-initiated character of human action, is forced to restrict the manner and scope of God's creature agency. A metaphysical difference of opinion concerning whether or not certain sorts of being produce self-initiated motions, a difference about putative facts that could be spanned by the same rules for discourse, turns into a dispute of theological principle.[66]

Although Banez assumes on a priori theological grounds, then, that a creature cannot have a power for action sufficient to permit it to move itself to act, he does not want to say that the creature is moved to its act simply by God. There must be some immediate created correlative of God's will for the creature's movement, received within the operative potency of the creature and bringing it to act. If there were not, Banez would have to infer, on the basis of his usual either/or between God's working and the creature's working, that the creature is not producing an act that is its own.[67]

To avoid this implication, Banez says God cannot bring the human will to act apart from a certain created motion which is distinct from the act of the human will itself. Banez talks of a physical premotion of the act of the human will by God. God's will for a person's act must issue in an extraordinary secondary created cause, having an 'intentional' existence or '*esse viale*' within the human agent. It is by its means that God moves the human will to act.

This account violates, however, the rule for talk of God's agency as immediate. To move a creature to its own act, God cannot do without the extraordinary created motion that physically premoves it. That physical premotion is therefore a third thing within the created order mediating between the divine will for the creature's act and that act itself.

The assumption of a Pelagian structure of discourse begins to break through Banez's affirmations of divine sovereignty. Although God is said to work on the human agent rather than simply with that agent's acts as in Molinism, God is not immediately creative of the human act of the will itself – only of the created physical premotion which brings the human will to its act. God is said to work on the human agent but the human act of will nevertheless escapes the direct creative determination of God.[68] In Molinism, God directly produces the created effect of the human will by acting with that will's own absolutely self-originating acts. In Banezian Thomism, God directly effects the created physical premotion which brings about acts of the human will within the created order; God does not effect in the same direct manner, however, those human acts themselves. In either case, the integrity of the act of the human will is assured in a naturalistic way by granting it an independence from the direct creative will of God.

Since a created physical premotion intervenes between the divine will and a human act, God's will for that act can be infallibly efficacious of it only if created physical premotion is also.[69] This conclusion would not have been necessary had Banez abided by our rules for talk of God's agency and transcendence. We saw in chapter 2 that if God's creative agency is said to extend directly to every aspect of created existence, God's will is necessarily effective whether or not its effects have necessary created causes. The rule for talk of God's transcendence blocks any inference that necessary efficacy must characterize created causes because divine agency is itself necessarily efficacious. As it is, Banez must assign properly divine functions to created causes. The transcendent working of God is confounded with a finite act. God operates as one agent among others in the mode of a peculiar sort of supernatural secondary cause.[70]

The requirement of infallibly effective created causes is also the implication of Banez's account of the medium in which God foreknows contingent events. God knows infallibly the contingent effect of a created cause. This knowledge, according to Banez, does not require the contingent effect's eternal 'presentiality' to the divine intellect, which results from God's will for it. God's knowledge would still be certain even if God knew contingent effects simply in knowing their created causes.[71] For that to be the case, however, these causes would have to be taken to be certain of themselves to produce those effects. God's infallible knowledge would require, once again, infallible created causes.

This obviously appears to conflict, however, with the genuine contingency of the effects. For physical premotion, for example, to be an infallible created means by which the divine will for human agency is executed, it would seem to have to force the human will to an act of a particular sort. Physical premotion, as a created causality, cannot be talked about using the rules appropriate for talk of God's own transcendence and agency; those rules are what permit talk of an infallible agency with contingent or free effects. God's influence on the human will by means of such a physical premotion can only appear, therefore, to be a tyrannical one. God seems to work on human agents by way of an oppressive, deterministic constraint. Banez's initial refusal to use the language of *divinis concursus*, because of a mistaken impression about what such a use implies, ultimately results in a distortion of Christian discourse characteristic of an unrestrained use of the negative side of the rules.

The usual Banezian defence against this accusation involves an appeal to the scholastic distinction between composed and divided senses: chance, contingency and freedom apply to created beings viewed apart from their determination by divine agency (divided sense): the same predicates are not appropriate when created beings are viewed with respect to the divine will for them (composed sense).[72] This strategy is sufficient to show the genuine reality, and not simply the appearance, of created contingency and freedom only if it is possible, however, to assume that created beings in some degree really exist apart from any determination by the divine will. If no created being actually exists in any respect apart from its determination by divine agency, then there is no created reality corresponding to the divided sense in Banez's argument; contingency and created freedom are just appearances to be corrected by the knowledge of God's universally effective agency. In the traditional scholastic use (Thomas), composed and divided senses distinguish affirmations that God determines creatures to be contingent and free. Contingency or freedom in their divided sense refer to the relation of created effects to proximate created causes. That contingency or freedom is real because a created order of that sort is what God wills. Contingency and freedom are not applicable in a composed sense to cover the manner in which contingent and free effects within the created order result from God's will; they proceed necessarily from the divine will for them. That simply means, however, that contingent or free effects have to exist if God wills them to. The

Banezian version of the distinction comes about because of a subtle transposition in line with assumptions shared with Molinism: the two orders of divine and created causality are collapsed into one so that contingency and freedom seem able to exist only in real independence of divine agency.[73]

THE GENERAL EFFECTS OF A MODERN FRAMEWORK ON THEOLOGY

In this section I refer back to the account of a modern framework in an attempt to deduce the distortions of theological language that are likely in a modern context. I will line up the results with what we have uncovered in the historical analyses of the last section. The historical examples are to confirm and fill out the deductions that will be produced here.

Although typical claims about human beings and the natural order were closely tied to modern methods of inquiry in our second section, we will take the two separately now in order to distinguish their effects. Modern claims promote improper implications in discourse according to the positive side of our rules. Biel's use of traditional scholastic notions is the primary case in point among our historical examples. Modern methods of inquiry are liable to undercut the entire structure of theological discourse according to our rules, so that traditional claims about God's sovereignty and the creature's powers become incoherent, and complementary theological positions stressing one claim or the other become mutually exclusive alternatives. The *de Auxiliis* controversy between Molinists and Banezian Thomists is illustrative in this regard.

A modern emphasis on autonomous human powers of self-determination and self-assertion, and a modern tendency to perceive and comprehend the world apart from any reference to God, would seem to pose a clear danger for discourse according to the positive side of our rules. In this sort of cultural context, use of the positive side of our rules to talk about what the creature has, God's beneficent generosity as an agent, or the non-competitive concurrence of divine and created agencies, is likely to be especially susceptible of improper inference. The more human freedom is defined as freedom from outside interference the more a theological consideration of human powers and self-initiated action in themselves will suggest their real independence of God. Where the world tends to be nothing more than the object of the human subject's projects of cultivation and control, where the world is primarily viewed as mere material to be transformed according to the human agent's creative will, theological language emphasizing God's gift of power to human beings may easily find itself serving as a witness to the absolute self-sufficiency of the 'horizontal' progress enacted by human agents. A modern preoccupation with human achievement is likely to suggest in talk of divine *concursus* that the operations of human agents proceed independently of God. The theologian's provisional focus on creatures in the abstract, apart from a reference to the divine agent upon whom they depend, can easily be transformed, according to a modern consideration of the world 'in itself', into a description of their real existence apart from God. The modern propensity to restrict the understanding of nature to immanent explanations will promote an improper use of talk about sufficient created causes in which those causes are no longer subordinated to the overarching agency of God. These probabilities are instantiated in the second section by Biel's 'domed' naturalism, his optimistic assessment of human capacities to earn salvation and his tendency to reverse the priority between Thomas's two causal orders.

If these are the likely dangers for misconstrual that the characteristic claims of a modern context pose, they should set the corrective rhetorical stress of modern theology. To block the danger of improper inferences from discourse according to the positive side of our rules the theologian presumably should stress discourse according to the negative side of the rules. The claims about human persons and the world that we have mentioned figure prominently and from early on within discourse that defines itself as modern. The likely distortion of the positive side of the rules is suggested quite directly from those sorts of claims. It is very curious, then, how often modern theologians seem oblivious to the danger. In the theological trend represented by Biel, for instance, we saw an overwhelming emphasis on discourse associated with the positive side of our rules and a skewing of discourse associated with the negative side to confirm rather than counter improper inferences from that emphasis.

Even more curious, however, is the lack of success shown by theologies that do use discourse associated with the negative side of the rules in an attempt to block a perceived danger. A stress on divine sovereignty and the creature's direct dependence upon God blocks the immediate danger from discourse according to the positive side of our rules. But this function always seems liable to reversal: the illicit implications of talk according to the positive side of the rules always seem ultimately to reappear. We saw, for example, how Banez, by talk about God's working what the creature cannot, attempted to counter Molina's affirmation of human operations proceeding independently of God's agency for them; his own account of physical premotion assumed, however, that a created motion is an intermediary for the divine will, that divine agency is conditioned by the character of this created intermediary, that human acts themselves escape the direct creative agency of God, and that genuine contingency and freedom within the created order require a real independence of God. The case of Banez can sum up the historical reversals of Reformation Protestantism. We saw at the end of the last chapter how Luther and Calvin stress divine sovereignty according to the negative side of our rules; Reformation Protestantism was designed to rebut the very theological trend that Gabriel Biel represents. Eventually, however, Protestant culture and theology are marked by unabashed Pelagianism of one sort or other: God tends to aid or respond to human actions that proceed independently of God's creative will for them.[74]

This tactical failure of discourse associated with the negative side of our rules suggests that the problems posed by a modern framework are of a more general nature. Modern methods of inquiry prompt, I will argue, a distortion of both sides of the rules. If all the rules are prone to deformation they lose their function. Christian discourse becomes incoherent, whether it stresses their positive or negative sides. Traditional claims for God's sovereignty seem to exclude the creature's power and freedom; the creature's power and freedom seem to exclude God's sovereignty. The mechanism for this distortion makes clear the inevitably Pelagian results.

Let us suppose modern methods of inquiry supply the hermeneutic principles for modern theology's appropriation of traditional theological language. What is likely to happen? Our account will divide according to the two features of a modern method of inquiry as we have described it: (1) its emphasis on the referential adequacy of discourse; and (2) its tendency to reify the distinctions of abstract analysis.

A focus on referential adequacy forces a decontextualized reading of traditional theological discourse. Traditional theological affirmations are considered the result of a 'pure' inquiry into the nature of God and the world, uninfluenced by practical theological agendas or attempts to meet the needs of particular audiences. The theologian's task in appropriating that discourse is simply to further such a search for statements as descriptively adequate as possible for those referents. The theologian carries on the tradition of Christian discourse without sufficient regard for the fact that previous formulations were conditioned by functions they were designed to serve within the context of Christian communities and by the exigencies of particular circumstances.

When appropriating discourse that follows the positive side of our rules the theologian ignores its rhetorical dangers in a modern situation. The result is an uncritical accommodation to the improper inferences a modern context suggests. If the theologian takes over traditional discourse formed according to the negative side of our rules, it will happen that the rhetorical force of that language is suitable for heading off the dangers of distortion posed by modern claims. Interpreted, however, as providing accurate ontological descriptions, discourse according to the negative side of the rules will be 'absolutized' as generally adequate apart from the need for any consideration of the context of its formulation. It will never seem appropriate, whatever the circumstances, to affirm, according to the positive side of our rules, the power and free action of creatures. These sorts of affirmation are unavailable for blocking the improper inferences that talk of God's sovereignty might suggest. The result is an overwhelming stress on the negative side of the rules without any precautionary measures taken to prevent its own attendant dangers. Both sides of the rules are liable, then, to distortion.

Viewed as ontological descriptions, traditional statements according to the negative side of the rules become difficult to reconcile with statements according to the positive side; traditional Christian discourse lapses into incoherence. It is proper to say that the creature is nothing in itself – without power and freedom, an empty vessel to show forth transparently the will of God – when addressing an opponent who presumes the creature is something independent of the will of God. Taken as simple referential discourse, such statements appear to conflict with affirmations of the creature's own existence, power and operations under a loving, creator God: the creature is simply nothing at all. Improper inferences are drawn from statements according to the negative side of the rules: God becomes a tyrant – one who acts only to keep down and deny.

In good Hegelian fashion, these distortions of discourse according to the negative side of the rules serve indirectly to foster the illicit inferences of a stress on the positive side. If the creature is to be anything at all under these circumstances it must appear to be so in independence of God. If the creature has its own power, it can only have it in opposing God's tyranny. It may be that a theologian like Banez, who affirms the necessary impoverishment of human power and suggests a divine determinism, is unwilling to give up altogether talk of God's gifts to the creature. His discourse will tend to veer around, then, in claims for physical premotion that require secondary created causes and isolate human action from God's direct creative influence. Moderns who refuse for their own reasons to concede human power to an oppressive divine rule are forced to take the stand of an irreligious humanism. Talk of God's power that would otherwise be suitable for preventing assumptions of the independent being and power of creatures promotes an ever more vigorous naturalism.

Where theology is accommodated to the second feature of a modern method of inquiry, it reifies the clear distinctions of abstract theological analysis. Those distinctions are taken to refer to essentially separate entities ordered in linear series. A Pelagian structure of discourse is the result.

Created being which can be analysed abstractly apart from God's will for it is assumed actually to exist independently of any relation to God. These independently constituted beings are then externally related to divinity, within a one-dimensional plane like all orderings of phenomena subject to the blueprint of modern methods of inquiry: God and creatures are brought together secondarily, according to a linear syntax. Biel's account of salvation in terms of a single order of mutual action and reaction on the part of God and humans is a classic case in point. Banez's account of physical premotion as a kind of billiard ball causality, Molina's version of divine *concursus* as the conjoint operation of parallel agencies, follow the same structure.

God's gifts to the creature that are the result of the creature's relation to God form a similarly secondary addition. The stratigraphic configuration of being that follows from the reification of analytico-referential discourse is reproduced within a theological account of created reality. The 'real' characteristics of creatures which they have apart from a relationship with God constitute a separate sphere. To them is merely appended an additional layer of qualities effected by that relationship. The *dignitas* of human acts is added on to their *bonitas*, according to Biel. The supernatural order of grace is appended to a self-sufficient and self-enclosed natural order within the extrinsicist structure of discourse shared by Molinism and Banezian Thomism. A similar naturalistic structure of discourse occurs within Protestant theology: the absolute gratuity of God's grace vis-à-vis a radically corrupt human order has the unintended consequence of suggesting that humans operate entirely on their own, sealed off from God's will for their salvation.

If the structure of modern theological discourse is Pelagian, our general rules for talk of God's transcendence and creative agency cannot be followed. Something escapes the direct creative agency of God; one cannot talk of God's creative agency applying directly everywhere. God must work alongside or on what pre-exists it within a single order of being and causality: in that way our rule for talk of God's transcendence is abrogated in discussing divine agency. God and the creature must have a certain parity as partial causes within a common causal nexus or plane – Molina's two horses pulling a barge, Banez's physical premotion as a created intermediary within the causal line that runs from God's will to human action.

The complex predication relations that hold by the rule for talk of God as transcendent will flatten out, accordingly, into linear relations of either direct contrast or identity. What characterizes God's agency for the created order must also characterize creatures within that order. If God's will for the creature is necessarily efficacious, created causes must be themselves necessary; the apparent freedom and contingency of created happenings are spurious. Banez's account of physical premotion has these implications. Qualities attributed to created being themselves must also characterize created being in relation to divine agency. If the creature is free, the creature must also be free from God; if the creature has power, that must be a power that may be exercised with respect to divinity. The creature's freedom and power are therefore potential limitations on God's. The creature gains at God's expense.

Because the creature is not entirely dependent upon God's creative agency for it, an inverse proportion between God's working and the creature's results. This violates our rule of a direct proportion in talk of what the creature has in relation to God's agency. The more extreme the affirmations of God's power the more inconsequential must the creature's own capacities be. The more formidable the creature's power the more God's appears limited and conditional. Traditional affirmations of God's unlimited and unconditioned sovereignty are no longer compatible with claims about the genuine power, operations and efficacy of creatures.

Finally, because something escapes God's creative agency for it, God's transcendence tends to be defined negatively vis-à-vis an already given factuality. This violates our rule for talk of God's transcendence and thereby suggests the incompatibility of that transcendence with God's immediate involvement with the world. God is simply not what the world is; too close a connection with it would seem to threaten a transcendence of that sort. The Greek problematic set out in chapter 2 infiltrates modern theology. God is imprisoned by a transcendence negatively defined: God is either isolated over against a basically self-sufficient nexus of created causes and effects, or may operate in the way a finite being would within a single causal order shared with others. We have seen both these results in the *de Auxiliis* controversy that follows an extrinsicist account of the relation between the natural and the supernatural. Biel is a very good case of the first. That an effect of this sort could come about because of a negative definition of transcendence is supported by the history of Protestant culture. The otherness of God in power and purpose suggests distance: God would not seem in the main, therefore, to be directly present or influential. The world is de-sacralized, disenchanted; men and women are abandoned by God, left to the devices of their own making.[75]

These are the general rule violations that lead to the incoherence of traditional theological claims about God and the world. The Pelagian assumptions of a modern theological structure of discourse also infect our body of more specific rules for talk about God's agency and the power of creatures. Whether one uses the positive side of those rules in stressing the creature's power and freedom or the negative side in stressing the sovereign power of God, they are distorted in line with the assumption of the creature's independence from God's creative agency.

The distortion caused by Pelagian assumptions is more obvious where the positive side of the rules comes to the fore. Our rules for talk of a divine *concursus* will be violated: as in Molinism, God will be understood to work with created operations not themselves directly dependent or influenced by divine agency. Independent causal lines converge in the establishing of a created effect. God works as a partial cause of the effects a creature also works to produce. When it is said God acts to supplement the power of created causes, for example in grace, the theologian distinguishes between what is and what is not the direct effect of God's creative agency. The converse of talk of supplementation is permitted rather than restricted; the adequacy of created causes apart from the operation of God's agency is understood to imply the inadequacy of God's own agency apart from the independent operation of created causes. As in Molinist uses of *scientia media*, created agents condition God's agency for them.

That Pelagian assumptions are also behind the drawing of improper inferences in discourse according to the negative side of the rules is not quite so obvious. It is because created freedom is assumed to be a freedom from God that Banez's account of the sovereignty of God's power suggests a divine determinism. It is because created power must be a power with the potential to condition God's agency that Banez believes God's sovereignty requires the denial of created causes with the power to move themselves to act. It is only when created reality has an existence apart from God's creative agency that God is certain to have his way only where necessarily effective created mechanisms exist. If an independent domain is reserved for creatures, God's working on them must take the shape of an after-the-fact intervention. God must be working from without, altering the course of the creature's activity on its own. If that influence is to be sure, God must use an inexorable might, unbreakable constraints, or an infallibly effective mode of persuasion which takes away the creature's ability to do otherwise. When it is asumed God's agency does not extend directly to everything, God's working without sufficient created causes must mean that God enters within the created sphere in the form of a supernatural force – in Banez's case, physical premotion.

These improper implications of discourse associated with the negative side of our rules cannot be blocked by discourse according to the positive: the theologian who talks of divine sovereignty in this way has already ceded the positive side of the rules to the improper implications that a modern context suggests. He or she cannot talk of the creature's own capacities without taking such talk to imply their independence of God's creative agency. If the theologian is unwilling to renounce talk about the gifts the creature receives from God, the theologian will tend therefore to draw the same improper implications that his or her opponent has. The theologian cannot combat Pelagianism by a stress on God's sovereignty since the theologian is making the same Pelagian assumptions. The theologian cannot combat Pelagianism by a stress on God's sovereignty because he or she is not making that sovereignty radical enough: God exercises power in the manner of a finite agent who must meet the prima facie constraints on its own operation posed by other beings.

A Strategy for Faithfulness

In the last two chapters I showed how traditional Christian claims about God and the world are coherent. In this chapter I have shown how Christian theology becomes incoherent in a modern context. The rules are deformed and their function lost. What can a theologian do to remedy the situation? Our account of the mechanism of this deformation points the way towards over-coming it.

If the theologian wishes to remain faithful to our rules, the first step must be to formulate discourse with a stress appropriate for a modern context. The theologian must block the Pelagian impli-cations that modern claims about the world and humans will suggest in talk about the creature's own capacities. The theologian must avoid, therefore, discourse marked by a predominant use of the positive side of the rules. The theologian should stress God's sovereignty and talk of the creature with a constant thematic reference to God's direct creative agency for it. To counter theological trends like that instantiated by Gabriel Biel, the theologian can talk of the nothingness of the creature, eschew discussion of created causes and speak of how God must work without us to remedy our frailty and impotence. This is the rhetorical emphasis of the Reformers. We must be convicted of sin before being given any word of comfort. Everything must be taken away before it is given back by God.

Talk according to the negative side of our rules should not cut off, however, the possibility of using the positive side. The rhetorical stance of the theologian should be recognized *as* a rhetorical stance, as the proper response to an over-riding need posed by a modern context. The theologian should admit the propriety of talk according to the positive side of the rules where a stress on the negative side of the rules suggests improper impli-cations of its own – the absolute nothingness of the creature, a divine determinism, a tyrannical divine rule. The theologian should not be deceived by the referential focus of a modern method of inquiry into assuming that discourse according to the negative side of the rules conflicts with discourse on the positive side.

The theological response to the modern cultural climate cannot stop, however, with discourse that accords with the negative side of the rules, even when that discourse is recognized as a rhetorical posture appropriate for a particular context. To stop there is to accept the modern tendency to understand creaturely freedom as freedom from God, and creaturely competence as competence apart from the creative will of God. Theologians who do nothing more than deny to the creature freedom and power of that sort argue on the same grounds as their opponents. They are ultimately unsuccessful, therefore, in countering the influence on theology of modern claims about the world and human persons.

Faithful adherence to our rules requires, then, not merely a proper rhetorical emphasis; it also demands a critical revision of those distortions of talk about the creature's capacities that a modern cultural climate promotes. The theologian must correct the assumption that freedom and power are had by the creature only in independence of God's creative agency for them. The theologian must talk of creaturely freedom and agency as freedom and agency *under God.* And that requires the actual reinstatement of the positive side of the subsidiary rules – in talk, for example, of the creature's capacities and of God's working with them. This second step finds historical representation in Roman Catholic theology (though to my knowledge never with adequate attention to the first step).

Although theological discourse according to the positive side of the rules is to be reinstated, the priority of discourse according to the negative side must remain. Talk of the creature's capacities in themselves is never to come first. God's sovereignty must be the basis for an affirmation of what the creature has in dependence upon God. The order of exposition, if you will, must follow the order of reality. The creature is nothing without God. There is therefore nothing to say about the creature without talk of God first. So long as this sort of priority is constantly maintained, the theologian can go on to affirm modern claims for the productive powers of human agents, their rights of self-determination, and the sufficiency of explanations of natural events in terms of natural causes.

This second step of reinstating the positive side of the rules may still not be enough, however. Both sides of the rules remain liable to deformation through the surreptitious influence of a Pelagian structure of discourse that accords with modern methods of inquiry. To provide a defence against this, an explicitly meta-level analysis is necessary. It is not enough to use both sides of the rules. One must mention what they are and point out the ways in which they are prone to subversion in modern times. Our analyses in the last three chapters are a contribution towards that effort.

In my concluding remarks I will have more to say on this score. What are the prospects for avoiding in modern times the general subversion of our rules for coherent discourse?

Conclusion

Interpretation [is]. . . the violent or surreptitious appropriation of a system of rules . . . in order to impose a direction, to bend it to a new will, to force its participation in a different game, and to subject it to secondary rules.

Michel Foucault, 'Nietzsche, Genealogy and History'[1]

In the second and third chapters I made a positive case for the coherence of Christian talk about a transcendent God who effects beings with their own powers and operations: I specified rules for discourse according to which such talk hangs together intelligibly. In the last chapter I made a negative case for the coherence of Christian talk according to those rules: I demonstrated how incoherent discourse arises from the systematic violation of those rules in modern times. Traditional theological claims supposing God's universal, direct creative agency and the creature's utter dependence upon God are compatible with talk of the creature's own power and efficacy, affirmations of God's sovereign and unconditioned agency imply no tyrannical rule, when discourse follows our rules. Such talk becomes incoherent when these traditional sorts of claim about divine agency and the creature are made without following the traditional usage rules for their elaboration. The theologian may affirm, for example, that God is the creator of all that is but exempt some aspect of the non-divine order from the direct creative efficacy of God in continuing the account. We can conclude, then, that those who dispute the coherence of the traditional claims are similarly misconstruing them. Their charges have merit only where traditional affirmations about divine agency and the creature are carried over while violating the rules for their proper use.

We have seen, however, how prone theologians are in fact to deform these rules in modern times; charges of incoherence find a target. In such a circumstance, the theologian has two options in the interest of maintaining Christian coherence. The theologian can adjust the claims made for divine sovereignty and the creature's capacities so that they fit the violations of the usage rules that occur in a modern context. Accepting the sort of violation of the rules we have recounted, the theologian becomes a revisionist theologian: he or she gives up the traditional claims for a transcendent creator God. Or the theologian can try to sustain the coherence of the traditional claims about God and the world according to the traditional rules for their elaboration; the theologian works to block, in this case, the initial violation of those rules in the first place.

The revisionist theologian alters claims for divine agency to reflect the deformation in a modern context of our rules for talk of God's transcendence and God's universal direct efficacy. This may be done in one of two very general ways. In the first way, God is talked about as one supreme but ultimately limited power among others; the theologian gives up claims for an unconditioned sovereignty based upon the universal and direct efficacy of God as a creator. God may start the self-maintaining mechanism of a world machine (e.g., in Enlightenment Deism), or ground our independent acts of ontogenesis (e.g., in the religious philosophy of Henry Duméry), or provide the lure for the good by which the creature determines itself (e.g., in Alfred North Whitehead's account of the primordial nature of God), or cooperate with the creature as a necessary, even fundamental, condition in the emergence of its operations (e.g., according to the English philosopher of religion J. R. Lucas).[2] These sorts of claim for divine agency obviously cohere with the genuine power of creatures since they suppose from the start an operation of the creature independent of God's agency for it. To make sure the supremacy of God's power cannot become a tyrannical rule under these conditions, talk of God's immediate efficacy with respect to the creature's own working is avoided: God is simply an enabler, a persuader or a cooperative partner.

In the second way, God's efficacy is said to have a direct and universal range, but only in virtue of the fact that, in violation of our rule for talk of God as transcendent, the creature is said to be some sort of part of divinity or moment in the divine life (e.g., in the philosophical theology of a Charles Hartshorne or G. W. F. Hegel).[3] By giving up the traditional Christian claim that the creature is not God, these theologians avert the oppression of the creature that is possible when the universal agency of God is understood according to Pelagian assumptions. The unconditioned sovereignty of God is now easily reconciled with the power of the creature since the creature is not ultimately other than divine. Suspicions that divine tyranny may remain in the form of a cunning of Reason are dispelled with the raising of the finite to the level of divinity: the finite attains thereby the true freedom of an unconstrained self-determination.

Because a theologian of this stripe is willing to alter traditional sorts of theological claim, he or she is not impelled to work over established linguistic habits for discourse borrowed from other contexts for theological purposes. Instead of working to realign non-theological language habits to head off potential problems of coherence among traditional theological claims, the revisionist theologican realigns traditional theological claims to fit those habits. Revisionist theology inclines, therefore, towards univocity in its account of God and creatures. Non-theological discourse tends to undergo only a quantitative extension of the sort that Whitehead made methodologically explicit in his requirement that divinity be the supreme exemplification of what typifies every finite being.[4] God works as a supremely powerful finite agent would, in a single order of causality, doing more of what a finite agent could, or supplying what no other agent can, but in the usual mode of an agent who acts alongside others. God becomes, for someone like Hegel, the all-encompassing instantiation of processes the philosopher is competent to describe – in Hegel's case, organic developments and human reflection in particular.[5]

As a result of this sort of univocity, revisionist accounts of God's agency in relation to creatures with their own powers and efficacy gain a kind of obvious coherence, i.e., a coherence that follows directly from the non-theological sense of the language employed. Because the coherence of theological claims is so obvious (as obvious as the relations of implication making up the discourse borrowed), the revisionist theologian need not be preoccupied with it. Concern over whether traditional theological claims about God and the world are consistent with one another tends to be replaced by concern over whether and to what extent an obvious coherent revisionist position is still compatible with a traditional one.

Revisionist theologians with an interest in maintaining continuity with traditional theological claims produce a kind of modern idiom that approximates the traditional rules for their use even while violating them. We have seen something like this in Molina's construction of a middle knowledge for God: talk of a *scientia media* allows Molinists to approximate the sovereign efficaciousness of the divine will while violating our rule for talk of God's universal and direct creative agency. Talk of God's cooperating with or aiding the creature's own independent activity approximates our rule for a direct proportion between the creature's working and God's working even as it restricts the arena of God's direct creative agency. Talk of the interaction between God and the creature as a relation of care and affection between separate persons approaches our rule that the creature be empowered by its dependence upon God: the creature is fulfilled only in a loving response to divine concern. Talk of an infinite patience that ultimately achieves its ends approximates the infallible efficacy of God's creative agency. Even though they include God and the creature within a single order of causality, Process philosophers can approximate our rule that the creature's freedom be the result of God's creative agency for it by saying that any genuine novelty and transcendence of the past requires the reception of possibilities from the primordial nature of God. Hegelian talk of God and the creature in terms of a relation between a self-identical process and its moments approximates our rule for talk of God as transcendent – a moment is neither simply identical nor simply other than the process that takes it up – even as it violates that rule by requiring a much stronger identity between God and the creature than the rule allows.

On the second option, the theologian attempts to prevent the Pelagian rupture that prompts these sorts of realignment in the interest of Christian coherence. We are raising again the question posed at the end of the last chapter – how to remain faithful to our rules for Christian coherence in the face of the distortive influence exercised by a modern context.

Certain problems of distortion may be peculiar to a modern circumstance but the potential for subverted rules is a general problem with which theologians of very different times and places must contend. Whenever theologians borrow discourse they must fight against previously established linguistic habits which suggest what it is inappropriate to say about God. Rules for theological discourse are always liable to subversion by expectations channeled by prior patterns of inference. As an instance of a general problem, the distortive influence of a modern context has a general solution: the recognition that theological discourse is a fracturing discourse, that theological rules for discourse are critical principles for reworking those in force elsewhere. Where established linguistic habits become intractable, God's transcendence should be invoked; talk of God is not the same as talk of the creature. Our rule for talk of God's transcendence is the rule that makes the fracturing capabilities of the others clear.

This function of this rule has an analogue in a modern context. A modern sensitivity to historical change and cultural diversity points up the conditioned, revisable character of what is taken for granted at any particular time and place. A recognition, at least since Ludwig Wittgenstein, of the varying requirements of different fields of discourse hampers any one's over-generalization. The willingness to revise previous linguistic habits, which faithfulness to rules for theological discourse demands, is therefore encouraged by certain developments of a modern context that in other respects proves so dangerous.

The specific features of a modern context that lead to the distortion of the structure of theological discourse – its emphasis on referential language and its confusion of the abstract with the concrete – also find modern opponents. The modern framework for discourse was never monolithic. The aspects I described are perhaps those now on the wane. The sources for our discussion were in fact twentieth-century critics of the modern modes of inquiry I pinpointed.

Thus, the decontextualization of language that comes about because of a stress on referential adequacy has been effectively undercut, at least since the influential work of Wittgenstein and J. L. Austin,[6] by a more inclusive respect for the various uses of language requiring attention to speaker and circumstances, and by the recognition of the way communication is furthered by the 'vague' or 'open-textured' character of language in use.[7] The once-and-for-all character of statements that are reputedly descriptively adequate is attenuated by a heightened regard for the connection between statements and their contexts of utterance. Criticism of the tendency to confuse abstract distinctions with ontological differences between essentially separate and subsequently related units is the common thread joining, for all their very major differences, Ernst Cassirer's attack on 'thing-concepts',[8] George Lukács's critique of reification,[9] Martin Heidegger's reproach to scientific method and Enlightenment common sense,[10] Alfred North Whitehead's repudiation of the fallacy of misplaced concreteness,[11] John Dewey's diagnosis of the problems requiring a genuinely empirical method,[12] and Gilbert Ryle's analysis of Cartesian 'para-mechanical' category mistakes.[13] The specific theological project of countering the distortive influence of these two features of a modern context is therefore furthered by developments of that cultural climate itself. Direct philosophical attack on the modern framework for discourse I have described facilitates the theologian's own projects of language revision in a modern context while helping those unfamiliar with theology to follow its linguistic manoeuvres more readily.

In the end, however, countering the subversive effects of modern modes of inquiry is an internal matter: the theologian needs to understand the theological enterprise better. The theologian who is to avoid the modern subversion of our rules for discourse must know the theological tradition of which he or she is a part: how traditional theological claims have been used within their discourse contexts – the apparent implications that are to be permitted or restricted, the functions they can serve. Principled reflection on the way theologians have talked – our own enterprise in this book – aids the theologian in the continuation of an established theological practice.

Principled reflection cannot, however, take the place of sound judgement. In the first place, the rules we have specified provide no decision-procedure for constructing theological statements that conform to the rules or for avoiding the dangers of their misuse or misapprehension that a particular historical context may pose. In the second place, our rules simply try to encapsulate the moves of a theological practice that is itself the result of training; our principled reflection is an after-the-fact attempt to sum up the sort of fracturing of discourse that occurs for the most part without the theologian's explicit recourse to rules. The principles we have adumbrated are therefore parasitic upon the unreflective skills of theologians, which in turn presuppose – if our account of the theological enterprise in chapter 1 is correct – the unselfconscious know-how that Christians exhibit in their day-to-day lives. The rules will not work apart from these skills. If modern theologians are peculiarly prone to break our rules for Christian coherence, this may find its final source, then, in a failure of socialization.[14] While principled reflection is not sufficient to remedy such a failure, it can nevertheless be an invaluable aid in the correction of mistake-prone practitioners; selfconsciousness is the necessary companion of error. This task of principled reflection, which a faltering theological practice generates of itself, finds support once again in a modern cultural context; the theologian's own project of selfconsciousness about language use finds support in the linguistic turn of modern philosophy.

Our own account of the uses and abuses of traditional theological claims in terms of rules for discourse is a contribution, then, to the recovery of the coherence of those claims. The recovery of a tradition of coherent discourse about a transcendent God who brings to be all that is, including created powers and efficacy, should be a real possibility at the present time. The actual recovery of that tradition is of course a matter for first-order theological construction. Such a tradition is not actually reinstated by a meta-level analysis of the sort undertaken here, however helpful it may be as a critical propaedeutic. It is up to modern theologians, convinced by arguments like those presented here, to fracture anew the language of the ordinary, so that traditional affirmations about God and the world come to hang together intelligibly once again.

Notes

INTRODUCTION

1 Section 334, trans. W. Kaufmann, (New York: Random House, 1974).
2 Trans. based on that of J. Baillie (New York: Harper and Row, 1967), p. 92, following revisions made by G. Spivak in her introduction to J. Derrida, *Of Grammatology* (Baltimore: Johns Hopkins, 1974), p. xiii.
3 This is at least Karl Barth's charge which I am considering representative of anti-Roman Catholic polemics in Protestant theology for present purposes. See his *Church Dogmatics*, trans. G. W. Bromiley et al. (Edinburgh: T. and T. Clark, 1957–75), 1:1 (second ed).
4 See Louis Bouyer, *The Spirit and Forms of Protestantism*, trans. A. Littledale (Westminster, Maryland: Newman Press, 1961), ch. 8.
5 See Richard Bernstein, *Beyond Objectivism and Relativism* (Philadelphia: University of Pennsylvania, 1983), for an interpretation of Peter Winch's notion of practical wisdom as an essential moment of hermeneutics. See Hans-George Gadamer, *Truth and Method* (New York: Seabury, 1975), for this re-evaluation of the Enlightenment opinion of prejudice.

CHAPTER 1   METHOD IN THE STUDY OF THEOLOGY

1 (Oxford: Clarendon, 1930), p. xii.
2 Trans. E.G. Salter (New York: Dutton, 1928), p. 83.
3 See Willard van Orman Quine, *Word and Object* (Cambridge, Mass.: MIT Press, 1960), ch. vii, section 56, for the notion of semantic ascent. Richard Rorty popularized the expression 'linguistic turn' by making it the title of an anthology of essays in philosophical method which he introduced and edited. See his *The Linguistic Turn* (Chicago:

Chicago University Press, 1967). On p. 8 of his introduction he gives Gustav Bergmann the credit for coining the phrase. See Gustav Bergmann, *Logic and Reality* (Madison : University of Wisconsin Press, 1964), p. 177.

4 I am using the terminology of Rudolf Carnap here. See his 'Empiricism, Semantics and Ontology' in *Semantics and the Philosophy of Language*, ed. L. Linsky, (Urbana, Illinois: University of Illinois Press, 1972), pp. 208–28.

5 The present work is not the first employing this general strategy for understanding theological statements and making the apophatic or agnostic assumptions about theological language congruent with it. I am following the lines laid down by David Burrell and Victor Preller in their studies of Thomas Aquinas. See David Burrell, *Aquinas* (Notre Dame, Indiana: Notre Dame University Press, 1976); also his *Exercises in Religious Understanding* (Notre Dame, Indiana: Notre Dame University Press, 1974); and Victor Preller, *Divine Science and the Science of God* (Princeton, NJ: Princeton University Press, 1967). The two of them concentrate, however, on preliminary epistemological questions, questions about how talk of God is possible at all and under what linguistic conditions. The present study tries to determine rules for discourse at work in a specific theological locus and the way in which those rules provide a coherent structure for basic theological claims made there.

6 The linguistic turn of analytic philsophy exhibits the same pragmatist tendencies. See Carnap, 'Empiricism, Semantics, and Ontology'; Quine, *Word and Object*. John E. Smith situates this development within the history of modern analysis in his 'The Reflexive Turn, the Linguistic Turn and the Pragmatic Outcome', *The Monist* 53 (1969), pp. 588–605.

7 My appreciation for the variety of things that religious statements can do has been furthered by reading a manuscript version of William Christian's *Doctrines of Religious Communities* (New Haven: Yale University Press, 1987).

8 Maurice Wiles, *The Making of Christian Doctrine* (Cambridge: Cambridge University Press, 1967), pp. 84ff.

9 See Jaroslav Pelikan, *The Christian Tradition*: vol. 2, *The Spirit of Eastern Christendom* (Chicago: University of Chicago Press, 1974), pp. 183ff.

10 See Nicholas Rescher, *Methodological Pragmatism* (New York: New York University Press, 1977), pp. 259ff. The suggestion here of a feedback structure within a pragmatist theory of theological language is an application of ideas developed by Rescher with regard to

logic and epistemology.

11 For this general pragmatist perspective see Peirce's 'The Fixation of Belief' and 'How to Make Ideas Clear', in *Charles Peirce : Selected Writings*, ed. P. Wiener (New York : Dover, 1966), pp. 91–136.

12 See Robert Nozick, *Philosophical Explanations* (Cambridge, Mass.: Harvard University Press, 1981).

13 See Edmund Schlink, 'The Structure of Dogmatic Statements as an Ecumenical Problem', trans. G. Overlach and D. B. Simmonds, in *The Coming Christ and the Coming Church* (Philadelphia: Fortress Press, 1968), pp. 16–84, for a contrary view. Schlink argues that in elevating them to a theoretical plane presumptions of Christian practice are distorted to produce unnecessary problems.

14 See Stephan Körner, 'The Impossibility of Transcendental Deductions', *The Monist* 51(1967), pp. 317–31; also A. P. Griffiths, 'Transcendental Arguments', *Proceedings of the Aristotelian Society*, suppl. vol. 43 (1969), p. 171.

15 This is what P. F. Strawson is doing in *Individuals* (New York: Doubleday, 1963).

16 See Ludwig Wittgenstein's *On Certainty* (Oxford: Basil Blackwell, 1969) for the sense in which claims essential to a form of life are 'foundational' in virtue of their place in a network, in virtue of how they are held up by everything else in a linguistic practice.

17 Quine, 'On Empirically Equivalent Systems of the World', *Erkenntnis* 9(1975), pp. 313–28.

18 See Nozick, *Philosophical Explanations*, pp. 12 – 3.

19 Ibid. p. 10; see Michael Dummett, *Truth and Other Enigmas* (Cambridge, Mass.: Harvard University Press, 1978), p. 311.

20 See Nozick's preference for philosophy's 'bureau of internal affairs' over 'foreign relations' in the attempt to meet the challenges of scepticism; *Philosophical Explanations*, pp. 15–6.

21 Ibid. p. 16; Dummett, *Truth*, p. 296.

22 See Nozick, *Philosophical Explanations* p. 15; Dummett, *Truth*, p. 296.

23 See John E. Smith, *Experience and God* (Oxford: Oxford University Press, 1968), ch. 5; and Louis Dupré, *A Dubious Heritage* (New York: Paulist Press, 1977), part 3, for the suggestion that even the traditional arguments for the existence of God move within the experience of Christian faith rather than bridge a gap between belief and unbelief.

24 See Karl-Otto Apel on Wittgenstein and transcendental argument in chapter 1 of his *Towards A Transformation of Philosophy*, trans.

G. Adey and D. Frisby (London: Routledge and Kegan Paul, 1980); also Strawson, *Individuals*.

25 See Austin Farrer, *Faith and Speculation* (New York: New York University Press, 1967)

26 See A. D. Sertillanges, *L'idée de Création et ses Retentissements en Philosophie* (Paris : Aubier, 1945), pp. 239f.

27 See Nicholas Rescher, *Many-Valued Logics* (New York: McGraw-Hill, 1969), pp. 122–9, 143–54; epistemological application of this distinction between meta- level rules and first-order propositions or between a meta- and intra-systematic use of propositions can be found in Rescher's *Methodological Pragmatism*, pp. 256ff.

28 See Rescher, *Methodological Pragmatism*, pp. 257–9, on the negative character of regulative principles of logic.

29 See the classic functionalist anthropological approach of Emile Durkheim, *The Division of Labor in Society* (New York: Macmillan, 1933); also Mary Douglas, *Purity and Danger* (London: Ark, 1984), ch. 5. See Robert Merton, *Social Theory and Social Structure* (New York: Free Press, 1968), ch. 3, for a general discussion of the notion of function in the social sciences. See especially his criticism of the 'postulate of indispensability' for a notion of functional alternatives in the social sciences.

30 See Nicholas Lash, *Change in Focus* (London: Sheed and Ward, 1973), for an antidote to the common assumption of a linear and cumulative development in the doctrinal history of the church.

31 There may be a historical shift in the use of this principle, particularly in its application to the case of created grace, from Ockham and Scotus, on the one hand, to Gabriel Biel, on the other. For Ockham and Scotus, see Gordon Leff, *The Dissolution of the Medieval Outlook* (New York: Harper and Row, 1976); *William of Ockham* (Manchester: Manchester University Press, 1975). For Biel, see Heiko Oberman, *The Harvest of Medieval Theology*, (Durham, N. Carolina: Labyrinth, 1983).

CHAPTER 2   THE TRANSCENDENCE AND CREATIVE AGENCY OF GOD

1 (Rome : Marietti, 1950), paragraph 661, p. 245. My attention was drawn to this passage by Robert Sokolowski. See his *The God of Faith and Reason* (Notre Dame, Indiana : Notre Dame University Press, 1982), p. 51, note one.

2 Trans. Cyril Richardson in *Christology of the Later Fathers*. (Philadel-

phia: Westminster, 1954), pp. 300f.

3 No references to Eastern Orthodox writings occur in this chapter. A reading of Gregory Palamas's *The Triads*, trans. N. Grendle (New York: Paulist Press, 1983) convinces me , however, that an analysis of God's transcendence and creative agency similar to the one found here can be made of Gregory's distinction between the essence and energies of God. This impression is confirmed by the interpretation of that distinction provided in the works of John Meyendorff, *A Study of Gregory Palamas* (London: Faith Press, 1974); *St. Gregory Palamas and Orthodox Spirituality* (Crestwood, New York: St Vladimir's, 1974); *Byzantine Theology* (New York, 1979).

4 See David Burrell's treatment of the notion of transcendence as a fundamental formal feature of Christian discourse in his 'A Response to Louis Dupré,' *Proceedings of the Thirty-First Annual Convention of the Catholic Theological Society of America*, 31 (1976), p. 11.

5 The terms 'contrary' and 'contrast' are not being used in a technical logical sense distinct from 'opposite'; they are used as synonyms of that term, as in 'on the contrary' or 'in contrast to'.

6 See R.G. Collingwood's treatment of Plato's theory of Forms in chapter 2, section 2, of *The Idea of Nature* (Oxford: Oxford University Press, 1960), pp. 55 ff.

7 See Richard Norris, *God and World in Early Christian Theology* (New York: Seabury, 1962), p. 60. My interpretation of the Greek milieu of theological thinking is generally informed by Norris's work.

8 Plotinus, *Enneads*, V i. 7, in *The Philosophy of Plotinus*, trans. Joseph Katz (New York: Appleton-Century-Crofts, 1950).

9 Plotinus, *Enneads*, VI ix.1,2.

10 Plotinus, *Enneads* VI ix.8, in Katz, *The Philosophy of Plotinus*, p. 152.

11 Note well my argument does not assume the historical importance of Plotinus for the development of Christian theology and does not depend for its force upon such a connection. Plotinus is a conceptual foil in the present context for the purposes of my own argument.

12 Note well that it is axiomatic that God creates only what is good. Questions of sin and evil are left out of account in what follows; the intelligibility of evil if a theologian follows our rules is a further question not addressed in this work. It may very well be that evil is not intelligible on that score but perhaps it should not be. Sin is an impossible possibility, as Karl Barth says. To claim its inexplicability, as Barth does, is not to trivialize its existence but to stress its horror as something with no right to exist, no place within a divinely instituted order.

13 See George Lindbeck, *The Nature of Doctrine* (Philadelphia: Westminster Press, 1984), pp. 18–19.

14 See Lindbeck, *The Nature of Doctrine*; Bernard Lonergan, 'The De-Hellenization of Dogma', *Theological Studies* 28 (1967), pp. 336–51; Ian Ramsey, *Religious Language* (London: SCM, 1973).

15 Lonergan, 'The De-Hellenization of Dogma', p. 347; Ramsey, *Religious Language*, pp. 166ff.

16 Bernard Lonergan, *Method in Theology* (New York: Seabury Press, 1972), p. 307; and 'The De-Hellenization of Dogma', pp. 344–5. See Ramsey, *Religious Language*, pp. 173ff.

17 See Lonergan, 'The De-Hellenization of Dogma', pp. 345–7; Ramsey, *Religious Language*, pp. 169, 170.

18 See his introduction to *The Concept of Mind* (New York: Barnes and Noble, 1949).

19 Note that this account does not specify any particular class of term appropriate for analogical use. Compare David Burrell, *Analogy and Philosophical Language* (New Haven: Yale University Press, 1973).

20 I am interested in forms of speech capable of producing a structure of discourse isomorphic with that which rules for coherent discourse would generate. Grammatical peculiarities of forms of language, more than the conceptual content of terms favoured for theological use, come in for special attention, therefore. Here the present proposal differs from those philosophical analyses stressing the use of models in theology (e.g. the models of 'king', 'friend' etc.). See Ian Ramsey, *Models for Divine Activity*, (London: SCM, 1973); Sallie McFague, *Metaphorical Theology* (Philadelphia: Fortress, 1982); John MacIntyre, *The Shape of Christology* (London: SCM, 1966).

21 Norris, *God and World*, p. 86.

22 I am providing here an analysis of Tertullian's argument in 'On the Flesh of Christ', ch. IV. A modern version of this argument is presented by Robert Sokolowski in his *The God of Faith and Reason*, ch. 4.

23 David Burrell, *Aquinas* (Notre Dame, Indiana: Notre Dame University Press, 1976), pp. 4ff. I am generally indebted in this chapter to Burrell's analysis of Aquinas.

24 See Karl Barth, *Church Dogmatics*, trans. G.W. Bromiley et al. (Edinburgh: T. and T. Clark, 1957–75), 2:1, pp. 260ff, 299ff, 334f etc.

25 See Burrell, *Aquinas*, pp. 4ff, 21ff, 31ff.

26 Ibid. pp. 5–6, 21–2.

27 See David Burrell, *Exercises in Religious Understanding* (Notre Dame, Indiana: Notre Dame University Press, 1974), pp. 94ff; *Aquinas*, pp. 32–3 etc.

28 We will see shortly that alternative readings of Aquinas, those that stress his reworking of Aristotelian metaphysics or his affinities with nineteenth- and twentieth-century German philosophy, also conform to what would be expected from a theologian following our rules for discourse. In the latter case, we have in mind Karl Rahner's interpretation of Thomas. See, e.g., his *Hearers of the Word* (New York: Seabury Press, 1968).

29 See the summary of Thomas's position given by R. Garrigou-Lagrange, *God: His Existence and Nature*, trans. B. Rose (St Louis: B. Herder, 1939), vol. 2, pp. 312–8.

30 For this interpretation of Thomas's metaphysic see Cornelius Fabro, *Participation et Causalité* (Louvain: Publications Universitaires de Louvain, 1961), esp. pp. 357ff, 372ff.

31 See Johann Gottlieb Fichte, *Science of Knowledge*, ed. and trans. P. Heath and J. Lachs (New York: Appleton-Century-Crofts, 1970).

32 See Karl Rahner, *Foundations of Christian Faith* (New York: Seabury, 1978), p. 78.

33 Ibid. pp. 75–81.

34 Friedrich Schleiermacher, first section of the first part of the System of Doctrine in *The Christian Faith* (Philadelphia: Fortress Press, 1976).

35 Schleiermacher, *The Christian Faith*, paragraphs 8.2 and 35.

36 Rahner, *Foundations*, p. 62; *Theological Investigations*, trans. K. Smyth (New York: Crossroad, 1982), vol. IV, p. 51.

37 Ibid.

38 Rahner, *Foundations*, pp. 58, 62 – 3.

39 See Henry Duméry's Plotinian affirmation of this implication in a philosophical theology condemned by the Roman Catholic Magisterium in 1958. Discussed by René F. de Brabander, *Religion and Human Autonomy* (The Hague: Martinus Nijhoff, 1972).

40 See, e.g., Paul Tillich, *Systematic Theology* (Chicago: University of Chicago Press, 1951), vol. one, p. 223.

41 Peter Geach, *Logic Matters* (Berkeley, Calif.: University of California Press, 1972), pp. 323–4.

42 See *Summa Theologica* (hereafter abbreviated as *ST*), q. 19, a. 4.

43 See *On the Power of God* (hereafter abbreviated as *OP*), q. 3, a. 15; *ST*, q. 19, a. 4.

44 See *Summa contra Gentiles* (hereafter abbreviated as *ScG*), book 2, chs 32–8.

45 See *ScG*, book 2, ch. 30

46 See *ST*, q. 19, a. 7.

47 See *ST*, q. 19, a. 8; q. 22, a. 4, ad. 1.
48 *Church Dogmatics*, 2:1, pp. 314–16, 496ff etc.
49 See Barth's rejection of a theology organized according to general notions in favour of one that centres on God's self-revelation in Jesus Christ; see also his rejection of a division of divine attributes between those assumed on a priori grounds to apply properly to God in 'himself', and those assumed to apply improperly to God because they directly concern divine acts in relation to us; ibid., esp. pp. 334–5, 345.
50 See, for instance, ibid. pp. 564–6.
51 Ibid. p. 260
52 See ibid. pp. 275–6, 281, 300, 337, 564–6 etc.
53 See ibid. pp. 467, 333, 335 etc.
54 Ibid. pp. 301ff.
55 Ibid. pp. 307ff.
56 Ibid. p. 303.
57 Ibid. pp. 311, 313.
58 Ibid. p. 314.
59 Ibid. p. 467.
60 See ibid. pp. 339, 343–5, 351–2, 358–9 etc.

CHAPTER 3   GOD AND THE EFFICACY OF CREATURES

1 Entry 616 in *The Journals of Søren Kierkegaard*, ed. and trans. Alexander Drue (London: Oxford University Press, 1938).
2 For the distinction between consistency and coherence of belief systems see Michael Williams, 'Coherence, Justification, and Truth', *Review of Metaphysics*, 34 (Dec. 1980), pp. 246f.
3 See Karl Barth's theological anthropology in *Church Dogmatics*, trans. G. W. Bromiley et al. (Edinburgh: T. and T. Clark, 1957–75), 3:2.
4 See *Theological Investigations*, trans. C. Ernst (New York: Crossroad, 1982), vol. 1, pp. 162, 188; *Theological Investigations*, trans. K. Smyth (New York: Crossroad, 1982), vol. IV, p. 117; *Foundations of Christian Faith* (New York: Seabury, 1976), pp. 78ff, 226 etc.
5 See R. Garrigou-Lagrange, *God: His Existence and Nature*, trans. B. Rose (St Louis: B.Herder, 1939), vol. 2, p. 522; and A. Sertillanges, *L'idée de Création et ses Retentissements en Philosophie* (Paris: Aubier, 1945), p. 190, for examples of what seems to be a commonplace Roman Catholic argument at least since Bossuet.

6   See Louis Bouyer, *The Spirit and Forms of Protestantism*, trans. A. Littledale (Westminster, Maryland: Newman Press, 1961), pp. 140, 146, 148, 159 etc., for a strong affirmation of this as a fundamental principle in Roman Catholic theology.

7   *Church Dogmatics*, 2:1, p. 410.

8   Ibid. 4:1, p. 89.

9   Ibid. 3:3, p. 130.

10 Garrigou-Lagrange, *God*, pp. 503, 387 note. See A. Sertillanges, *La Philosophie de S. Thomas d'Aquin* (Paris: Aubier, 1945), vol. 1, pp. 235–7, and *L'idée de Création*, for an argument that dependence upon God is a formal or meta-empirical characterization in the sense that it is compatible with any empirical determination of things and their relations.

11 I leave open here the question of what sorts of description of the creature's freedom require such theological judgements. Disputes in the Christian tradition centre on freedom of choice. If a person is really absolutely free to do one thing or another, does this not require a freedom from God? If God's creative will extends to my choice for a particular created effect, am I really free to do otherwise? Thomas answers, I am: the creature retains the *power* to do otherwise even if it is not exercised, since no created object of the will is able to constrain a decision for it. God's creative founding of my choice for a certain end does not alter that fact (see *ScG* book 1, ch. 68; *De Malo*, q. 6, a. 1, ad. 3). Martin Luther and John Calvin would argue this is no *real* power to do otherwise. One must deny the existence, then, of freedom of choice in abiding by our rules for discourse about divine agency and the creature (see esp. Luther's *Bondage of the Will*).

12 *Church Dogmatics*, 3:3 p. 92.

13 Ibid.

14 Ibid. p. 93.

15 Ibid. p. 13.

16 See *ST*, q. 22, a. 3; q. 23, a. 8.

17 See *OP*, q. 3, a. 7.

18 This expression 'two total subordinated causes' is the one used by Garrigou-Lagrange in *God*. The Banezian twist of his account is not my own; see below, ch. 4, note 66.

19 *ScG*, book 3, ch. 70, section 8, trans. V. Bourke (Notre Dame, Indiana: Notre Dame University Press), p. 237.

20 From Bernard's 'De Gratia et Libero Arbitrio', quoted by Hans Küng, *Justification* (Philadelphia: Westminster, 1964), p. 266.

21 See Barth, *Church Dogmatics*, 3:3, p. 133, agreeing with Thomas.

22 See Thomas, *ScG*, book 3, ch. 70, section 6.

23 Ibid. section 8.
24 *Church Dogmatics*, 3:1, p. 133. See Friedrich Schleiermacher, *The Christian Faith* (Philadelphia: Fortress Press, 1976), p. 176, for this same restriction on the meaning of divine cooperation.
25 See Cornelius Fabro, *Participation et Causalité* (Louvain: Publications Universitaires de Louvain, 1961), pp. 507ff. This interpretation of Thomas is contrary to twentieth-century Molinist variants like those found in Théodore de Régnon, *La Métaphysique des Causes d'après Saint Thomas et Albert le Grand* (Paris: Victor Retaux, 1906), and Johann von Stufler, 'Ergebnis der Kontroverse über die thomistische Konkurslehre', *Zeitschrift für Katholische Theologie*, 51 (1927), pp. 329–69, and 'Das Wirken Gottes in den Geschöpfen nach dem hl. Thomas', *Zeitschrift für Katholische Theologie*, 49 (1925), pp. 62–86, 186–219.
26 Thomas, *ScG*, book 3, chs 88, 89.
27 *ScG*, book 3, ch. 92, section 2, trans. Bourke, p. 42 (part 2).
28 *ScG*, book 3, ch. 89, section 1, trans. Bourke, p. 35 (part 2).
29 Luther and Calvin seem to disagree with Thomas here: under God's rule, persons act voluntarily but without freedom of choice. See Luther's *Bondage of the Will*, ch. 2, section 7; Calvins' *Institutes of the Christian Religion*, book 2, ch. 2, section 7. They may, however, be claiming only that we lack freedom of choice vis-à-vis God's own decisions for us; we retain it with respect to things of this world (see Luther's *Bondage of the Will*, ch. 2, section 9; ch. 7, section 14). Thomas would not disagree.
30 Peter Fransen, *Divine Grace and Man*, trans. G. Dupont (New York: New American Library, 1965), p. 172, in the particular tradition of Flemish Trinitarian mysticism. An appreciation of this point informs the dialectical analysis of religious experience which Louis Dupré offers. See his *The Other Dimension* (New York: Doubleday, 1972), and his 'Transcendence and Immanence as Theological Categories', *Proceedings of the Thirty-first Annual Convention of the Catholic Theological Society*, 31 (1976), pp. 1–10.
31 See Thomas, *ScG*, book 3, ch. 98, section 1.
32 See Thomas, *ST*, q. 19, a. 5; q. 21, a. 1. Also *ScG*, book 1, ch. 67; book 3, ch. 96 etc.
33 *Church Dogmatics*, 3:3, p. 139.
34 Ibid. p. 285. This is a common thread of *Church Dogmatics* 2:1.
35 See *ScG*, book 1, ch. 87, section 3. See also *ST*. q. 19, a. 8, ad. 2.
36 In talk of people acting intentionally, the order of execution generally reverses the order of intention. Supralapsarian theologies often make use of this. Thereby the primary significance of Christ

can be maintained even though Christ's coming occurs last in the order of creation, fall and covenant. Karl Barth's account of election in Christ and of the relations among the orders of creation, covenant and reconciliation avails itself of this structure of the language of intentionality.

37 See Thomas, *ScG*, book 3, ch. 96; and St Augustine, *The City of God*, book 5, ch. 10.

38 *Church Dogmatics*, 3:3, p. 173.

39 *OP*, trans. L. Shapcote (London: Burns Oates, 1932), q. 6, a. 1.

40 See the last chapter of David Griffin's *God, Power and Evil* (Philadelphia: Westminster Press, 1976), for an argument about omnipotence which disputes this distinction between impossibility within a certain created order and absolute impossibility.

41 Augustine, *Enchiridion*, ch. 32, trans. F. Shaw in *The Nicene and Post-Nicene Fathers*, ed. P. Schaff (Grand Rapids, Michigan: Eerdmans, 1956), vol. III, p. 248.

42 See Sertillanges, *L'idée de Création*, pp. 185ff.

43 Gustav Siewerth in his *Die Menschliche Willensfreiheit* (Düsseldorf: L. Schwann, 1954), esp. pp. 131ff, seems to provide an example within Roman Catholic theology of this claim that God cannot work without created causes.

44 Schleiermacher, *The Christian Faith*, is the case in point.

45 See Thomas, *ScG*, book 2, ch. 4.

46 See Thomas Mullaney, *Suarez on Human Freedom* (Baltimore: Carroll Press, 1950), ch. 2, for an account of Suarez's metaphysics.

47 See ch. 4 for an illicit transformation of this metaphysical difference of opinion into a theological controversy which violates the coherence of Christian discourse.

48 See G. Moeller and G. Philips, *The Theology of Grace* (London: A.R. Mowbray and Co., 1961), chs 1 and 2, for this general contrast.

49 See *ST*, II.II, q.23, a.2. For similar metaphysical arguments excluding a creature's acting by the creative power of God see *OP*, q.3, a.4.

50 See Gerhard Ebeling, *Luther* (Philiadelphia: Fortress Press, 1964); Karl Barth, 'No!', trans. P. Fraenkel, in *Natural Theology*, ed. J. Baillie (London: Centenary Press, 1946), pp. 67–128; Henri de Lubac, *Surnaturel* (Paris: Aubier, 1946), or Karl Rahner, *Foundations of Christian Faith*.

51 See *ST*, q.1. I am following Otto Pesch's account of the programme of the *Summa Theologica* in his *Die Theologie der Rechtfertigung bei Martin Luther und Thomas von Aquin* (Mainz: Mattias Grünewald, 1967), ch. 16, section one.

52 The theology of Karl Barth is a case in point. See esp. statements like those found in '*No!*' against Emil Brunner.
53 See Pesch, *Die Theologie der Rechtfertigung*, esp. ch. 16.
54 *Bondage of the Will*. ch. 7, section 18.
55 Calvin's *Institutes*, book one, ch. 17, section 10; see also sections 7, 8, 11.
56 Cited by George Lindbeck, *The Nature of Doctrine* (Philadelphia: Westminster Press, 1984), p. 75
57 See, e.g., J.N.D. Kelly, *Early Christian Doctrines* (New York: Harper and Row, 1978), pp. 178–83, 348–53.
58 This is the explanation suggested by Henri Bouillard's *Conversion et Grâce chez S. Thomas d'Aquin* (Paris: Aubier, 1944), ch. 2 esp; and by C. Moeller and G. Philips in their *The Theology of Grace* (London: A.R. Mowbray, 1961), ch. 2.

CHAPTER 4   THE MODERN BREAKDOWN OF THEOLOGICAL DISCOURSE

1 Commentators on modernity who have influenced my account include: Hans Blumenberg, *The Legitimacy of the Modern Age*, trans. R. Wallace (Cambridge, Mass.: MIT Press, 1983). Ernst Cassirer, *The Individual and the Cosmos in Renaissance Philosophy*, trans. M. Domandi (Philadelphia: University of Pennsylvania Press, 1963). Louis Dupré in his lectures on 'The Shape of Modernity' given at Yale University 1982–3. Michel Foucault, *Discipline and Punish*, trans. A. Sheridan (New York: Pantheon, 1977); *The Order of Things* (New York: Vintage Books, 1973). Russell Fraser *The Language of Adam* (New York: Columbia University Press, 1977). Hans Frei, *The Eclipse of Biblical Narrative* (New Haven: Yale University Press, 1974). Martin Heidegger, *The Question concerning Technology and other Essays*, trans. W. Lovitt (New York: Harper and Row, 1977); *What is a Thing?*, trans. E. Gendlin (South Bend, Indiana: Gateway, 1967). R. Jones, *Ancients and Moderns* (St Louis: Washington University Studies, 1936). G. Lukács, *History and Class Consciousness*, trans. R. Livingstone (Cambridge, Mass.: MIT Press, 1968). Timothy Reiss, *Discourse of Modernism* (Ithaca, New York: Cornell University Press, 1982). Gilbert Ryle, *The Concept of Mind* (New York: Barnes and Noble, 1949). Alfred North Whitehead, *Science and the Modern World* (New York: Macmillan, 1925).
2 See his Reply to Objections, V, in his *Meditations on First Philosophy* (1641).

3   See his *Novum Organum* (1620).

4   See Louis Dupré, 'The Problem of Divine Transcendence in Secular Theology', in *The Spirit and Power of Christian Secularity*, ed. A. Schlitzer (Notre Dame, Indiana: Notre Dame University Press, 1969), pp. 100–12, for the importance of the notion of human autonomy in promoting secularization.

5   See the sonnet 'Pentimento' in the *Canzoniere* of Petrarch discussed by M. Domandi in his introduction to Cassirer, *The Individual and the Cosmos*, p. xi.

6   John Webster, *Academarium Examen* (1653), p. 86, discussed by Fraser, *The Language of Adam*, p. 77.

7   See Johann Sturm and Petrus Ramus discussed by Fraser, ibid. p. 52; or Bacon discussed by Reiss, *Discourse of Modernism*, p. 215.

8   See Fraser, *The Language of Adam*, p. 5, citing Webster.

9   See Reiss, *Discourse of Modernism*, on this characteristic of analytico-referential discourse; and Hans Frei, *The Eclipse of Biblical Narrative*, on the priority of reference in modern hermeneutics.

10 Blumenberg, *The Legitimacy of the Modern Age*, p. 136.

11 René Descartes, 'Discourse on the Method of Rightly Conducting the Reason and Seeking Truth in the Sciences', part II, trans. J. Veitch, in *The Rationalists* (New York: Anchor, 1974), pp. 39–96, esp. p. 51

12 See Leibniz, discussed by Ernst Cassirer in *The Philosophy of Symbolic Forms* (New Haven: Yale University Press, 1955): vol. 1, *Language*, p. 130.

13 See Heidegger, esp. *The Question concerning Technology*.

14 See Reiss, *Discourse of Modernism*, pp. 26–42, 215–26, 238–51, 282–8.

15 Le Père Dominique Bouhours (1671) cited by Reiss, ibid. p. 282.

16 See John Dewey, *Experience and Nature* (New York: Dover, 1958), esp. pp. 135ff.

17 See Cassirer for an extended treatment of this tendency in modern philosophy and science, esp. his *Substance and Function*, trans. W. Swabey (New York: Dover, 1953), and the introductions to *The Philosophy of Symbolic Forms* in three vols.

18 This is the phrase of Alfred N. Whitehead. See his *Science and the Modern World*, ch. 3; and *Process and Reality* (New York: Free Press, 1969), p. 10, where he defines the fallacy this way: 'This fallacy consists in neglecting the degree of abstraction involved when an actual entity is considered merely so far as it exemplifies certain categories of thought.'

19 See Cassirer, *Substance and Function*; and *The Philosophy of Symbolic*

Forms, on 'substantialist' modes of interpretation. Whitehead, *Science and the Modern World*, on the fallacy of misplaced concreteness. Heidegger, *What is a Thing?*, and the helpful account of this work given in Charles Guignon, *Heidegger and the Problem of Knowledge* (Indianapolis: Hackett, 1983), pp. 34ff, 161ff. Dewey, *Experience and Nature*, esp. the introduction. Ryle, *The Concept of Mind*. Austin Farrer, *Freedom of the Will* (London: Adams and Charles Black, 1958). Ludwig Wittgenstein, *Philosophical Investigations*, trans. G.E.M. Anscombe (New York: Macmillan, 1953).

20 See Dewey's remark, *Experience and Nature*, p. 9.
21 Whitehead, *Science and the Modern World*, p. 55.
22 Ryle, *The Concept of Mind*, pp. 18ff.
23 Farrer, *Freedom of the Will*, ch. VI, section ii.
24 Ibid. ch. XI, section iii.
25 The trend to be documented is also associated with William of Ockham. Heiko Oberman in *The Harvest of Medieval Theology* (Durham, N. Carolina: Labyrinth, 1978), p. 4, simply terms the late medieval current of thought to be discussed 'the Ockham–Biel School'. I am using Biel for illustrative purposes rather than Ockham because I believe a fuller account has been made in the historical literature to support the idea that Biel's theology moves in the direction under consideration. The following commentators would dispute Ockham's 'complicity' with Biel on the interpretation I will be giving: Werner Dettloff, *Die Entwicklung der Akzeptations- und Verdienstlehre von Duns Scotus bis Luther* (Münster: Aschendorf, 1963), p. 268. Wolfhart Pannenberg, *Die Praedestinationslehre des Duns Skotus* (Göttingen: Vandenhoeck und Ruprecht, 1954), p. 143. Paul Vignaux, *Justification et Prédestination au XIVe Siècle* (Paris: Librairie E. Leroux, 1935), pp. 137, 185ff. Gordon Leff in his *The Dissolution of the Medieval Outlook* (New York: Harper and Row, 1976), and *William of Ockham* (Manchester: Manchester University Press, 1975), seems to be classing Ockham with Scotus as an anti-naturalistic response to the Condemnation of 1277.
26 See e.g. Oberman, *Harvest*; and H. McSorley, *Luther–Right or Wrong?* (New York: Newman Press, 1968). I am following Oberman's interpretation fairly closely. The analysis in terms of rules for discourse is of course my own contribution. For primary textual support see the citations of Biel's texts in Latin in Oberman's footnotes on the pages referred to below.

McSorley and Oberman argue effectively in support of their interpretation of Biel against the dissenting voices of : F. Clark, 'A

New Appraisal of Late-Medieval Theology', *Gregorianum*, 46 (1965), pp. 741–51; Lief Grane, *Contra Gabrielem* (Denmark: Aaehus, 1962), pp. 218–21 (see McSorley's remarks in *Luther*, p. 204, note 105); Paul Vignaux, *Luther Commentateur des Sentences* (Paris: Libraire Philosophique J. Vrin, 1935), pp. 52ff, 89ff (see the response of Oberman in *Harvest*, pp. 177, 209ff); Reynold Weijenborg, 'La Charité dans la Première Théologie de Luther', *Revue D'histoire Ecclesiastique* 45 (1950), pp. 629f.

Note, too, for purposes of our argument that Biel was a highly respected and influential theologian in late medievel theology (see McSorley, *Luther*, p . 199), if not the chief exponent of a school which represented the majority opinion of theologians (see ibid. p. 213f).

27 The same basic distinctions find a central place in the theology of the Franciscan Scotus without, it is generally agreed, a Pelagian consequence (see e.g., Heiko Oberman, *Forerunners of the Reformation* (Philadelphia: Fortress, 1966), p. 130; McSorley, *Luther*, p. 170). There is a Nominalist wing which is anti-Pelagian: Gregory of Rimini is the best case; also Heinrich Totting of Oyta, Heinrich Heinbuche of Hessen, Marsilius of Inghen, and John Mairo (see McSorley, *Luther*, pp. 196–9; Oberman, *Harvest*, pp. 196ff).

28 See Heiko Oberman, 'Some Notes on the Theology of Nominalism with Attention to its Relation to the Renaissance', *Harvard Theological Review* 53 (1960), pp. 47–76, esp. pp. 63ff.

29 See 'The Condemnation of 219 Propositions' (1277) (excerpted in *Philosophy in the Middle Ages*, eds A. Hyman and J. Walsh (Indianapolis: Hackett, 1967), pp. 542–9): Propositions 17 and 23 (versus a necessary natural order constraining divine agency), Propositions 68 and 69 (versus necessary intermediary causes), Propositions 96 and 100 (versus naturalism).

30 Oberman, *Harvest*, ch. 2, pp. 30–57, 186 etc; 'Some Notes'.

31 Ibid. pp. 46, 47, 97f, 100, 168, 170, 186 etc.

32 See McSorley, *Luther*, p. 209. It appears to be a common tendency of the time to alter the import of the traditional scholastic distinction between necessity of consequence and consequent in this way: see McSorley; ch. 7.

33 See Oberman, *Harvest*, p. 186.

34 Ibid. pp. 50, 139, 164.

35 Ibid.

36 Ibid. pp. 48, 156, 162, 116, etc; and Oberman, 'Some Notes', pp. 65–7.

37 For the historical arguments that created grace was conceived prior

to the sixteenth century as the very grace of God in its immediate effect upon humans see Henri Bouillard, *Conversion et Grâce chez S. Thomas d'Aquin* (Paris: Aubier, 1944), esp. pp. 194ff. See also Otto Pesch, *Die Theologie der Rechtfertigung bei Martin Luther und Thomas von Aquin* (Mainz: Mattias Grünewald, 1967), on grace as a quality in Thomas, esp. pp. 620ff, where grace for Thomas is interpreted as 'the immediate created resonance of the personal salvific action of God for man.'

38   See Oberman, *Harvest*, p 184.

39   See Pesch, *Die Theologie der Rechtfertigung*, on the use of 'merit' by Thomas, pp. 775, 777 etc.

40   See Oberman, *Harvest*, pp. 168, 170, 172.

41   See Pesch, *Die Theologie der Rechtfertigung*, pp. 782ff.

42   See Oberman, *Harvest*, pp. 135–8; McSorley, *Luther*, pp. 199ff.

43   See Bouillard's interpretation of Thomas's use of form/matter language in discussing God's grace and its reception, in *Conversion et Grâce*.

44   The following quotation from Biel, cited by Oberman, *Harvest*, p. 174, shows clearly the degree to which God becomes the debtor of even that human activity which is only meritorious *de congruo*: '"God cannot deny himself". Because he is just, he cannot deny his justice. Therefore, because he is compassionate, he cannot negate his own goodness and mercy, since he is more prone to give out of mercy and goodness than to punish out of justice. Now, if he is not able to deny his justice to malefactors, much less is he able to deny his goodness and compassion to those who beg for it. But he who does his very best begs for goodness and compassion. Therefore, God grants this to him. This gift is the infusion of grace. . . . God takes notice of those who seek their refuge with him. Otherwise there would be inquity in him. But it is impossible that there be iniquity in him. Therefore, it is impossible that he would not receive those who take refuge with him. But if one does his very best, one does take refuge with him. Therefore, it is necessary that God receive him. This reception, now, is the infusion of grace.'

45   Ibid. pp. 160ff.

46   Ibid. p. 247.

47   For the rudiments of the Banezian Thomist/Molinist controversies see the following secondary sources: M. John Farrelly, *Predestination, Grace and Free Will* (Westminster, Maryland: Newman Press, 1964). R. Garrigou-Lagrange, *God: His Existence and Nature*, trans. B. Rose (St Louis: B. Herder, 1939), vol. 2: *Predestination*, trans. B.

Rose (St Louis: B. Herder, 1937). Gallus Manser, *Das Wesen des Thomismus* (Freiburg: Paulus, 1949). Thomas Mullaney, *Suarez on Human Freedom* (Baltimore, Maryland: Carroll Press, 1950). Anton Pegis, 'Molina and Human Liberty', in *Jesuit Thinkers of the Renaissance*, ed. Gerald Smith, (Milwaukee: Marquette University Press, 1939), pp. 75–131. Théodore de Régnon, *La Métaphysique des Causes d'après Saint Thomas et Albert le Grand* (Paris: Victor Retaux, 1906). Henri Rondet, *The Grace of Christ*, trans. T. Guzie (New York: Newman Press, 1966). Gerald Smith, *Freedom in Molina* (Chicago: Chicago University Press, 1966).
For primary text support see these endnotes.

48   See Pope Paul V's declaration to this effect in August, 1607, quoted by Garrigou-Lagrange, *Predestination*, p. 151.

49   See Robert W. Jenson, *Lutheranism* (Philadelphia: Fortress Press, 1976), p. 66, for a short argument about the presuppositions of the Philippist/Gnesio-Lutheran controversy that conforms to that given below for the *de Auxiliis* disputes: 'Both sides assumed the basic question, what can man in and of himself do about fulfillment? The Philippists answered: "A little bit" ; and the Gnesio-Lutherans answered: "Nothing". But the trouble was the interpretation hidden in the question, that there is any such reality as man-in-himself.'

50   See Robert Scharlemann, *Thomas Aquinas and John Gerhard* (New Haven: Yale University Press, 1961), pp. 13–22, for a summation of the historical scholarship supporting the claim that this Jesuit work was the basic textbook for Protestant scholastic polemics.

51   For this point and an analysis of the two-storey view discussed below see esp. Henri de Lubac, *Surnaturel* (Paris: Aubier, 1946); Henri Rondet, 'Le Probleme de la Nature Pure et la Théologie du XVIe Siècle', *Recherches de Science Religieuse*; 35 (1948), pp. 481–521; Karl Rahner, 'Concerning the Relationship between Nature and Grace', in *Theological Investigations*, trans. C. Ernst (New York: Crossroad, 1982), vol. I, pp. 297–318, and 'Nature and Grace', in *Theological Investigations*, trans. K. Smyth (New York: Crossroad, 1982), vol. IV, pp. 165–88.

52   Henri de Lubac, *The Mystery of the Supernatural*, trans. R. Sheed (New York: Herder and Herder, 1967), pp. 97–102. See A. Sertillanges on speaking of the act of creation, in *L'idée de Création et ses Retentissements en Philosophie* (Paris: Aubier, 1945), esp. pp. 59ff, and *La Philosophie de S. Thomas d'Aquin* (Paris: Aubier, 1940), vol 1, pp. 264–5

53   This is Gallus Manser's Type A solution to God's working without jeopardizing created freedom, *Das Wesen des Thomismus*, pp. 604f;

see Farrelly, *Predestination*, p. 21 and note 44.

54 Manser's Type B, *Das Wesen des Thomismus*, pp. 606f; Farrelly, *Predestination*, pp. 20f.

'The total effect, indeed, comes from both from God and from the secondary cause; but it comes neither from God nor from secondary causes, as total but as partial cause, which at the same time demands the concurrence and influx of the other, just as when two men are pulling a boat. . . . Moreover, from what has been said it is clear that, when causes are subordinated to one another, so that some are more, some less universal, others are particular, it is not necessary that the higher in that order always moves the lower, even if they are essentially subordinated one to the other and are mutually dependent on one another in producing some effect; but it suffices if they immediately exert an influence on the effect'. (Molina, *Concordia* on Thomas's *ST*, q. 14, a. 13, disp. 26; Paris edn, 1876, p. 158; trans. in Garrigou-Lagrange, *God*, p. 469, note 2).

55 On Molina's general *concursus* see Smith, *Freedom in Molina*, p. 155; and de Régnon, *La Metaphysique des Causes*, pp. 594–8.

56 On Molina's general and special *concursus* in grace, see Smith, *Freedom in Molina*, pp. 153, 156–60; and Farrelly, *Predestination*, p. 22.

'The helps of prevenient and adjuvant graces. . . depend upon the free cooperation of our will with them, and so it is freely within our power either to make them efficacious by our consent . . . or inefficacious by withholding this consent' (Molina, *Concordia*, q. 14, a. 13, disp. 40, pp. 230–1; trans. in Garrigou-Lagrange, *Predestination*, p. 129).

'Wherefore it can happen that of two persons who are called by God, each receiving an equal interior grace, one of them of his own freewill is converted, and the other remains an unbeliever' (Molina, *Concordia*, q. 14, a. 13, disp. 12, p. 51; trans. in *Predestination*, p. 129).

See 'Certainly that we perform our acts well or badly, which we can do by the faculty alone of our free will and God's general *concursus*, must be referred not to God, but to ourselves as to a particular and free cause. . . God is not, therefore, the cause of virtue and vice in us, but it is proposed and willed by us' (Molina, *Concordia*, q. 14, a. 13, disp. 23, p. 196; trans. in Garrigou-Lagrange, *God*, p. 471).

57 This dissociation of God's knowledge from God's creative will in the *scientia media* is presupposed in the following: 'It was not in God's power to know by this knowledge [*scientia media*] anything else than he actually knew. If the created free will were to do the

opposite of what it did as it truly can do, God would have known this very act by the same knowledge' (Molina, *Concordia*, q. 14, a. 13, disp. 52, p. 318; trans. in Garrigou-Lagrange, *God*, p. 477).

58   See Garrigou Lagrange, *Predestination*, pp. 134f; Farrelly, *Predestination*, p. 26.

59   See Farrelly, ibid. pp. 26–7, note 53.

60   See Garrigou-Lagrange, *God*, pp. 368f; and *Predestination*, pp. 153ff.

61   See Garrigou-Lagrange, *God*, pp. 478f.

62   Ibid.

63   See Garrigou-Lagrange, *Predestination*, p. 159.

64   Ibid. pp. 147ff.

65   De Régnon, *La Métaphysique des Causes*, pp. 565ff.

66   See Sertillanges, *La Philosophie de S. Thomas d'Aquin*, pp. 238–9, 268–9, on the improper mix of the theological and the metaphysical in Banez and Molina.

67   See Garrigou-Lagrange, *Predestination*, pp. 250–60. This is Garrigou-Lagrange's own position as a twentieth-century Banezian Thomist.

68   This is the objection that Molina makes to Thomas in disputing the interpretation of Banez; see Smith, *Freedom in Molina*, p. 154.
     'There is [a]. . . difficulty. According to this doctrine, God does not concur immediately in the action and in the effect of secondary causes, but only through the intermediary of these causes' (Molina, *Concordia*, q. 105, a.5, pp. 152ff; trans in Garrigou-Lagrange, *God*, p. 153).

69   Garrigou-Lagrange, *Predestination*, pp.268, 282 and elsewhere. See Farrelly, *Predestination*, p 10.

70   See Gustav Siewerth, *Die Menschliche Willensfreiheit* (Düsseldorf: L.Schwann, 1954), pp. 110f, 131, for this objection.

71   See Smith, *Freedom in Molina*, pp. 134ff; Pegis, 'Molina and Human Liberty', pp. 98, 99; Farrelly, *Predestination*, p. 9.
     'Etiam si Deus non cognosceret futura contingentia tamquam praesentia in sua aeternitate, sed solum in causis ipsorom, eius cognitio esset certa et infallibilis' is the crucial text from Banez's commentary on Thomas's *ST* 1a, cited by Pegis ('Molina and Human Liberty', p. 98, following Fr Stegmüller, *Geschichte des Molinismus* (Münster i W: Aschendorff, 1935), vol. 1, *Neue Molinaschriften*, p. 403).

72   'God knows future contingents in their particular causes, in so far as these particular causes are subject to the determination and disposition of the divine knowledge and will which is the first cause. But

particular causes of future contingents in so far as they are subject to the determination of the divine knowledge and will, are determined and completed, and not impeded in the production of their contingent effects. God therefore knows future contingents in so far as they exist in determined and completed causes, and not impeded ones. The minor is unquestionably true. Proof of the major: God knows all created causes through his own essence, in so far as he is a first cause giving existence and power and determination to all causes. *Ergo.* But as concerns this argument, notice: although contingent causes, in so far as they are subject to the determination of the first cause, are determined and completed in act *in sensu composito*, absolutely speaking and *in sensu diviso*, they remain contingent and indeterminate and incompleted. Hence, their effects must be strictly called future contingents.' (Banez, from his commentary on Thomas's *ST* 1a, cited by Molina, *Summa Haeresium Maior*, in Fr Stegmüller, *Geschichte des Molinismus*, vol. 1, pp. 402–3; trans. Pegis, 'Molina and Human Liberty', p. 93).

73   See Sertillanges, *L'idée de Création*, pp. 181–2.
74   For the opinion that Protestant theology tends to become predominantly Semi-Pelagian or Arminian, see, e.g., Karl Barth, *Church Dogmatics*, trans. G. W. Bromiley et al. (Edinburgh: T. and T. Clark, 1957–75), 1:1 (second ed); and Louis Bouyer, *The Spirit and Forms of Protestantism*, trans. A. Littledale (Westminster, Maryland: Newman Press, 1961).
75   See Max Weber's analysis of the unintended consequences of Reformation theology in *The Protestant Ethic and the Spirit of Capitalism* (New York: Scribner, 1958); also, Peter Berger, *The Sacred Canopy* (New York: Doubleday, 1967), ch. 5, 'The Process of Secularization'.

CONCLUSION

1   In *Language, Counter-memory, Practice*, ed. D. Bouchard (Ithaca, New York: Cornell University Press, 1977), pp. 151–2.
2   Henry Duméry, *Philosophie de la Religion*, (Paris: Presses Universitaires de France, 1957). Alfred North Whitehead, *Process and Reality* (New York: Macmillan, 1969). J. R. Lucas, *Freedom and Grace* (Grand Rapids, Michigan: Eerdmans, 1976), ch 1. and 2.
3   See Charles Hartshorne, *The Divine Relativity* (New Haven: Yale University Press, 1948); G.W.F. Hegel, *The Phenomenology of Mind*, trans. J. Baillie (New York: Harper and Row, 1967).

4   This requirement follows from the general methodological prin-
    ciples of Whitehead's metaphysic; see *Process and Reality*, part 1.

5   Joseph Maréchal makes this point about Hegel in his *Point de Départ
    de la Métaphysique*. See the excerpts from this work translated by J.
    Donceel in *A Maréchal Reader* (New York: Herder and Herder,
    1970).

6   See J. L. Austin, *How to Do Things with Words* (Cambridge, Mass.:
    Harvard University Press, 1962); Lugwig Wittgenstein, *Philosophi-
    cal Investigations*, trans. G.E.M. Anscombe (New York: Macmillan,
    1953). On the many uses of linguistic forms of expression see, e.g.
    Philosophical Investigations, section 11: 'Think of the tools in a
    tool-box: there is a hammer, pliers, a saw, a screwdriver, a rule, a
    glue-pot, glue, nails and screws. The functions of words are as
    diverse as the functions of these objects.'

7   On the functional character of vagueness see, e.g., *Philosophical
    Investigations*, section 99: 'The sense of a sentence – one would like to
    say – may, of course, leave this or that open, but the sentence must
    nevertheless have a definite sense. An indefinite sense – that would
    really not be a sense at all. . . But is that true?'; and section 71 'Is it
    even always an advantage to replace an indistinct picture by a sharp
    one? Isn't the indistinct one often exactly what we need?' On the
    open texture of language according to Friedrich Waismann see his
    'Verifiability' in *Logic and Language*, ed. A. Flew (Oxford: Basil
    Blackwell, 1951), (first series).

8   See esp. his *Structure and Function*, trans. W. Swabey (New York:
    Dover, 1953).

9   See his 'Reification and the Consciousness of the Proletariat' in
    History and Class Consciousness, trans. R. Livingstone (Cambridge,
    Mass.: MIT Press, 1968).

10 See esp. *Being and Time*, trans. J. Macquarrie and E. Robinson (New
    York: Harper and Row, 1962); and *What is a Thing?* trans. E.
    Gendlin (South Bend, Indiana: Gateway, 1967).

11 See his *Science and the Modern World* (New York: Macmillan, 1925).

12 See his *Experience and Nature* (New York: Dover, 1958).

13 See his *The Concept of Mind* (New York: Barnes and Noble, 1949).

14 See George Lindbeck's case for this and his proposal of a modern
    variant of ancient forms of catachesis in his *The Nature of Doctrine*
    (Philadelphia: Westminster, 1984), ch. 6; see also his 'Ecumenism
    and the Future of Belief', *Una Sancta 25/3 (1968)*, pp. 3–17, and his
    'The Sectarian Future of the Church' in *The God Experience*, ed. J.
    Whelan (Westminster, Maryland: Newman Press, 1971), pp.
    226–43.

Index

act of existence, *see* existence, act
    of
act/potency, 63–4
Albinus, 41
analogy, 54–5, 175 n. 19; *see also*
    rules of Christian discourse
Apel, Karl-Otto, 173 n. 24
apophasis, 12, 171 n. 5
Aquinas, Thomas, *see* Thomas
    Aquinas
Arianism, 15
Aristotle (Aristotelian), 2, 38, 40,
    41, 58, 62, 63, 71, 72, 107,
    109, 117, 176 n. 28
Arminianism, 142, 189 n. 74
Athanasius, 50
audience, *see* rhetoric
Augustine, 17, 101–2, 117, 143
Austin, J. L., 167
authenticity of Christian
    language, 17, 38
de Auxiliis controversies, 132,
    141–52, 158, 185–6 n. 47

Bacon, Francis, 124, 182 n. 7
Baius, 144
Banez, Dominic, 141–52 (esp.
    147–52), 154, 156, 157, 158,
    159, 160, 179 n. 18, 185 n.
    47
Barth, Karl, 58, 59, 77–80, 83,

    85, 87–8, 91, 94, 96, 97, 99,
    109, 175 n. 12, 177 n. 49,
    180 n. 36, 189 n. 74
Bellarmine, Cardinal, 146
Berger, Peter, 189 n. 75
Bergmann, Gustav, 11, 171 n. 3
Bernard of Clairveaux, 92–3
Bernstein, Richard, 170 n. 5
Biel, Gabriel, 132–41, 152, 153,
    154, 157, 158, 161, 173 n.
    31, 183 n. 25, 184 n. 26, 185
    n. 44
Blumenburg, Hans, 181 n. 1, 182
    n. 10
Bonaventure, 107
Bouhours, Dominique, 182 n. 15
Bouillard, Henri, 181 n. 58, 185
    nn. 37, 43
Bouyer, Louis, 170 n. 4, 178 n.
    6, 189 n. 74
de Brabander, René F., 176 n. 39
Bradley, F. H., 10
Brunner, Emil, 181 n. 52
Burrell, David, 61, 171 n. 5, 174
    n. 4, 175 nn. 19, 23

Cajetan, Cardinal, 143
Calvin, John (Calvinism), 114,
    117, 142, 154, 178, n. 11,
    179 n. 29
Carnap, Rudolph, 171 nn. 4, 6

Cassirer, Ernst, 168, 181 n. 1,
    182 nn. 12, 17, 183 n. 19
Catholicism, 2–3, 5, 103, 107–8,
    109, 113, 142, 144, 162
causality
    Aristotelian, 63–4, 71
    natural vs. intentional, 71–2
    primary and secondary, 91–2
Christian, William, 171 n. 7
Clark, F., 184 n. 26
coherence/incoherence, 1–9,
    18–19, 23, 26, 45–8, 81–90,
    122, 152–60, 163–4, 165
    distinguished from consistency,
    81–2
Collingwood, R. G., 174 n. 6
complements, *see* functional
    complements
complexity, *see* diversity in
    theological statements,
    functional complements,
    rules as two-sided
composed and divided senses,
    151–2
Congruism, 146
creation, creature, *see* God,
    creative agency of integrity
    of, 84–5, 105, 106, 113,
    117–18

decontextualization, 124–8,
    155–6, 167
de dicto/de re, 73–4
deism, 87, 88, 89, 164
Derrida, Jacques, 11
Descartes, René, 100, 124, 127
Dettloff, Werner, 183 n. 25
Dewey, John, 11, 168, 182 n. 16,
    183 nn. 19, 20
discourse, Christian, *see* rules of
    Christian discourse
diversity in theological

statements, 29, 32, 34, 37,
    48, 83, 105; *see also*
    functional complements
Docetism, 57
Donne, John, 120
Douglas, Mary, 173 n. 29
Duméry, Henry, 164, 176 n. 39
Dummett, Michael, 172 nn. 19,
    21, 22
Duns Scotus, John, 133, 137, 173
    n. 31, 184 n. 27
Dupré, Louis, 172 n. 23, 174 n.
    4., 179 n. 30, 181 n. 1, 182
    n. 4
Durkheim, Emile, 173 n. 29

Eastern Orthodoxy, 174 n. 3
Ebeling, Gerhard, 109
ethics, *see* practice, Christian
existence, act of, 58, 60, 63–4, 84
extrinsicism, 143–5, 157, 158

Fabro, Cornelius, 176 n. 30, 179
    n. 25
facere quod in se est, 136, 140
Farrelly, John M., 186 n. 47, 187
    n. 56, 188 nn. 59, 69, 71
Farrer, Austin, 26, 173 n. 25, 183
    nn. 19, 23, 24
Fichte, Johann Gottlieb, 65
filioque, 15–16
form-itself schema, 58–60
Foucault, Michel, 163, 181 n. 1
Fransen, Peter, 179 n. 30
Fraser, Russell, 181 n. 1, 182 nn.
    6, 7, 8
freedom of the human will, 7, 24,
    35, 63, 81–119 *passim*, 131,
    144, 145–53, 158, 159, 178 n.
    11, 179 n. 29; *see also* Biel, *de
    Auxiliis* controversies
Frei, Hans, 181 n. 1, 182 n. 9

functional complements, 32–3, 84, 104–19

functional equivalents, 30, 31, 32, 36, 83

Gadamer, Hans-Georg, 6, 170 n. 5

Galileo Galilei, 128

Garrigou-Lagrange, R., 176 n. 29, 178 nn. 5, 10, 18, 186 n. 47, 188 nn. 58, 60, 61, 62, 63, 64, 67, 69

Geach, Peter, 176 n. 41

Gnesio-Lutheranism, 142, 186 n. 49

Gnosticism, 56, 117

God

creative agency of, 36–80 *passim* (esp. 36, 47, 62–4, 65–6, 72–3), 81–119 *passim*; working with creatures, 90–8; working without creatures, 98–104

and the existence of creatures with power, 84–90

as Father, Son, Spirit, 15–16, 38, 50

power of, 36, 81; *see also* God, creative agency of; absolute vs. ordained, 133–7; nonviolent, 95–6; total-working, 101–2; unconditioned, 96–8

sovereignty of, 25, 33, 34, 35, 113, 114, 117, 122, 134, 144, 146, 160, 162, 165

transcendence of, 36–80 *passim*; *see also* Irenaeus, Plotinus, Tertullian; contrastive and non-contrastive, 40–8, 56–8, 64, 67, 72–3, 77–80; in Hellenism, 39–45; and

personalist categories, 68–80; and transcendental categories, 65–8

as tyrant, 2, 122, 156, 161, 163, 165

grace, created, 108, 112, 118, 136–9, 140, 173 n. 31, 185 nn. 37, 43

grammar, 8, 15, 26, 27, 29; *see also* rules

Grane, Lief, 184 n. 26

Gregory of Nyssa, 36

Gregory Palamas, *see* Palamas, Gregory

Gregory of Rimini, 184 n. 27

Griffin, David, 180 n. 40

Guignon, Charles, 183 n. 19

Hartshorne, Charles, 165, 189 n. 3

Hegel, G. W. F., 1, 11, 165, 166, 189 n. 3

Heidegger, Martin, 65, 168, 181 n. 1, 182 n. 13, 183 n. 19

Heinbuche, Heinrich, 184 n. 27

Hellenism, 37, 38–45, 59, 117, 158

history, *see* rules and history

Hugh of St Victor, 133

Hume, David, 107

intentionality, 69–71, 102–3

Irenaeus, 56–7

Jenson, Robert W., 186 n. 49

Jesus Christ, 50, 57, 85, 88, 111, 177 n. 49, 180 n. 36; *see also* God, as Father, Son, Spirit

Jones, R., 181 n. 1

Kant, Immanuel, 20–3, 26, 65

Kierkegaard, Søren, 81

Kelly, J. N. D., 181 n. 57
Körner, Stephen, 22, 172 n. 14
Küng, Hans, 179 n. 20

Lash, Nicholas, 173 n. 30
Leff, Gordon, 173 n. 31, 183 n. 25
Leibniz, Gottfried Wilhelm von, 182 n. 12
Lindbeck, George, 50, 181 n. 56, 190 n. 14
Locke, John, 127, 131
Lombard, Peter, 108
Lonergan, Bernard, 50, 51
de Lubac, Henri, 181 n. 50, 186 nn. 51, 52
Lucas, J. R., 164
Lukács, G., 168, 182 n. 1
Luther, Martin, 17, 111–12, 113–14, 116, 154, 178 n. 11, 179 n. 29

McFague, Sally, 175 n. 20
MacIntyre, John, 175 n. 20
McSorley, H., 183–4 n. 26, 184 n. 32
Manser, Gallus, 186 n. 47, 187 nn. 53, 54
Mairo, John, 184 n. 27
Marcion, 57
Maréchal, Joseph, 190 n. 5
Marsilius of Inghen, 184 n. 27
merit, 113, 137, 139–41, 146, 185 n. 44
Merton, Robert, 173 n. 29
Meyendorff, John, 174 n. 3
middle knowledge, *see scientia media*
miracles, 99–100, 103–4
modernity, 1–2, 4, 7–8, 9, 103, 120–62 *passim* (esp. 124–32), 167–8, 169

modus significandi, 12
Moeller, G., 180 n. 48, 181 n. 58
Molina, Luís de, 141–52 (esp. 145–7), 154, 157, 159, 166, 179 n. 25, 185 n. 47, 187 nn. 55, 56, 188 n. 68
Mullaney, Thomas, 180 n. 46, 186 n. 47
mysticism, 179 n. 30

Nicholas of Cusa, 10
Nietzsche, Friedrich, 1, 11
nominalism, 2, 107, 133, 184 n. 27
Norris, Richard, 174 n. 7
nouvelle theologie, 109
Nozick, Robert, 172 nn. 12, 18, 20, 21, 22
Nyssa, Gregory of, *see* Gregory of Nyssa

Oberman, Heiko, 173 n. 31, 183 nn. 25, 26, 27, 28
occasionalism, 86–7, 88, 100
Ockham, William of, 107, 133, 173 n. 31, 183 n. 25

Palamas, Gregory, 174 n. 3
Pannenberg, Wolfhart, 183 n. 25
Paris Articles, 134, 184 n. 29
Paul V, Pope, 186 n. 48
Pegis, Anton, 186 n. 47, 188 n. 71
Pelagianism, 17, 121, 122–3, 143, 145, 149, 154, 156, 157, 159, 160, 161, 165, 166, 184 n. 27, 189 n. 74
Pelikan, Jaroslav, 171 n. 9
Pesch, Otto, 181 nn. 51, 53; 185 nn. 37, 39
Petrarch, 125, 182 n. 5
Philippism, 142, 186 n. 49

Philips, G., 180 n. 48, 181 n. 58
Pico della Mirandola, Gian Francesco, 125
Pierce, Charles, 16, 172 n. 11
Plata (Platonism), 38, 40, 41, 42, 59–60, 84, 106–7, 117
Plotinus, 42–5
potentia absoluta/ordinata, see God, power of
practice, Christian, 13–20, 26, 32, 37–8, 113–15, 169
predestination
  in Biel, 135–6
  in *de Auxiliis* controversies, *see scientia media*
Preller, Victor, 171 n. 5
premotion, physical, 149, 150–1, 157, 158, 160
Protestantism, 2–3, 5, 103, 108, 112, 142–3, 144, 154, 158–9, 161, 186 n. 50, 189 nn. 74, 75

Quine, Willard van Orman, 11, 171 n. 6, 172 n. 17

Rahner, Karl, 65–8, 85, 109, 176 n. 28, 186 n. 51
Ramsay, Ian, 50, 51, 175 n. 20
Ramus, Petrus, 182 n. 7
reference, 11, 122, 155–6, 157; *see also* decontextualization
reification, 129–31, 155, 156, 157, 168
de Régnon, Théodore, 179 n. 25, 186 n. 47, 187 n. 55, 188 n. 65
Reiss, Timothy, 182 nn. 1, 7, 9, 14
Rescher, Nicholas, 171 n. 10, 173 nn. 27, 28
res significata, 12

revisionist theology, 1–2, 4–5, 164–6
rhetoric, 7, 32, 34, 54, 115–19, 120–1, 155, 161–2, *see also* rules and history, rules as two-sided
Roman Catholicism, *see* Catholicism
Rondet, Henri, 186, nn. 47, 51
Rorty, Richard, 11, 170–1 n. 3
rules of Christian discourse, 47–8, 81, 84, 90–104, 167; *see also* grammar
  not conclusively derived, 31, 53
  deformation of, 123, 152–60, 164; *see also de Auxiliis* controversies, Banez, Biel, Molina
  faithful use of, 160–2, 166–9
  and first-order statements, 27–9, 31, 49–50, 173 n. 27
  as formal, 29, 178 n. 10
  and history, 33–5, 52–3, 116–18, 120
  as 'logical geography', 52
  as negative, 29, 173 n. 28
  and paradigms, 50
  and meta-level talk, 49–50, 51, 60–1
  as transcendental preconditions, 25–7
  as transformation rules, 26–7, 54, 167
  as two-sided, 105–19; *see also* rhetoric
  how to uncover, 48, 52–5, 62
Ryle, Gilbert, 52, 131, 168, 182 n. 1, 183 n. 19, 190 n. 13

Scharlemann, Robert, 186, n. 50
Schleiermacher, Friedrich, 65–6, 179 n. 24, 180 n. 44

Schlink, Edmund, 172 n. 13
scientia media, 145–7, 159, 166
Sertillanges, A., 173 n. 26, 178
    nn. 5, 10, 180 n. 42, 186 n.
    52, 188 n. 66, 189 n. 73
Siewerth, Gustav, 180 n. 43, 188
    n. 70
sin, 103, 116–17, 161, 174–5 n. 12
Smith, Gerald, 186 n. 47, 187 nn.
    55, 56
Smith, John E., 171 n. 6, 172 n.
    23
Socinianism, 142
Sokolowski, Robert, 175 n. 22
Stoicism, 40, 41
Strawson, P. F., 172 n. 15
Stufler, Johann von, 179 n. 25
Sturm, Johann, 182 n. 7
Suarez, Francisco, 108, 143, 146,
    147, 180 n. 46, 186 n. 50

Tertullian, 57, 175 n. 22
Tillich, Paul, 176 n. 40
Thomas Aquinas, 12, 36, 58, 60,
    61, 62–4, 71–6, 83, 84, 91–2,
    93, 95, 96, 100, 103, 108,

110, 112, 118, 133, 137, 140,
    143, 151, 153, 175 n. 23, 176
    n. 28, 178 n. 11, 179 nn. 25,
    29, 181 n. 51, 185 n. 37, 188
    n. 68
Totting, Heinrich, 184 n. 27
transcendental arguments, 20–6,
    30, 31
    compared with other forms of
        argument, 23–6
    two forms of, 20–3

Vignaux, Paul, 183 n. 25, 184 n.
    26

Waismann, Friedrich, 190 n. 7
Weber, Max, 189 n. 75
Webster, John, 182 n. 6
Weijenborg, Reynold, 184 n. 26
Wiles, Maurice, 171 n. 8
William of Ockham, *see* Ockham
Williams, Michael, 177 n. 2
Winch, Peter, 170 n. 5
Wittgenstein, Ludwig, 8, 11, 167,
    172 n. 16, 173 n. 24, 183 n. 19

Errata

10, line 2 of first paragraph: *transformed*
22, middle of first full paragraph: *transcendental*
29, line 5 from bottom: *concerning*
41, line 7 from bottom: change *independence* to *dependence.*
46, line 5: *influence*
53, line 8: *are*
57, middle of second paragraph: *therefore*
89, last sentence of first full paragraph: *then* should be *than*
95, near end of first paragraph: *constraint*
121, 4 lines from bottom: *vis*
183, first word: *Forms* should be italic

CPSIA information can be obtained at www.ICGtesting.com

226923LV00002B/15/A